In The Palm

LONGING

MY NEED TO BELONG

A MEMOIR

Beverly Bernard

First Published 2025 by Beverly Bernard

ISBN 978-1-0682295-0-3 (Print)
ISBN 978-1-0682295-1-0 (eBook)

Cover Design and Interior Formatting by Gregg Davies Media (Pty) Ltd
www.greggdavies.com

To my God, who has held me in the palm of His hand throughout my life, guiding and sustaining me with His endless grace.

To my husband, my steadfast companion, whose love and unwavering support have been my anchor.

And to my children, my greatest blessings, who fill my life with joy and inspire me to be the best version of myself daily.

With all my love and gratitude.

__11__ In him we were also chosen, having been predestined according to the plan of him who works out everything in conformity with the purpose of his will, __12__ in order that we, who were the first to put our hope in Christ, might be for the praise of his glory. __11__ In him we were also chosen, having been predestined according to the plan of him who works out everything in conformity with the purpose of his will, __12__ in order that we, who were the first to put our hope in Christ, might be for the praise of his glory.

— EPHESIANS 1:11-12

And we know that in all things God works for the good of those who love him, who have been called according to his purpose. __29__ For those God foreknew he also predestined to be conformed to the image of his Son, that he might be the firstborn among many brothers and sisters. __30__ And those he predestined, he also called; those he called, he also justified; those he justified, he also glorified.

— ROMANS 8:28-30

Your beginnings will seem humble, so prosperous will your future be.

— JOB 8: 7

"Can a mother forget the baby at her breast
and have no compassion on the child she has borne?
Though she may forget,
I will not forget you!
16 See, I have engraved you on the palms of my hands;

— ISAIAH 49: 15-16

Chapter One

You don't belong in this family, get out! My aunt's words rang in my head when the screech of the teacher's chair yanked me out of my thoughts—breaking the silence, the stillness, and the palpable sense of dread in the room. She picked up the stack of neatly folded report cards. It drew everyone's attention and we perked up, now on our best behavior. As if the mere act of going into good behavior mode would somehow magically produce good grades.

Mouths shut, heads up, backs straight as Miss Pearl, with her slender build and chocolate skin, leaned against the desk to address the class.

"I will give you your report cards, and I want you to take them to your parents. And you, Beverly…"

Her full attention on me drew all eyes in my direction, and I froze in dismay.

"Give your report card to your guardian."

"Miss Pearl, what's a guardian?" a little voice asked.

"The term *guardian* is given to someone who takes care of a child if the child doesn't have a father or a mother."

All eyes glanced toward me.

"As Bev doesn't have a father or a mother, she will have to give her report card to her guardian."

Crouched over like a pill bug in my effort to disappear, I sank into my chair. I wished I could get her to take her words back or make them evaporate by sheer might.

We collected our report cards, and the bell rang. A welcome sound, one of freedom. I rushed outside, but so did everyone else. I was surrounded by inquisitive five-year-olds hurling questions as if they were high-profile reporters and I, a noble queen.

"How come you don't have a father or a mother?"

"Sure, I have a father and a mother, but they don't live here."

"Where they live then?"

"I don't know," I said, taking a few steps while pressing through the mob.

"So, who you live with, then?"

In my effort to suppress my thoughts and my desire to blurt out, *Mind your own business, and leave me alone*! I sighed and said, "I live with my granny and my grandpa." At this point, they were almost running to keep up with me.

"But do you have brothers and sisters?"

Bringing myself to a stop and a slow swivel to face my audience, I leaned forward as if about to spill a secret. "Ok, let me tell you."

Their eyes fixed on my lips as they drew closer.

"Ask no questions, hear no lies." A frown veiled their faces. Wide-eyed and mouths open, they stared.

"I have to go," I said, breaking away from the pack. "A guardian," I mumbled as I kicked the pebbles in my way. "I don't have a *guardian*. I have a granny and a grandpa. Not a guardian. What does she know?"

A sense of sadness floated over me like a dark cloud, slowing my steps to a crawl. Nevertheless, it was Friday, and the thought of not having to face anyone at school, at least for a couple of days, was a relief. The walk along the dusty road cemented my frustration and the uncomfortable experience I had been exposed to. Thoughts of my absentee parents called for answers to the questions floating in my head.

The green wooden house perched on concrete stilts caught my eye. I was home. I marched into the yard, eager to see Granny. I stepped into the dining room and placed my bag on the shelf.

"Granny, who is my mother and father?"

"You forget your name before you forget your manners. Now you take that bag and go straight back to where you came from, and when you remember your manners, then you can come back. Do you hear me?"

"Yes, ma'am."

Moving as if in a backward film, I snatched my bag and retraced my steps out of the yard and back up the road toward my school, this time dragging my steps. Halfway there, I turned around and retraced my steps back home.

"One of these days, I goin' meet my mother and father, and they will love me," I grumbled.

A few minutes later, I reentered the dining room.

"Good evening, Granny."

"Good evening."

Easing my bag onto the shelf, I turned and quietly drifted out of the kitchen, no longer wanting to ask my questions. Hoping for an opportune moment when she would be in a better mood. While the absence of my father and mother differed from the norm, being called out on it in class was embarrassing.

The following evening, after a hectic run in the yard, I stepped into the dining room. A spread of ingredients lined the table: eggs, sugar, butter, spices, and a stainless-steel dish pan.

"What you making?" I asked.

"A cake. I need you to rub the sugar and butter for me because rubbing that sugar will hurt my elbow."

"Okay."

Granny put the butter and the sugar in the pan and handed me a big spoon. With the dishpan on my lap, slowly I incorporated the sugar and butter. While stiff at first, it got easier after a while.

"When the sugar melts in the butter, we will add the eggs. Sunday will be the second Sunday in April, so this is your birthday cake."

"Yes!" I said gleefully. "Did you find out yet when it's my real birthday?"

"No. I know it's in April, but I don't know the date," said Granny. "I need to trim those bangs of yours soon," Granny said, referring to a short bang I wore on my forehead.

"Why do you have to cut it? Let it grow."

"I have to cover that spot at the top of your head where the hair don't grow."

I rubbed my finger over the bareness and felt the indentation in my skull just above my hairline.

"Why do I have this spot?"

"You were stabbed with a knife when you were smaller."

"Who stabbed me?"

"I don't know. It was when you were in Bluefields with your mother. When your father brought you to us, you came with a big bandage wrapped around your head. Your father said they had taken you to the hospital for the doctor to remove the knife. The knife was standing straight up in your head when you were taken in. But when he asked what happened, they said that you fell and the knife got stuck at the top of your head."

"Who took me to the hospital?"

"I don't know," Granny said.

Even though my birthplace was Managua, Nicaragua, I had lived in Bluefields for a while. This was far from my recall.

As far as I understood, I was not yet two years old when I came to live in Corn Island. I often wondered about my mother when I watched kids interact with their mothers at school, at church, and around the neighborhood.

"What's my mother's name?"

"I can't remember her name. Pay attention to what you doing."

"What does my mother look like?"

"I don't know. I can't explain to you how someone looks."

"Do I have any brothers or sisters?"

"I am told you have one brother, but I don't know if you have any sisters."

"Granny, can I have an Orange Crush for my birthday?"

"Okay, I'll ask your grandfather to get one."

"Ooh." Having tasted an Orange Crush drink a long time before, I longed for one again, and I could not wait.

After Granny emptied the batter into the baking pan, I licked my fingers and left the bowl clean.

A few minutes later, the glorious smell of freshly baked cake filled the kitchen. Granny placed the finished tube cake on the six-seater wooden rectangular table, which was pushed against the wall, to cool.

The next day, the golden-brown deliciousness adorned the table. Next to it was a brown glass bottle with the words Orange Crush written in bold white and orange letters. I smiled with excitement. When she held the bottle, I perked up in anticipation. It popped when she removed the metal topper, and she proceeded to pour the orange beverage into my red plastic glass. It foamed and fizzed and my mouth watered, at which time, Granny proceeded to pour water into my drink.

"Nooo!" I moaned as if in pain.

"This drink is full of acid, and it's not good for you. That's why I have to dilute it," she said.

The fizz came out of me, as it did the drink, and I was crushed. I sat back in the chair with folded arms and pouted.

The flavor of the drink was no longer there. It was ruined. Almost in tears, I sulked, but knew not to cry or I would ruin my birthday. Grandpa would be mad.

Blinking away my tears, I turned my attention to the cake.

We had just finished lunch when Grandpa said, "Okay, it is your birthday, so I have to give you six smacks with the belt. One for each year."

"No, that's not fair," I giggled.

"Well, there will be no cake if there are no smacks. What do you say, Ivy?" he asked Granny.

"That's right."

I jumped to my feet and said, "Okay, fine."

Grandpa held my hand, turned me around, and fondly started the tradition. He gave me a smack on my skirt with the belt.

"One," Granny joined in the counting.

"Two . . ." And after the last smack, "Six!"

"Happy birthday!" he said.

We laughed. Granny put a slice of the golden yellow cake on my plate and I dove in. The splendid aroma and delicious taste made up for the lack of icing or candles. It was the best birthday cake ever.

"Time to go inside and get your rest," Granny said.

Sunday evenings were no fun, as playing on that day was forbidden. According to Granny, Sunday was a day of rest, but in my opinion, a day of punishment was more like it. Staring at the ceiling from the confines of my bed was a complete waste of my precious time, while outside a number of activities screamed for my presence. It didn't matter how I asked, the answer was always the same.

"No. You can run and play during the week, but Sunday is a day of rest," she said.

"Like I need any rest," I mumbled, wishing for a book to read.

As in previous years, my thoughts went to my parents,

whom I could not remember. I was one year older and still, there was no news. I thought because it was my birthday, they would come looking for me. Silly girl. Holding onto a dream, longing for a miracle. As my birthday only fell on a Sunday, I found myself in the same predicament every year, having lots of time to lay in bed and think.

How could birthdays be so exciting for others, yet for me, it was dull and quiet but for the whispers in my mind? Whispers that said, *You are not loved, you are not special, you are not wanted.* I longed for the day to end when I would step out from under the dark clouds and be discharged from my punishment.

Some Sunday nights, we went to a different church. Granny got her flashlight and her umbrella, just in case it rained. Up the road we went, in the pitch-black night. The congregation was smaller, but the singing was nice. On the nights we didn't go to church, we sat on the porch and watched the people pass by. While on the stairs, the dark-blue sky sprinkled with stars twinkled overhead, and we listened to music on BBC Radio.

But the most fun was playing riddle mi riddle with Grandpa.

"Grandpa, give me a riddle," I said.

"Riddle mi riddle, guess me this riddle. House full, kitchen full, and I can't get a spoonful. What is it?" Grandpa asked.

"Water," I blurted.

"No, you can't have a kitchen full of water."

"Mmm, I know, I know, smoke."

"You got it."

"Give me another one," I said.

"Riddle mi riddle, guess me this riddle. Outside green, inside red, and I have a whole lot of black men."

"I know, I know, a watermelon."

Grandpa had lots of riddles. Granny sat and listened while

I tried to guess the answers until Grandpa said, "It's time to hit the sack."

The next day at school, Miss Pearl tested our penmanship skills by asking each of us to write our last names on the board. Some students were assisted by Miss Pearl to get it right.

I went up and wrote "Williams." Before I could put down the chalk, I heard, "Look, look, she wrote a bunch of I's." Giggles echoed and someone said, "Yeah, she can't even write her name." I turned around and addressed the classroom.

"These are not a bunch of I's, it is the way my last name is written."

"She is right, these are not all I's. Her last name is written with two i's and two I's."

You could hear a pin drop as I strolled back to my desk. My chest up, my head held high with a smile of sweet vindication.

A few days later, Miss Pearl recorded our birthdays. She asked each student to provide her with their birth date. This went on with no glitches.

"Beverly," she said.

"The second Sunday in April," I replied.

"Okay," said Miss Pearl. "It is in April, but what date in April?"

"I don't know the date; I only know that we celebrate it on the second Sunday in April."

Whispers ensued all over the classroom. I heard someone say, "They claim she's so smart, and she don't even know when her birthday is."

"Yeah," others echoed.

Addressing the whispers, I said, "Granny don't know the exact date, but she is goin' to find out, then I will know."

"Okay, that's enough. She can let me know the date when she finds out," the teacher said.

Staring at my notebook, I wished to be anywhere but there and waited in silence for class to be over.

We lived in Brig Bay. Everyone knew each other. People were friendly for the most part, but things could become difficult for a six-year-old because all grown-ups had a license to mind every child's business in the neighborhood. Grandpa said it was like having eyes behind his head, and anything I did or said behind his back got back to him in living colors.

On the road, I had to be on my best behavior and was reminded of this often. This included when we had visitors to the house—visitors like our neighbor, Ms. Yorda.

One evening, while playing in the yard, my skinny legs dangled in the air as I tried to perfect my cartwheels. From the corner of my eyes, I saw them—the dogs. One after the other, they came down the dusty road. The brown one, then the white one, and lastly, the black one. I recognized them. Yeah, they were Ms. Yorda's dogs. I was not afraid of the dogs though, but of the owner, Ms. Yorda Downs. She was a mean, tall, meager woman who lived up the road and visited Granny far too often. She came in her flip-flops. Her long, skeletal arms dangled back and forth, and she wore a ruffled ponytail with whiffs of curls framing her drawn, freckled face.

What do I do? I asked myself.

I ran for cover in an effort to keep out of her sight. Each time she visited, I ended up in trouble or being punished. I knelt on the wooden floor in the dining room next to the door with my face practically touching the green wall, staring at the cracks in the doorframe, shuffling from one knee to the other to attain comfort.

The time before, she said, "Tit Ive"—Ivy was Granny's

name, but some people had no regard for names; they called you whatever they liked, hence "Tit Ive"—"Do you know Beverly is out there in the front yard doing cartwheels wit' her dress over her head and completely exposing herself to the world?"

"Beverly!" Granny yelled.

There it was, trouble again. The time before, I had her figured out, or so I thought. I ran and sat on the stairs as soon as the dogs came into sight, pretending to mind my own business. Her accusing eyes glanced at me as she went to the dining room.

She can't say anything now, I thought, seated innocently on the step. But oh, how wrong I was.

"Tit Ive, do you know Beverly is sitting on the stairs out front with her legs sprawled open to the world?"

There it was again.

"Beverly!"

Sure enough, it was punishment again. Then Granny got the idea that to solve this problem, she would have me wear shorts.

"Put these on," she said as she handed me the pair of blue shorts.

Not only did I have to put on a pair of shorts, but she handed me some white straps with four big buttons at the end too.

"What's these?" I asked.

"Braces," she said as she strapped them on. "These shorts nah goin' hold up on their own." After fastening the buttons to the suspenders, she handed me the blouse. "Now you can go and play."

I wondered what these straps would do that an elastic waistband couldn't, but I learned the hard way. At times, it's better to keep my thoughts to myself and to keep my mouth shut.

Granny said if I was fresh—the term she used for me

speaking my mind—she would slap my teeth down my throat or to kingdom come.

Grandpa didn't go to church and wasn't very religious, but I was convinced he was well-versed in the Bible. He was of the firm belief that you did not save the rod and spoil the child, and he had no problem applying the rod of correction to my derrière. I could testify to that.

Hence, as the saying went, "En boca cerrada no entran moscas" (in closed mouth, no flies enter).

In my new dress code, minding my own business, I made a stop at the toilet. It was an outhouse consisting of two holes parallel to each other, the use of which required the removal of my blouse. When done, to my shock, I realized I had set the blouse precisely where the other hole was. It was gone. *Now what?* This solution was nothing but a nuisance, but what else was I to do? Wearing only my shorts and suspenders, I confidently stepped out and a familiar scream jolted me to attention.

"Beverly! What are you doing out there without a blouse? Where is your blouse?" Granny shouted at the top of her voice.

"I had to use the toilet, and it fell in."

"Get in here this minute and get yourself a blouse. I don't know what I goin' do with you."

Trouble followed me everywhere, but this time, I would perfect my strategy to sabotage Ms. Yorda's plans. Tall, concrete posts supported the house. The concrete stairs provided the perfect hiding place. I made a dash for it. Granny went the usual way to the dining room at the back of the house.

"Tit Ive."

What she goin' say now? I thought.

"Where is Beverly? I don't see her anywhere."

My back leaned against the concrete wall—the back of the stairs. The two pink ribbons at the end of my braids rested on my shoulders as I hugged my knees, waiting for the racing in my chest to settle down. *Please don't let her call me. Please, please.*

Then Granny replied, "I don't know where she is. She is out there playing somewhere."

Relieved not to hear my name called, I stared at my tanned skin and the dirt ground, making sure not to move. The unpainted floor panels overhead witnessed my ordeal. The crevices at the edge of the floor—my secret hiding place—held my small bag of marbles. While eager to get them, I could not risk being caught.

"Granny always believes everything Yorda tells her, but when I meet my mother, I will tell her about Yorda. I bet she will not punish me_for everything Yorda says, as Granny does," I mumbled.

Time went at a crawl and I wondered when she would ever leave. She resurfaced and began looking around, her eyes searching.

"Tit Ive. You know, I still don't see her anywhere."

"She has to be out there somewhere," Granny said.

Her eyes searched around as she dawdled out the yard and up the street, surrounded by her dogs. It was a relief to watch her fade away in the distance. My fists went up as I jumped for joy, yes! I laughed. *I did it!* A sweet moment of victory indeed.

Avoiding her on a consistent basis proved difficult, since Corn Island was only six square miles in size. In my view, it was huge, but I knew then how to avoid her in the future.

Grandpa came home and I overheard him say Aunt Edna would be visiting soon. This news put me on edge.

Chapter Two

My two aunts and cousins visited now and then. Aunt Edna lived in León, and Aunt Delcy in Chinandega, on the Pacific side of Nicaragua. Granny and Grandpa busied themselves in anticipation of her arrival. Grandpa picked her up at the airport. She gave Granny a big hug as she entered the dining room, and Grandpa brought a big box and rested it on the floor. After the giggles and chitchats, she got a shirt from her suitcase and gave it to Grandpa.

"Here, Papá, I brought this for you."

"Your gift is in this box," she said to Granny.

"You must have brought half of Managua in there," Granny laughed.

Eager to see what was in such a big box, I stared. One by one, Granny and Grandpa placed the items on the table. It was a complete set of apple-green melamine dishes, all matching, with dinner plates, cups and saucers, creamer, a butter dish, a sugar bowl, and even salt and pepper shakers. It was like Christmas in the middle of the year! Aunt Edna looked on and smiled, watching Granny's and Grandpa's faces light up as they unpacked each item.

My aunt saw me standing at the door watching.

"What you looking at?" she barked. "No one invited you, move!"

My arm slid down the doorjamb, joy replaced by gloom. On my way to the yard, I reached for my bag of marbles, but the heaviness that drained down my arms was not conducive to play. The window drew my attention repeatedly, curious about what may be happening inside; an outsider looking in.

The next day, Aunt Edna sat at the table with Granny as I entered the dining room.

"Get out. Can't you see you don't belong in this family? All you are doing is dragging my mother down," Aunt Edna said with disdain, her tone thunderous.

"Go outside and play," Granny said softly. As I drifted out the door, tears welled up in my eyes. Granny's calm words were still at ear's reach.

"Why don't you leave her alone? You know she has no one but me."

"She is not your responsibility. Let her go and look for her people."

With my head held low and a crumbling feeling inside, I went outside to the mango tree. How can she be so mean? I didn't do anything to her. Why does she hate me so? As I wiped away my tears, the words, *"Let her go look for her people,"* rebounded in my head.

Who are my people? Are Granny and Grandpa not my people? How could I go look for them? Does she mean my mother's people? I don't even know who they are. And I don't drag Granny down. I help her. *She* doesn't help her, *I* do! My thoughts of running the errands, gathering the fruits, sweeping the house, and doing various chores came to mind. Always trying to do my best to earn my keep. Despite this, my efforts always fell short. I glanced at the kitchen as if the answers to all my questions could come floating through.

The cool breeze brushed against my skin as if making an effort to calm my anger and soothe my sadness as my arms hugged the coarse bark of the mango tree. The chirp of a pine warbler interrupted my thoughts. The leaves swayed ever so softly. There, on a branch, was the yellow bird. It moved swiftly and its tail swayed as it hopped from branch to branch. A movement so graceful and soothing to my turbulent and conflicted mind. Needless to say, I spent a lot of time outside gazing at the trees during my aunt's visits.

"Bev!" Granny called. "Go and see if you can find some mameys!"

Across the road and down the narrow lane I went.

The enormity of the tree trunk was impressive. Even with both hands extended, I could not be seen on the other side. The branches extended wide. Glimpses of blue sky and sunlight peeped through the foliage, draping the path with dappled shade. The crackling sound of the dry leaves under my feet broke the silence.

I gathered some young mameys of different sizes that were scattered about, to add to my collection of pretend gigs. Oftentimes, I sat on the porch and challenged myself to keep several spinning at the same time.

My eyes roamed around in search of a mamey. Their brown color amidst the dry leaves made them hard to spot. Startled by a brisk shuffle of the leaves, I jumped. A huge iguana, perched high on his front legs, caught my eye. The spikes on its back were sharp and fierce. Black-and-white rectangles perfectly spaced apart like strips of a checkered board formed his tail wrapped in a semicircle around him. The dewlap under his neck flashed as he shook his head up and down, his eyes fixed on me as if saying, "I see you. I have my eyes on you. Don't you dare come near me!"

Keeping my eyes on the creature, slowly in a sideways move I reached for a piece of branch, just in case. What color is it? I thought. Is it green? No, brown? No, gray? No, it had all those colors. Another perfect camouflage in the midst of the foliage. He looked more like a prehistoric creature.

Then a sound in the distance caught my attention. "Peck, peck, peck." *What is that?* I wondered, drawn towards the sound that floated down from high in the trees. But where? In between the slender trunks, I meandered. "Peck, peck, peck." Up the bark of a tall tree, my glance trailed, and something red caught my eye. It was a woodpecker! It looked as if it was wearing a red Nutcracker soldier hat, the brightest and most beautiful red my eyes had ever seen. His body was lean and black, with pale yellow streaks on the side of his neck. His claws gripped the bark of the trunk. "Peck, peck, peck." His beak was sharp and as strong as nails. *Do they ever get a headache?* The thought brought a smile to my face and joy filled my being, the cares of the world erased by the magic of nature.

The bright sunlight painted the scene in golden yellow to allow for a perfect view, when, as fast as a flash, he flew away. *No! Come back. Where did he go?* I could watch him all day. The magical image was fixed in my mind.

Then, it dawned on me: the mamey. The iguana was now gone. Around the tree I roamed when a big one caught my eye. I pinched off the very tip, as Grandpa showed me to do, and saw the reddish hue just under the skin. This was an indication the fruit was fit.

Eager to show Granny my awesome find and tell her of the beautiful woodpecker I spotted, I skipped home in glee. But at the door, my body froze and dread filled my thoughts as if landing back on Earth. *What will my aunt say if she sees me?* Cautiously, I peeped in and let go of a sigh, relieved she was not there. The coast was clear, at least for now.

A few days later, she was gone, leaving with me the thought of ever seeing my mother and meeting those she called my people.

Ms. Zena came by to collect the weekly dirty laundry and

stood waiting on the step. Granny handed her the clothes, all tied up in a white sheet. This was a weekly event. It was funny and odd that her name was the same as the colorful flowers in the yard next to the post office. A smile brushed my face at the thought of such a coincidence. She collected the clothes one day, which she would return a few days later all washed and ironed. She lifted the big bundle and placed it on her head.

"See you on Tuesday, Tit Ive!" she shouted as she left.

Granny got the small items she did not give to Ms. Zena and placed them in a galvanized wash pan propped up on a wooden stool, followed by her wooden washboard. Well sod with blue soap, she rubbed them on the board. While she rinsed and hung the clothes on the line, I stood on a stool and washed my socks and underwear as well. The white garments were laid out in the sunshine to get rid of stains and dipped in pre-powdered blue water to bring out the white. On the line, they billowed in the soft island breeze. Learning to wash my clothes would serve me well for years to come.

A few weeks later, on the porch, I rocked back and forth in the little rocking chair.

"Next week, those children goin' be here," Grandpa said.

"Which children?"

"Ivania, Juanita, and them."

"Is Henningston comin'?" I asked.

"No. Not this time. Frank is coming this time."

Henningston was the eldest of my cousins. I liked it when he came because he was nice to me. The following week, the house was full.

"Ivania, you want to play marbles?" I asked.

"No, she don't want to play with you, caterpillar, 'cause you are black and ugly like the hairy black caterpillars on the pepper trees outside," said Frank, Ivania's elder brother, fair-skinned, tall, and slender, his thin lips in a sly smile.

They all laughed.

"And don't call my grandpa 'Grandpa' either, 'cause he is not your grandpa. He is not your father's dad, and you don't belong here. Go and look for your people, but aah, yes, not even them want you."

His expressions mimicked his mother's sentiments. It was as if she spoke through him. I turned and walked away, leaving them sitting around the table, feeling less than others, as if I had no voice, and they had the license to point out I did not belong. But his comments went even further and cut like a knife. *Not even them want me? How did he know that? Is that what my aunt said as well?* But his tone, cold as ice, screamed out louder than his words. His eyes glanced down at me as though his look had to reach down to see me down there, beneath him, beneath all of them, tugging at my emotions, leaving me bare and listless—an orphan among family.

Who are my people? And why are they not here? They were a unit. *They* had each other. But I was the misfit, the odd one out, the outcast.

At midday, Granny called, "Go and set the table, then come and serve your cousins!"

"Why can't they serve themselves?" I asked.

"They are your guests and therefore, you must serve them."

Not satisfied with that explanation, and wanting to tell Granny they were not my guests because I didn't invite them, I resisted and kept my thoughts to myself to avoid punishment, especially with them around.

At the table, my cousin Juanita—the eldest—sat at the head of the table, and Frank, who was a year older than Ivania, sat at the other end. Ivania, who was my age, and Cecilia and Monica, the two youngest, respectively, sat across from each other.

After placing the forks and drinks on the table, I came back with one plate of food in each hand. About to put the plates on the table, I stumbled and almost dropped the food. They all laughed out in chorus. Frank sat back in his chair, holding his belly as he chuckled. He had intentionally pushed his leg in front of me.

Grateful the food did not spill and cause me undue trouble, I sighed. After several trips, I cautiously approached the table, surveying my surroundings to avoid their tricks. Once the meal was served, they condescended to have me join them at the table. I always had my own plate and my own red plastic glass. Their breakable plates were all matching, and their breaking glasses too.

Cecilia asked, "Why are your plate and glass different from ours?"

"Because she has germs, and Granny and Grandpa don't want to get any of her germs. That's why she has to use a separate plate and glass," said Frank, grinning.

My glance took in their reaction, the sly smiles on their faces. *How could they be so mean?* I had no germs; of this, I was certain. Their opinion was of no consequence, but their rejection produced a hollow feeling inside this was real, and it was them versus me. They had each other. I had no one.

Later that day, in the passageway to the dining room, Frank approached.

"Get out of my way," he said as he pulled back and punched me in the stomach. The force of the blow took my breath away and darkness covered my eyes. To my knees, I fell, curled over, and held my stomach while gasping for breath. He laughed and walked away.

After composing myself, I sat in the doorway and watched the Guinea hens scratch around. One lifted its blue head as if acknowledging my presence. In their dark-grey plumage sprinkled with tiny white polka dots, they looked dressed as though they were ready to attend a ball. The quietness of their world was enviable. A place where no one called them names or treated them as though they were unworthy or less than others.

Keeping away and trying to make myself invisible didn't always work. Frank approached me one evening with a machete in his hand. The look of rage and disgust was written all over his face.

"Get out of my way before I chop you," he said as he lifted the machete and chopped at me. With my hands in the air, I jumped back to avoid the machete, but it caught me on my right hand just below my thumb. Squeezing my hand in shock, I dashed off to the room, grabbed a rag, and pressed it over my wound to stop the bleeding.

Backed into the dark corner like a helpless, injured kitten, I nursed the ache of my bleeding heart. Tears rolled freely down my face as the blood trickled down my arm. I felt insignificant, destitute, and devoid of defense, wondering who would look out for me.

Stifling the desire to sob or to scream to let out the rage I felt inside, I kept quiet to avoid drawing attention to my hiding place. Not wanting to believe he actually cut me, I cried not so much for the pain in my hand, but the pain in my being, knowing he could do whatever he wanted and not be in trouble. He belonged. He was a part of this family, but I was merely a misplaced alien in their world.

Curled in a dark corner under the cot, I stayed for a while, fearing that this would somehow be my fault. The bleeding took a long time to stop, but I waited patiently and longed for his quick departure.

It was the middle of the week, but because we were on holiday and my cousins were visiting, we were allowed to go to the beach. The girls dressed for the occasion in their nice bathing suits with dainty flowers, all made with stretchy material that hugged their bodies in beautiful, bright colors, each with their big, colorful towels in hand. A far cry from what mine looked like. Green with envy, I stared.

Granny had the seamstress sew mine, but it was made of the most hideous dark moss-green cotton cloth I had ever seen, and it did not stretch. It had elastic at the legs and ballooned all the way up to the yellow straps at my shoulders. The neck opened wide, to allow me to enter the thing. A tie of the straps over my shoulders completed the process. In my effort to hide it, I pulled a dress on over it and stepped out. At the beach, I removed my dress hesitantly, trying to avoid being seen before I could get in the water to camouflage myself.

"Caterpillar!" Frank said at the top of his voice. "Wha' you wearing?" He pointed at me, laughing. Everyone's attention turned to me. Giggles erupted. I marched into the water, ignoring the surrounding scene, and hid.

After a while, thankfully, I blended in with the other kids. Some jumped off small boats anchored near the shore, others dived under and so did I. While on the beach, some buried themselves in the sand and others made castles. The chatter and laughter filled the air.

The days went by and they left, but their words stayed with me. The sense of estrangement lingered and my deep desire to prove them wrong grew, along with the longing for an opportunity to meet those they claimed were my people. How awesome that would be!

What would it be like to meet my mother? How would that day be? Did I have brothers and sisters? How would we get along? Would they accept me? Or would I be an alien in their world also?

One day, I would show them how wrong they were. That those they called my people did want me. I imagined myself standing tall, feeling vindicated as I felt in class when I had the right answer, being able to one day show them I was accepted and I belonged after all. I wondered if that day would ever come. The day I could let them eat their words. Even though they saw me as a caterpillar, I saw the possibility of someday being a butterfly.

Granny was in the dining room, her favorite spot in the whole house. Most of her days were spent there, preparing meals for us, or sitting in her favorite chair at the head of the table. She gazed through the window while cutting up coconuts to feed the chickens, enjoying the cool breeze that emitted from the shade of the huge avocado tree. She was a little on the plump side, with distinct Chinese features, an eggnog complexion, and slanted eyes. Her silky, jet-black hair was worn slicked back in a huge bun.

Even though she spent most of her time secluded in the confines of the kitchen or dining room, she was always well-dressed before starting her day. Her pristine white apron with two pockets at the sides was always neatly pressed. This went over her head as soon as she put her foot in the dining room. If a visitor came and she had to go outside to greet them, her apron immediately slipped off, and voilà, she was dressed for the occasion.

"Beverly!" Granny called.

"Yes, ma'am?"

"Come and fill this bucket with water." Bucket in hand, I skipped to the well.

"Can I help you to wash the dishes?" I asked as I put down the bucket of water on the floor.

"No, I don't want you breaking my bowls. What I want you to do is go to Ms. Flora's shop for me."

She gave me the money and barely hearing what she asked me to buy, I took the money and ran outside.

"Just a minute, young lady."

I pulled my brakes and stopped at once.

"Yes, sir?"

"What does a needle look like?" Grandpa asked. Puzzled at this weird question, I answered hesitantly, "Straight?"

"That's how you go, and that's how you come back. Straight."

"Yes, sir," I replied.

With the frame of my old bicycle wheel in hand and the piece of wire I used to steer it, up the road I went, trying to avoid the big rocks while keeping the wheel from falling. The wheel bounced on the rocks and up off the road. It was a balancing act, but I had it down pat.

At the steps of Ms. Flora's house, perched on a hill sustained by long stilts, I parked my wheel and entered the shop on her porch. A cage fitted on the veranda rail drew me. It housed the prettiest squirrel I had ever seen. In fact, it was the *only* squirrel I had ever seen. The furry beauty was propped up on its back legs, munching on a nut. It twiddled its nose and chewed and held its paws together as if praying. Its big, fluffy tail caressed the curve of its back as it prayed.

"Hi, Bev," Ms. Flora interrupted.

She looked so much like Granny they could pass as sisters, but she was a bit slimmer.

"Hi, Ms. Flora." I handed her the money. "Granny asked if you could please sell her one rotten egg."

Ms. Flora frowned.

"One what?"

"One rotten egg."

Ms. Flora laughed.

"Wait, let me call Mr. Boosy."

She stepped away and called her husband.

"Boosy, come here."

He appeared at the door, tall, full-bodied, and of a caramel complexion.

"Ask Bev what she wants."

He asked, and I repeated my request.

"Granny said if you could please sell her one rotten egg."

Now they were both laughing.

"Bev, you mean one nutmeg?" Ms. Flora asked.

"Oh, okay." I had no idea what that was and wondered why Granny wanted a rotten egg, but that's what she said. I shrugged.

She handed me a little bag and off I went, rolling my wheel.

My father lived in Managua, way before my arrival on the island, and I couldn't remember ever meeting him. I didn't think he liked the island life very much because he never came back. I longed for the day he would visit. I daydreamed of spending time with him, of him embracing me and telling me he loves me. But I started to lose hope after such a long wait.

I was in the dining room when a short, brown-skinned man with slanted eyes came in. Granny jumped up and gave him a big hug.

"Boy, you want to give me a heart attack? Why didn't you tell us you were coming?"

"Then it wouldn't be a surprise now, would it?"

"How long you here for?"

"Just for a day. It's a short visit," he said.

"You mean to tell me that after all this time, you're only giving me a doctor's visit?"

At the door, I gazed at the visitor, wondering who he was. Granny was so happy to greet him.

"Come and say hi to your father," Granny said.

Was I hearing right? It was the shock of my life. My mouth dropped as I stared. A rainbow of emotions colored my being; seven years old, and seeing my father for the first time. Paralyzed with apprehension and fear of what his reaction would be, it quelled my urge to run and embrace him. Not knowing the correct protocol for meeting a parent fed my hesitation. Trying hard to control my excitement and inner turmoil, I thought, should I burst out in laughter? Run and hug him and have him twirl with me in excitement? No, that may not be appropriate either. I erred on the side of caution, and so, I drifted awkwardly toward him.

"Hi," I said.

"Hi, big girl," he replied, and gave me a hug.

Shyly, I returned the hug.

"Go outside and play," Granny said.

Glancing back, I did not want to go outside, not now. Was I dreaming? Or was that really my father? Why wouldn't Granny leave me to stay there and gaze at him? My father, my very own father, was standing right there in front of me, at arm's length. This was the moment I had been waiting for, dreaming about. The moment to finally embrace him, tell him of all my cares, and hear him say he loved me for the first time. Because that's what fathers do, surely.

Taking a deep breath I floated along, telling myself, he came to look for me and only me. My thoughts drifted to my classroom and a smile came over my face. I fantasized about telling my classmates all about my awesome experience; he was no longer a figment of my imagination, he was real.

Patiently I waited, giving him all the time he needed to speak to Granny. My time to have his undivided attention was at my fingertips. At the corner post, I sat and stared towards the kitchen, my eyes fixed on the dining room window, not wanting to go too far because maybe, just maybe, he would come outside and call me. Under my breath I repeated, it's my father, it's my father.

Glancing at my arm, I ran my hand over my skin and smiled. He is brown, like me. I hid my grin under my hand and sighed deeply.

A while passed, but nothing happened. My turn seemed to have been taking forever. *Did he not want to spend the time with me as I did with him? What could be keeping him so long?*

Cautiously, I eased my way back to the kitchen to eavesdrop at the door, since Granny always said, "If you hear grown-ups talking, you stay away. A child should not be a part of a grown-up's conversation."

Granny's scolding words reached me at the door.

"Take care of your children, I tell you. You may not need them now, but when you grow old, you will need them, and if you haven't done anything for them, they will not be there for you when you reach old age."

Why is Granny telling him that? I wondered. *Of course I am going to be there for him when I grow up.* I slid away quietly, trying not to interrupt.

After their conversation, he went out and came back late. He sat on the porch with Granny and Grandpa. I was sent to bed. Early the next morning, I dashed to the kitchen, eager to spend some time with him. It would be our time now, for sure.

"Good morning, Granny. Did my papá wake up already?" I asked chirpily, smiling from ear to ear.

"Yes, child, your father left already."

"He left already?" I heard myself ask deep down in my throat, not believing my ears.

"Yes, he had to catch an early flight."

My bubble burst and my smile vanished, replaced by a shrugged shoulder and a heavy heart.

"But he just got here!"

"Yes, but he only came for one day."

"Did he tell you when my birthday is?"

"Child, your father came and left so quickly, I forgot to ask him about that. I will ask him next time."

Breakfast was not appealing that morning; I found it hard to chew or swallow. My energy was somehow zapped. I pushed away my plate and excused myself from the table. My shoulders drooped as I placed one foot in front of the other. On the porch, I emptied my mammies and spun them one after the other.

It was as if a stranger had come by for a day and left. My mind whirled with thoughts, as fast as the mammies were spinning. He only came to look for Granny and Grandpa, not me. I knew it. "He doesn't love me," I said under my breath. I had been fooling myself, building up false hopes, only to be left as broken as my shattered dreams. I should have known better. If he wanted to spend time with me, he would have visited before, or he would have asked for me to go and spend some time with him. But no, I meant nothing to him. Even my thoughts of telling everyone about my father's visit were now silenced. I would keep everything to myself.

Chapter Three

I daydreamed about meeting my mother. Meeting her would be a different experience than with my father, for sure. If only I could get to meet her, she would get to know me. Surely, she would love me.

Running errands and doing chores kept me busy, but not always out of trouble. I sat on the step when Granny said, "Go and get me some limes, and after you do that, I need you to clean the coop."

I stooped carefully under the tree to avoid the sharp prickles on the branches, a blue plastic bowl in hand. There were golden-yellow limes scattered on the ground, and plump ripe ones peeped through the leaves. I noticed on a branch, curled in a loop like a coil of rope, a whipping snake. My heart skipped a beat. It had a grayish-brown back and pale-yellow stomach. Grandpa said if I wanted to kill a whipping snake, I could catch it from the tail, swing it over my head, and then hit it against a tree, so it would not bite me. But I wouldn't do that this time. He was sleeping, and that was fine with me. I stepped away on tiptoes, hoping not to disturb his slumber, get out of harm's way, and deliver the limes.

Like a slap in the face, the foul smell greeted me at the entrance to the coop. Aged planks of uneven wood with large seams formed the walls. Four bamboo-like sticks leaned from the middle to the back wall, and four across served as a roost. Three hens nested on dried banana leaves in the boxes fixed to the wall.

Cleaning the coop gave me the heebie-jeebies. Stepping around on fowl poop, my nose crunched, as I held my breath, quickly inching my way to the door and heaping the poop to the side. Out of the coop, I took a good breath of air and then shouted, "Granny, I am finished!"

"Okay, take those two buckets and go to the beach and bring some fresh sand to put in there. And you make sure and go straight there and get back here quickly."

"Yes, ma'am," I replied, trying hard to control my grin, elated at the notion of going to the beach on my own, which was a rare occurrence except for the times I went to buy fish.

Off I went, buckets swinging back and forth as I scampered under the shade of the huge mango trees along the way. I knew the perfect spot, an unspoiled secluded area. My steps stopped at the edge of the grassy rise. The view was magical, and a patch of gorgeous white sand greeted me. One step further, my toes were covered in its cool embrace.

The water had never been this clear and beautiful before, as still as water sitting in a bowl, with not even a ripple. The white sand peeped through the clear shallow surface as the sunlight bounced off the tiny crystals mingled in the grains of sand like shimmers of diamond dust. My gaze fixed on the water while filling the buckets; like magic, it seemed to draw me closer with each step.

The warm water caressed my feet, inviting me to venture a little further, and then a little more. Before I knew it, I was completely submerged, swimming away, floating on my back, gazing at the clear blue sky as I twirled in paradise.

After a while, it dawned on me, I must get back. Out of the water I waded through the sand. My dress stuck to my legs, and water dripped to my feet and off the blue ribbons at the end of my braids. My heart skipped a beat at the realization that I was soaking wet.

"What I goin' do? What I goin' tell Granny?"

The mere thought made me shiver. *Why didn't I take my clothes off before going in? What do I do now?* I wondered.

I slid out of my dress and wrang the water out as much as possible, but that didn't help much.

Perhaps if I walk slowly, by the time I get home, it will be dry, I reckoned. But I knew it would not be sufficient time for my clothes to dry. I strolled along the main road before taking the shortcut through the bushes. Tiny drizzles fell on my arm. Oh, this is perfect, I said with a smile. It was like a blessing from above. I would tell Granny I got wet in the rain. What a perfect solution. When—

"Hey!" someone called.

I glanced around and caught sight of the dark-chocolate skin and the cotton-white hair of Mr. Sherman Brooks waving on his porch.

"Come here, an' te'k this piece a plastic to cova you self from the rain."

"No, it's okay," I replied.

"No, come and get this. You grandmadda nah goin' be happy wid you gettin' wet in the rain."

"Why can't people mind their own business? I don't need his help," I whispered under my breath.

"You need to cova from the rain so you don't get sick."

"Sick? Sick never hurt anyone," I said to myself.

The last time I was sick with a fever, I tried to use it as an excuse not to go to school, but Granny said, "Well, you will still have to go to school, because if you stay home, you will still have the feva, and you would miss class. If you go to school, you will have the feva, but you will not miss school. So, go and get ready for school."

But if Mr. Sherman saw Grandpa, he would tell him about this incident, for sure. There was no way out. Subdued, I said, "Okay."

At that moment the drizzle stopped and the sense of helplessness was real. I had to come up with another idea. Handing the plastic back to Mr. Sherman, I continued on. My mind raced to come up with a better excuse. The best one that came to mind was to say I fell in a puddle and had to go into the sea to rinse off. Yes, that's what I would say.

As I approached the house, my pace slowed to a crawl. Maybe I would not have to come up with an excuse at all if I could avoid her. That would be the best thing. I would go straight to the coop and start to spread the sand before she saw me.

I picked up speed, but as I crossed the window, to my horror, I heard, "Why did it take you so long to get back here with that sand? And why are you so wet?"

Her words had a paralyzing effect. Even my neck had difficulty moving my head to face her, and the words I practiced got stuck on my tongue.

"I, I, I fell in a puddle and had to go in the sea to rinse off."

Relieved I finished my sentence, I paused for her response.

"You had to go in the sea to rinse off, eh?" she repeated.

"Yes, ma'am,"

"Who you think you trying to fool? I was not born yesterday. And you rememba one thing. When you hide behind the door and do wrong, you may think you all alone and no one is seeing you. But just rememba God is behind that door with you, and he sees and knows everything. You get in that coop and spread that sand, and as punishment for goin' in the sea, you will not be able to go to the beach on Sunday, nor anytime soon."

Her speech came out like a sermon at church to a congregation of one.

"But, Granny!"

"Don't but me! You get that sand spread and quickly!"

Needless to say, Sunday came around and all I could do was get ready for church and wish for a swim in the sea.

Chapter Four

After a day at school and a long stroll home, sweat trickled down the side of my face. Our two-toned green island-style home glistened in the sun. The adjacent well provided fresh, clean water to the neighborhood and never went dry. Someone left the cover open. The huge, smooth rock lying flat on the bottom peeped through the crystal-clear water. My reflection looked back at me like a mirror, reminding me of how thirsty I was.

"Good evening," I said, entering the dining room.

Wiping her hands in her apron, Granny greeted, *"Good evening. Change your clothes and come and cut these coconuts for the chickens. And be quick."*

I gulped down a glass of water and got to the task.

From the dining room window, she supervised as I tossed the coconuts to the chickens. On my way back to the kitchen, I whistled a tune.

"You stop that whistling right now," she said. *"A lady does not whistle."*

I thought it strange that she would think that a lady could not whistle.

"Why not? I can."

"There are some things a lady doesn't do, and whistling is one of them. Do you ever hear a chicken crowing?"

"No, ma'am"

"Well, that's why a lady should not whistle."

It was a strange notion to me, but I could not argue. My thoughts drifted back to the incident at school, teacher Pearl's detailed description of a guardian and me not having a mother or father, her words still rested on my mind.

"Granny, how come I don't live with my mother or my father? How come they don't want me?"

"Who says they don't want you?"

"I only saw my father once, and I have never seen my mother. She never came to look for me ever? That means they don't want me."

"Never mind."

"One of these days she will come and look for you. Now go and do your homework."

Her explanation was not convincing. I had been waiting for a long time for one of those days she referred to, to materialize, but they never did. As I took out my books, I realized I had another report card to give to Grandpa.

"Oh, Teacher said to give you this."

"Put it there on the table and rememba to give it to your grandfather."

In anticipation of Grandpa's arrival, I stared up the road, waiting for him to appear. In the distance, a glimpse of his khaki shirt came up the little rise. I took off running to meet him.

He waited for me to reach just close enough to grab him. He gave a sudden swerve and increased his pace as he zoomed away.

"Boy, you slow. Catch me if you can."

His movement was effortless. He wasn't even running, and yet I could not catch him.

About to reach the gate, he turned around. I ran into his arms and he whizzed me over his shoulder as I chuckled.

Granny handed him my report card, which he carefully reviewed.

"I want to see your grades always looking like this. But I want you to know one thing. The first thing I am going to look for in your report card is not the academic grades. It will be your conduct. And if you have a bad grade in conduct, it will be me and you."

Conduct appeared on our report card as a subject. It depicted our behavior at school and was graded like any other subject. Grandpa was a strict disciplinarian and gave high importance to my behavior in the community, as well as at school.

"If for some reason you don't get a good grade in a subject because you can't understand it, then I will help you to get a better grade. But the day you bring me a bad grade in conduct because you are not paying attention, you will be in trouble."

He continued solemnly. *"You see this belt?"*

I stared wide-eyed. *"Yes, sir."*

Pointing to one side, he asked, *"What color is this?"*

"Black," I said.

Then, pointing to the other side, he asked, *"And what color is this?"*

"Blue," I replied.

"And that's how I am going to leave your ass if you bring me a bad grade in conduct; black and blue." I stared in awe, not missing a single word.

"There is no excuse for getting a bad grade in conduct. All you have to do is sit and pay attention. If you want to talk to friends, you wait until recess time. That is why recess time is there. Just rememba what *I said."*

I nodded. *"Yes, sir."*

At the time, I was puzzled at being scolded despite bringing home good grades, but later on, the lesson learned served me well. By paying attention in class, I learned a lot, which reduced my need for extensive note-taking and improved my recall during examinations.

"Do you have any homework?"

"I did it already."

After reviewing my homework with Grandpa, permission was granted to visit the neighbors.

Through the darkness, I whizzed to Ms. Mary's house. The light shone through the windows and onto the grass. The street in front was pitch-black. My friend Quecha, Ms. Mary's daughter who was two years older than me, sat in the living room. Thump, thump, thump, came a sound from the kitchen. It was Quecha's older brother, Fernando—Nando for short. His movements, impaired by his deformed leg, caused him to drop heavily on his left leg as he hopped along. His left arm curled in, also deformed from polio.

"Let's play Macho Parado," Quecha said.

"Bring the ball," said Nando.

Nando could not open his left hand, but was a good catcher. He gripped the ball to his chest. Other kids in the neighborhood joined in.

After all the running and jumping to dodge the ball, it was time to get home and get ready for bed. After my nightly prayer, I asked, *"Grandpa, would you cover me with the sheet, please?"*

He lifted the sheet high as it billowed over me. I curled up in a ball and waited for the sheet to fall, cool and nice on my skin. This was my favorite nighttime routine. The sheet fell like a shower of love, softly as snowflakes seen through the eyes of a child experiencing the phenomenon for the first time. I embraced the soothing effect of the hug I longed for.

The island did not have an electric company. Grandpa had a big generator, and every evening he turned it on and shared electricity with a few people in the neighborhood. At bedtime, he turned it off. After covering me, he took his flashlight and went outside. The noise from the generator stopped. The glow from his flashlight searched through the darkness and entered the house as I hugged my pillow.

Early the next morning, Kitty, my ginger cat, jumped on

the bed. She gave me the best massage ever, her paws soft and soothing. It was the best way to start my morning.

The delicious aroma of freshly brewed coffee reached me in bed.

"Granny, what you made for breakfast? Is it eggs and fritters?"

"How many times do I have to tell you not to forget your manners? Did I sleep with you?"

"Sorry, good morning. Is it eggs and fritters?"

"No, you had eggs already on Monday and you are not having eggs again today,"

"But, Granny, there are lots of eggs there."

"That doesn't matter. Too much of anything is not good for you, and a little of everything is good for you."

"Man!" I grumbled and pulled the chair, gobbled down my refried rice and beans, and ran out to take my bath.

At school, Miriam, one of my schoolmates, greeted me at the door. Her wide smile boasted her perfectly white teeth, a beautiful contrast next to her dark chocolate complexion.

"Come by me. I don't want Mario sitting by me," she said.

At recess, Miriam and I ran out to play. Brett and Mario shared a tangerine. Miriam ran next to them.

"Brett, can I have a peg?"

"No, peg yuh egg," he replied. (Egg referring to the male parts.) The children nearby chuckled and teased.

"Peg yuh egg, Miriam."

"That's what yuh get. Yuh should learn not to beg," another girl said, grinning.

"Don't worry," I said, pulling her towards me.

"My grandpa has a tangerine tree, and it has lots of tangerines. I will bring you some tomorrow. You don't have to beg him for anything."

My friend was being teased and ridiculed, a feeling I knew too well. I would not have it. No, not on my watch.

The next morning, about to step out to school, the tangerines came to mind. I had forgotten to ask Grandpa for them. It was too late now; he had already left.

The orange tangerines glistened in the sunlight amidst the green foliage. There was no way I could go to school without those beauties. Granny stood at the window.

"Granny, I need to get some tangerines to take to school for a friend."

"You will have to ask your grandfather when he gets back. You can't get to the tree. It is in the middle of the pigpen, and you can't go in there."

"Yes, I can. I can climb over the wire."

"No, there is a sow with pigs, and it will come after you."

"It's okay. I nah 'fraid ah dah pig."

"Whether you are afraid of it or not, I don't want you goin' *in there."*

"But..."

"No buts, you heard what I said."

"Man!" I frowned and hissed, not wanting to accept my predicament.

Most days I walked to school, but today, I stood at the roadside waiting for the new bus to arrive. My school bag dangled from my shoulder, and I was well-dressed in my school uniform— a pleated navy-blue skirt and white blouse. I glanced back. Granny was no longer at the window.

It was my chance. Crouched forward like Pink Panther on the prowl, I dashed past the window to the back of the house.

At the fence, I put my bag on the ground, lifted the top wire, bent under, and squeezed myself in between the wires, being careful not to get scratched by the sharp protruding spurs. The path was clear. No pigs in sight. This would be a breeze.

A branch almost brushed the ground, bringing the tangerines to my reach. Three tangerines in hand, and a blood-curdling grunt stopped me in my tracks. A brown sow raced forward. The hairs on her back stood straight up like porcupine quills. I dashed for the fence, and the loud squeal trailed behind me as I raced ahead at full force.

"Oh no!" I threw the tangerines over the fence and sailed over the lower barbed wire while holding the upper wire away

from my head. My heart raced like a galloping horse and I shook like a leaf on a windy day.

A piece of blue fabric dangled from the jutted prangs on the fence, the color dreadfully familiar. My glance dropped to my skirt. The front was fine, but a swift twist to take a good look at the back revealed my biggest fear. I stared in horror at what was left of my once-perfect skirt, now ripped beyond repair.

Oh! My gosh! My eyes drifted to the window, hoping Granny had not seen anything.

I dashed to the front of the house, just in time to hop on the bus. At school, the children gazed. Miriam ran over and twirled me around for a good look.

"Bev, wha' happ'n? Did a dog attack you?"

"No, I was trying to get the tangerines. A pig chased me and I got hooked in the barbed wire."

The look on Miriam's face was priceless; her eyes blared, her mouth ajar.

"Gee."

"I got you the tangerines, don't worry. You don't have to beg Brett for anything."

"Thank you!" she said as she took a long sniff at the tangerines.

"But you goin' be in trouble."

"No, I goin' be okay," I said.

I continued trying to convince myself of that notion as I sneaked to my seat to avoid the teacher.

"Bev! Why is your skirt torn like that?" she asked.

"My skirt?" I asked as if wondering what she was talking about.

"Aam, it got hooked into a barbed wire."

"And how did you manage that?" Sheepishly, I looked at the floor.

"Make sure to go home straight to your grandmother. I am sure she will want an explanation for that."

On my way home, I dawdled along, practicing all the ways I could possibly explain the torn skirt to Granny.

"Good evening."

With a frown on her face, she asked, *"What happened to you?"*

"Aam, my skirt got hooked in a barbed wire at school, and it tore."

"You went in the pigpen, didn't you?" She must have magical powers to know everything, I thought. Not being able to find a quick enough answer, I came clean.

"I wanted to get a tangerine for my friend."

"Yes. But didn't I tell you not to go in that pen? I specifically told you to wait for your grandfather. And don't you ever lie to me again, because a liar is a thief, and a thief is a murderer. Do you hear me?"

"Yes, ma'am."

"Now you come here." She grabbed my hand and practically dragged me to the bedroom. She took her cloth belt.

"This is goin' to hurt me more than it will hurt you."

"So, don't do it then."

"You have to be punished for the things you do wrong. What you did, you know was not right. You were disobedient, and therefore, you have to accept the consequences."

Up went her hand and as she brought it down, she said, *"Don't, you, do, that, again, do, as, you, are, told!"* Each syllable, a whip.

Each time she brought her hand down it hit my skirt. I skipped, trying to avoid the swipes.

Out the door she went as the last syllable was said. Relieved the ordeal was over, I smiled. How different it was when Grandpa beat me with his heavy black and blue leather belt.

She reported me to Grandpa as soon as he got home.

"Beverly!" he called.

My heart raced. Wrapped in fear, I moseyed apprehensively to find out what he wanted.

"Your grandmother told me what you did. You make sure that doesn't

happen again. If you do that again, it won't be your grandmother who beats you, it will be me. Do you hear me?"

"Yes, sir," I replied as I scampered away in case he reconsidered. For the rest of the evening I moved cautiously, trying my best to keep out of trouble; at least until tomorrow.

Chapter Five

It was a new day for new adventures, marbles in hand. I tried to spin them into my pre-carved holes when a tall ladder leaning on the side of the outside bathroom caught my eye. The small structure faced the kitchen, where Granny washed the dishes. On closer inspection, my hands gripped the ladder and my eyes drifted upward; my feet followed suit, climbing the steps one after the other as my mind questioned, *I wonder what it looks like up there?*

Feeling the urge to go a bit further, I found myself at the top of the ladder. Resting my palms on the rippled metal zinc was another incentive to go a bit higher. Surely, I could get up there and stand, I assured myself. And so, I did.

On the top of the roof, with extended arms, I swirled around like a plane. I took a deep breath, filled my lungs with clean, fresh air, and exhaled, enjoying my sense of accomplishment and relishing in the achievement of my incredible feat, basking in victory. Everything was beautiful, new, and fresh from this point of view.

Overhead, the clouds drifted across the clear blue sky. The deep-green mango leaves were at my fingertips, and a tinge of yellow undertone on the leaves of the star apple tree produced an interesting contrast. The vibrant purple of the star apples swayed ever so gently with every burst of wind.

Mindlessly, I made my way to the edge of the roof and looked down to ascertain my altitude. *Wow! I am so tall!*

At that moment, Granny appeared at the window and excitedly I yelled, *"Granny, look at me, I am really tall!"*

"Oh! My God! What are you doing up there? You get down from there this minute!"

Her screams jolted me out of my moment of leisurely bliss and right back into reality. I dashed for the ladder and made my way down at double speed, in total shock at her uncalled-for reaction.

Man! Now I am in trouble again. I don't know why she gets frightened about everything.

She went off on a rampage. She was short in stature, but a real firecracker when she got mad.

"Don't you ever climb that ladder again! I never want to see you up on that rooftop again, do you hear me? Don't you know, you could have fallen from there and hurt yourself or worse yet, killed yourself? Now you go straight to your room. I will have this out with your grandfather as soon as he gets here."

The mention of Grandpa made this infraction very serious indeed. *What does Grandpa have to do with this?* I thought as I made my way to my assigned chamber of punishment, and out of Granny's sight. My bed was tucked in the corner, and Grandpa's favorite canvas cot stood directly across. Two doors divided the area, one on the right coming from the small dining room, and the door on the left leading to Granny's bedroom.

I sat on my bed and waited for my demise, gazing at the billowing, snow-white curtain hanging halfway down the small window frame over Grandpa's canvas cot. The almost sheer curtains swayed ever so softly. A ray of sunlight illuminated the pillow and folded covers.

How could I be in trouble again? It was ludicrous. Trouble

would not leave me alone. It was my constant companion. Avoiding its path was futile; it always managed to catch up with me.

On the bed, I sat scanning around for anything that would take my mind off my impending doom, but there was nothing. I lay on the floor and looked under the beds; there was nothing. My eyes wandered out to the little dining room outside the door. The dining table with its white top and brown abstract design stood empty in the almost dark room. One window was open, but the other closed. Up high on a wall, a slender shelf held a small toy monkey, dressed in a red drummer boy uniform with gold trim and a pair of bronze cymbals. A couple of times I had climbed on the chair and then on the windowsill to reach it, being careful not to touch the winding piece at the back because it clapped the cymbals and made a loud banging noise. Once I accidentally set it off, announcing my interference, and Granny went ballistic.

"Put that toy back this minute! I don't want you playing with that toy. It belongs to your aunt Edna and I don't want it destroyed. How did you reach it anyway? Look how high I have that thing!"

I better not touch that today; I am in enough trouble as it is.

Oh, how I wished for a book! On the shelf next to the monkey stood a Bible and a big blue dictionary. These were the only books I could find in the whole house, but they were in English. Attempting to read English was too much of a challenge. My classes at school were in Spanish, and so I sat nervously waiting for Grandpa to arrive and announce my fate, wondering how serious my infraction was this time. Based on Granny's reaction it was dire.

How many lashes would this transgression cost me? I wondered. The sound of Granny's voice reached my ear and I perked up. Grandpa had arrived, and Granny was having it out with him before he even reached the dining room door.

"Malcolm!" she exclaimed. *"How many times have I told you not to leave dangerous things lying around? You left that ladder leaning up*

against the bathroom, and do you know that child climbed that ladder and was standing on the edge of that roof? What would have happened if she had fallen from there today? God forbid. Please lay that ladder flat on the ground and don't leave it leaned up against that building again."

She scolded him as she would me and I feared the worst.

"Okay, old lady, she didn't get hurt, and that's all that matters."

His words were like manna from heaven, as if a chorus of angels were singing hallelujah and I found myself in the middle of their glorious light. His magnificent response lifted me out of my fear as if floating on clouds. My shoulders relaxed and I sighed in relief. It was a close call, but Grandpa was simply the best.

Through the door, I caught a glimpse of him. His head brushed the doorframe while Granny barely reached his shoulder. He slipped off his brown work boots and removed his khaki cap. His white hair molded to his head. I pulled back quickly to avoid being seen.

He went back outside to pick star apples using his beige fruit bag.

At the door, I stood in hopes of being released from my punishment. Not being ordered back inside was a good sign my punishment was over. Grandpa lowered the bag next to his milky white feet and emptied some star apples into the bucket just as I approached him.

"See, there is a purple one over there," I pointed.

"We don't need any more right now. We can leave those for another time."

He handed me one, bright purple fading into a light green at the stem. At the kitchen sink, I washed it well and brought it back to Grandpa to cut for me. He took out his pen knife and cut a deep circle, removing the stem at the green spot. A milky juice surfaced and I brought it to my mouth and squeezed, releasing the jelly-covered seed into my mouth.

"Mmm," I said, tasting the sweetness of the jelly as I

sucked the seed clean. I continued squeezing until there were no more seeds left in the fruit.

"Don't you eat too close to that skin or it will constipate you. That's enough," Granny said.

Grandpa sat on the step with a basin of water, washing his face and arms. He saw me watching him and said, "Look!" and pushed out his teeth, then quickly pulled them back. I looked closer.

"Do that again, Grandpa." And so, he did.

"Now you do it," he said, watching as I made every effort to push my teeth out with my tongue while he threw his head back and laughed.

"How do you do that?" I asked.

"It's magic," he said with a grin as he threw out the water. I kept trying to get my teeth out as he did, but my efforts were futile.

Being around Grandpa brought me joy. He didn't tell me I was in his way, and he didn't mind taking me with him to do things. Other children had a mother and a father, brothers and sisters, but I had Grandpa. I imagined it must be very nice to have siblings, but Grandpa was simply the best; better than all the rest.

Earlier in the week, Grandpa cut a big bunch of red bananas and hung them in the corner of the dining room. When the bananas were ripe, Granny picked one and gave it to me. It was delicious.

"Granny, can I have another ripe banana please?"

"No, you had one already. Be satisfied," she said.

A frown stiffened my face as I glanced at the bunch of forbidden fruit and back at Granny, making every effort to suppress my desire to say she was mean but could only sulk and mope my way back outside in silence. Later in the evening, a banana fell to the ground. I ran and grabbed it, reluctantly handing it to Granny.

"Go ahead and have it," she said.

"*Ooh!*" I peeled it bit by bit to quickly indulge in its sweetness while keeping my eyes on the nice, big, red bunch in the corner.

The next day, Granny gave me another one. Later that evening, my appetite for more was nudging but I didn't bother to ask, knowing very well what the response would be. I meandered into the living room and gazed at the lovely bunch, hoping it would be so kind as to let another one fall to the ground, but nothing.

Granny was busy in the kitchen. I sneaked along the wooden partition closer to the bunch, looked around to see if Granny was looking, then moved a little closer still. Pausing next to the bunch, I "accidentally" gave it a good bounce with my shoulder. To my surprise, bop, bop, bop, the bananas fell to the ground one after the other. Granny appeared at the door just as I dashed away from the bunch. She looked at the bananas on the floor and then back at me.

"They fell," I said, shrugging my shoulder, capturing the expression on her face and the eight bananas on the floor. I immediately scolded myself for being a tad too forceful with my bounce, which could have resulted in a catastrophic outcome. Acting quickly to right the situation and avoid an undesired outcome, I scurried to pick them up and demonstrate how helpful I could be.

"Put them on the table," she said, giving me a skeptical look. *"Take one and go outside and play."*

"Wow, that was close," I said as I dashed outside, relieved at having averted what I deemed to be an act for certain punishment, smiling as I peeled my banana.

It was customary every Saturday for Granny to bake some sort of pastry. This Saturday evening, while sitting outside, my nose caught the drift of a delicious smell coming from the kitchen. It was heavenly. Drawn to the kitchen, I asked, *"Granny, what you baking?"*

"I am baking a ripe banana heavy cake."

"Mmm," I said. *"Can I have a piece?"*

"No, it has to cool first. It's too hot."

Later that evening, I asked again, *"Granny, is it cool yet?"*

She went ahead and cut a piece and handed it to me.

"Mmm!" I took the first bite while inspecting the bits of yellow, mingled in with pink, and tiny threads of banana in the smooth texture. The spices enhanced the sweet smell of the bananas even more. It was sweetened to perfection; my taste buds celebrated every bite, as it was beyond delicious. The slice disappeared in three bites. I could not wait for tomorrow, to relive the experience again.

Chapter Six

Granny was seated at the table when I wrapped my arms around her.

"Judas!" she said.

It was her usual response to my hugs. "*Why does Granny always call me that old ugly English name?*" I asked myself as I stepped around and placed my hand softly on her head. She jerked away.

"Don't touch my hair. You know I don't like people playing with my hair. Go and ask Miss Mary if she can comb your hair for me."

My hair damp, dressed in my Sunday best, I headed up the road to our neighbor Miss Mary. Before long, I left with a head full of bouncing curls.

In the classroom, child-size wooden chairs neatly spaced apart on the wooden floor were all perfectly aligned. Large open windows lined the walls and brought in the morning light and island breeze. Quietly, we listened to the story our Sunday school teacher told, about a fellow who betrayed Jesus. His name was *Judas.*

My jaw dropped and my heart sank. The teacher described this horrible person. *How could Granny compare me with someone as horrible as this man?"*

After Sunday school, I avoided everyone, feeling as if they all knew my secret. I did not want anyone to see my tears, in my effort to suppress my emotions. Thankfully, Granny didn't come to church that Sunday.

On my way home, I stepped off the main road and onto the beach. The ugly brown seagrass was stacked in random rows on the shore. The sea breeze wiped the tears from my face. *Why would she call me Judas? It was as if she responded to every hug by saying, I despise you, you are repulsive and a horrible person. What did I do to cause everyone to push me away? It had to be bad when even my mother and father didn't want me, and now I knew what Granny thought of me too.*

On the trunk of a fallen coconut tree, I rested and gazed out over the ocean, my thoughts drifting out in the distance in search of answers. As if somehow the truth of my existence would float above the waves and bring me acceptance, love, and belonging. Sadness weighed heavily on my shoulders. There I was, surrounded by beautiful, powdery-white sand and azure-blue sea. Alone in paradise feeling gray within. But yes, there was freedom to cry. There was no one to witness my whimper, no shame to hide.

If only I could meet my mother, things would be different. If only I had some time with her, she would get to know me. What my relatives say are all lies. She does love me! My inner voice made its point. After all, they were my people. But how could I reach them? When would I be able to go?

As the days went by, the hugging stopped. I did not want to hear Granny call me Judas anymore. And as she never hugged me on her own accord, there were no more hugs.

One evening, with a piece of paper in hand and an old schoolbook, I wrote a letter in the best penmanship possible.

"Dear Mom, I hope you are well. I am your daughter,

Beverly. I would like to meet you one day. Would you come and look for me? Why did you give me away?"

On the bed, I sat and stared at my note. I had no way of sending my pretend letter, so I hid it under the mattress. "*Neither she nor my father even remember I exist anyway,*" I told myself, and walked out the door.

At Sunday school the following Sunday, my gaze drifted through the window. The palm leaves swayed under the golden rays of yet another sunny day on Corn Island and the sky was a dainty blue. It was chorus time, and we sang my favorite song:

"The birds up in the tree top sing their song
The flowers in the garden, all day long
The angels up in heaven, praise him too,
So why shouldn't I, why shouldn't you
Praise him too."

The teacher stood at the front of the class with the lesson book in her hand, about to start the message for the day. She paused and looked in my general direction.

"Do you know that Jesus loves you?"

I spun around to see who was so lucky.

Not being able to tell to whom she was talking, I looked back at her.

"Bev, I am talking to you. Do you know Jesus loves you?" she repeated.

"Me?"

"Yes, you. Jesus loves you."

What a revelation that was. No one had ever told me they loved me before. Nor had anyone said someone else loved me either. I could not believe my ears. My heart leaped as I stared at her, puzzled. That Sunday, I left Sunday school floating on air, repeating to myself,

"Jesus loves *me*, Jesus loves *me*." It did not matter if no one else loved me anymore. I knew Jesus loved me, and that was all that mattered.

In my room, I sang:

"Jesus, knock, knock, knock, at the door of my heart,
Jesus, knock, knock, knock, at the door of my heart,
Jesus, knock, knock, knock, at the door of my heart,
open and let him in."

After the song, I said,

"Jesus, you know, you need to open the door and come into my heart yourself 'cause I don't know how to open it. But I want you to come in."

I whispered, *"You know it is only me and you, 'cause you are the only one who loves me."*

Every once in a while, I traveled to that somber world. A sad and dreary place void of love that spoke of loneliness, rejection, and abandonment. It zapped my energy and stole my joy. It robbed me of my strength and made me weak, frail, and listless. Its atmosphere was dark and gloomy, where a smile was swapped for a frown, where tears were free to flow.

To be released required a deep breath, inner strength, and a desire to push forward as if rising from underwater to burst through into the light and gasp for air. To wipe away the tears and face a new day. Knowing Jesus loved me made all the difference in the world and gave me hope for a better tomorrow.

Granny called.

I went to the table, and lunch was set. The delicious aroma of stewed beef greeted me at the door. My favorite. On the table on my plate was a portion of rice and beans cooked in coconut milk, a boiled green banana resting in a pool of gravy from a delicious-looking portion of beef falling off the bone. In front of my plate was my red plastic glass filled with lemonade. As usual, there were so many bowls in front of Granny and Grandpa. One bowl with beef, one bowl with rice and beans, one bowl with banana, and an empty plate in front of them both. They also each had an empty glass and a mug of lemonade.

"Granny, why did you put so many bowls of food in front of Grandpa? Why you don't put the food on his plate like mine?"

"Because he is the head of the household, and he gets to choose what and how much he wants to eat. It is the way it is supposed to be done."

We proceeded to eat. The rice and beans and beef were lip-smacking. Granny was the best cook in the whole, wide world. Then I reached for my lemonade.

"No. Eat your food first," Granny said. *"You always drink your drink, then you don't finish your food."*

My glass was now a memory of Frank's words.

"Why do I have my own plate and glass?" I asked. Eager to disprove my cousin's remarks with Granny's response.

"Because it is best to have your own. It is not good to share your glass. That way, you don't get germs from other people."

There it was. She used the offending word, *germs*. They were right. Perhaps she did have this talk with them. Perhaps she also felt I had germs. The sinking feeling washed over me like a dark shadow.

"Can I have my drink now, please? I goin' to *choke if I don't get some drink."*

Tears welled up in my eyes. Grandpa saw and said, *"Do you want something to cry for?"*

"No, sir," I replied while wiping away my tears. He did not know that my tears weren't because I could not drink my drink, but because of what Frank had said. But I would not make him any wiser.

"Okay, take one sip," Granny said. After a nice, long sip, hoping it would wash away my sadness and help me to pull back my tears, I relaxed and finished everything on my plate. Afterward, Granny cut a nice big ripe mamey for dessert. It had two big, dark-brown seeds and the flesh was nice and red and deliciously sweet.

On yet another Sunday after church, people dressed in long white gowns strolled across the road and down the narrow pathway leading to the beach for the Baptism service. The bright, sunny sky mirrored the blue of the ocean. Giant-sized, smooth, black rocks lined the front of the beach while the water washed against them.

The younger folks opted to watch the immersion service from the top of the rocks. One by one the folks in white moseyed out to the ocean while the congregation sang:

"Yes, we'll gather at the river
The beautiful, the beautiful river
Gather with the saints at the river
That flows by the throne of God."

The pastor put one hand on a lady's back and the other on her elbow as she held her nose. The Pastor said, *"I baptize you in the name of the Father, of the Son, and of the Holy Spirit."* He ducked her under. When he brought her back up, the congregation clapped and shouted.

"Praise the Lord! Hallelujah!"

I touched Granny and said, *"I want to be baptized too. Can I ask the pastor to baptize me too?"*

"No."

"But why? I want to be baptized too."

"No, because you are too small, and you don't understand."

"Yes, I understand. The Bible says you are to be baptized, and so I want to be baptized."

"When you get bigger."

Folding my hands, I pouted. *"Granny thinks I don't understand anything, and I do,"* I grumbled.

At home, we had lunch. Blackie, our black Border Collie mix, sat up straight looking at Grandpa. He threw a piece of his chicken in the air and Blackie swiftly caught it. Popita, our brown Corgi mix, searched under the table for scraps. With a freshly eaten chicken leg in my hand, I teased her by pretending to hand her the bone, and each time she tried to take it, I pulled it back. I did this several times, then one of the times instead of trying to grab the bone, she grabbed my big toe. I threw her the bone and kicked and screamed.

"What happened?" Grandpa asked.

"Popita bit my toe." A tiny bubble of blood appeared on my toe.

"Look, look! I told you she bit me."

"Well, that will teach you not to tease her. I saw you teasing her. And if you can't hear, you will feel," Grandpa said.

"There is a saying that says, if you play with the puppy, the puppy will lick your mouth," Granny said.

Grandpa got up, cleaned my toe, and put a bandage on. I frowned at Popita as I went to the room.

One morning, I overheard Granny. *"I will get the spare room ready."*

"Why you goin' get *the spare room ready?"* I asked, worried that Frank would be visiting again.

"Your aunt Delcy and Victor will be here in a few days. We need to get the room ready for them."

I had mixed emotions about the news. *"Will it be like Aunt Edna's visit?"*

Grandpa went outside and I followed.

"Grandpa, where you goin'?"

"I'm going to get some bit an' sweet for your grandmother."

"Why they call it bit an' sweet?"

"Because it's a mix between lime and orange. It's big like an orange, but as sour as a lime. Some people call them Seville Orange."

"Oh, that's why you have a bag?"

"Yes. What did your grandmother give you to eat, parrot backside or something?"

"No, she gave me chicken."

I lifted my legs high to weave through the thick bush and keep up with Grandpa. It was a small tree, but it was loaded with bit an' sweet. We filled the bag and took them to Granny to make a bit an' sweet drink, which is similar to lemonade.

Granny and Grandpa liked to have visitors, especially my aunts and cousins. My aunts didn't visit often, which made Granny even more excited when they did. We dusted the vanity in the room, wiped the mirror, changed the curtains, swept and mopped the floor, changed the linens, and put clean towels in their room, all in anticipation of their arrival.

Chapter Seven

Grandpa went to the airport to meet Aunt Delcy and her husband, Victor. Aunt Delcy worked as a nurse in Chinandega. When she arrived, she sat with Granny around the dining room table and talked and talked. Her husband, Mr. Victor, like Granny, was also of Chinese descent. Her surname was Chang, and his surname was Siu. He sat on the porch with Grandpa while I strolled around in the yard.

Granny called, *"You rememba the lady we took the cloth to, to make your dress?"* Granny asked.

"Yes, ma'am."

"Do you think you can find where she lives?"

"Yes, ma'am."

"Go and ask her if the outfit she is making for you is ready. It better be ready, because I gave her that cloth over a year ago."

Running through the door, I heard her yell, *"And be careful on that road!"*

"Yes, ma'am."

The lady's house was what seemed miles away. I ran most of the journey. It was always better to run because you get wherever you wanted to go a lot faster. While crossing a bridge, I stopped and held onto the rail to take in the view.

The gold and orange hue of the setting sun peeped above the mangroves on the horizon and doubled in the reflection on the dark, murky water that mirrored the clouds in the sky. Seagulls floated above, complementing the view, and the ocean breeze permeated the atmosphere and the palpable smell of seaweed in the air.

I examined the water below and spotted the bubbles rising to the surface. My eyes searched to catch the view of a fish but only caught a glimpse of some passing jellyfish, so I continued my journey.

Granny was happy to see me carrying a bag when I returned.

"Well, it's about time it's ready," she said. *"You will wear that to church tomorrow."*

Grandpa was in the room, nailing a white sheet to the wall. Puzzled I asked, *"Grandpa, wha' you doing? Why you puttin' a sheet on the wall?"*

"This is so we can see some slides tonight."

Victor was busy setting up a contraption I had never seen before, with weird-looking wheels and shiny ribbons.

"Mr. Victor, what's that?"

"This is a projector," he said.

"A projector? Wha' you do with that?"

"This is for us to watch a picture on the wall later."

Eager to see this phenomenon, I stared.

Once everything was set up and ready, chairs were set facing the wall. I brought the small rocking chair and set it next to the rest. Victor rolled the tape.

My mouth dropped at the novelty. Aunt Delcy roamed around in a park wearing a baby pink jacket and bell foot pants; her hair nicely combed in a '60s vintage beehive with a line of pearls at the top, like a tiara fit for a princess. She laughed, her hands extended as she balanced herself on the edge of a water fountain. I could not believe my eyes. It was like in the movies, and she was the movie star.

Having been to the movies once before, to see a cowboy movie, this seemed even better. Wide-eyed, I watched in awe, to capture their every move. These were people I knew. How could they do that?

Then suddenly, across the screen, a huge creature appeared. I gasped and glared. My fingers gripped the rails, my back pressed against the back of the chair. The mouth of the huge creature opened wide, exposing its sharp white teeth, wide nostrils, and a long red tongue that looked like fire blazing from the mouth. Big, blaring eyes and two horns, then the huge, long body slithered across the screen like a gigantic snake.

"*What's that?*" I mumbled.

"It's a dragon. We attended a Chinese parade in New York City. We had a good time there," Victor said.

Grandpa saw the look on my face and said, *"Well, you know this dragon is going to come and get anyone who wets their bed tonight."*

"Now that's for sure," Granny said.

"I not goin' wet my bed," I said, but didn't want to go to bed either, just in case, but Granny sent me anyway.

"I not goin' sleep tonight," I said, seated on my bed.

"Let's see how long you can stay sitting there. Don't be silly. Go to your bed," Granny said.

I gave in and went to sleep.

The next morning, I was happy having not wet my bed and not being attacked by the dreadful dragon.

We got ready for church. Granny called, *"Bev, come here, let me see how your outfit looks on you."*

Proud of my new look, I posed. My brand-new white blouse tucked into my yellow skirt. The matching yellow straps fit nicely over my shoulders. A little black ribbon tied in a bow at the neck completed the look. Boasting a big smile, I waited to hear a compliment.

But instead, I heard, *"I don't believe that woman. I gave her that material over a year ago. And I can't believe that after waiting so long for this outfit, that lady didn't even take into consideration this child would have grown, after all this time. Look how short that hem is. How much wear will she get out of this? She should at least have let her try on the outfit before she gave it to her. Now, I watched her measure the length of that skirt, and it was surely not this short—"*

"Come on, let us take some pictures," Aunt Delcy interrupted. *"You can't cry over spilled milk. No need to send your pressure up."*

I wondered what the fuss was about. My new outfit seemed fine to me. A little short, yes, but who cared? I just wanted a compliment, which in the end didn't come, but all is well that ends well.

We went to the front of the house; the bright sunrays provided the perfect lighting. Aunt Delcy's tummy was big, but she was radiant in her baby-pink maternity dress. Granny in her light-blue Sunday dress and Grandpa and Victor also looking the part. Victor took a couple of pictures of Granny and Grandpa. Aunt Delcy joined them in a shot also, and Victor snapped the pictures.

Aunt Delcy was walking away when Granny said, *"Delcy, wait. I want a picture with Bev too."*

Aunt Delcy sighed.

"Come, Bev," Granny said. *"Stand next to me here."*

We posed as Victor took the picture.

"Victor, would you take a picture of Bev by herself, please?" I was already standing on the stairs.

"Look here," he said. I smiled and click! The picture was taken.

My very first picture—or at least the first one I knew about, as I had not seen myself in a picture before and could not wait to see what I would look like in a photo. After the photo shoot, we went to church, but Grandpa and Victor stayed at home. Later that evening, the guests were packed and ready to head back.

Aunt Delcy was a nurse, and that gave me the idea of becoming a doctor. I would have nurses like Auntie Delcy working for me. The notion brought a smile to my face.

In Sunday School, the teacher asked, *"Who would like to say your memory verse this Sunday?"*

Up went my hand. *"Me, me!"*

"No, Beverly, give someone else a chance."

Glancing around, I said, *"But they don't want to say it. I will."*

"You said it last Sunday."

With drooping shoulders and a sad face, I sank into my chair, watching my chance of winning another little Christmas book fade away. The teacher gave a tiny Christmas book as a reward to whoever knew their memory verse. This was my whole reason for making sure I knew my memory verse every Sunday. The little books only had a few pages, and sadly, they were written in English and not what I wanted. But anything is better than nothing. The last time I won *Rudolph the Red-Nosed Reindeer*. I hoped maybe this time it would be in Spanish, which was the language I read. Spanish was the official language in Nicaragua, and the language taught in the schools. There were no libraries at the school—or on the whole island, for that matter.

The islands are located 43 miles east of the Caribbean coast of Nicaragua and consist of two islands, Corn Island, the bigger of the two, and Little Island, the smallest. Corn Island, with a size of five square miles, boasted a population of around 2,500 inhabitants at the time.

The only book I had was my textbook *Paquito*, which I read repeatedly. The depictions at the beginning of each story pulled me in. I especially liked the chapter about a boy stepping on stones as he crossed a stream of running water. It seemed difficult for him to cross over to the other side, as the rocks were spaced far apart. The water splashed against the smooth rocks and they looked slippery. His short legs leaped, barely reaching the other rock as he landed on a slippery slope. He looked ahead at the river edge and made every effort to reach the other side.

I asked myself, "*Would he make it over?*" I thought of being in a similar predicament, looking ahead in expectation and wondering; would I make it over to that place I longed to be? A place to belong. The place where I would find my people.

To travel through pages of fantasy to distant lands, to a place like heaven, a place flowing with milk and honey, was a pleasant dream. A place filled with love and laughter, where children ran and played. To learn of other children's adventures in a book, I was free from my limitations, free from not being good enough. In a book, the possibilities were endless.

At church, the choir sang:

"Holy, Holy, Holy
Lord God almighty!
Early in the morning
Our song shall rise to thee.
Holy, Holy, Holy
Merciful and mighty,
God in three persons
Blessed Trinity."

It was my favorite hymn. Sitting next to Granny, I folded my handkerchief into a flower, then a hammock with two pretend babies in it, and rocked the two little babies back and forth. Granny whispered, *"Stop playing with that handkerchief and pay attention."*

On our way home, my arm wrapped around Granny's to gain the benefit of the shade under her umbrella.

"I told you before to stop playing with your handkerchief in church and pay attention to the pastor. One of these days, he goin' call to you for not paying attention."

At home, Grandpa had taken out the red-striped hammock. In the cool shade under the mango tree, he rocked.

"Hi, Grandpa, you want me to rock you?"

"No, I'm enjoying a little bit of tranquility. I don't need to be rocked."

I scampered inside to quickly change and come back to keep him company.

A few Sundays after, Pastor read the Scripture, and I went back to folding my handkerchief when, clearly, I heard him say, *"Beverly, Beverly, I say unto you."*

I jumped to my feet and shouted to the top of my voice, in a military style, *"Yes, sir!"*

The pastor laughed suddenly, and out onto the pulpit went his teeth. The whole congregation burst out in laughter; Granny included. It took a while before everyone composed themselves.

"You see? That's why I told you to pay attention. You were playing with that handkerchief again."

"But he called me," I said.

"No," Granny chuckled. *"He said, 'Verily, verily I say unto you.' But, as usual, you were not paying attention."*

I slid into the pew and looked around sheepishly with all eyes on me as the chuckle continued. Now even Pastor was laughing. I ducked lower. *Oh, how I wish the service would be over soon, to get away from the embarrassment.*

It took a while before the chuckles subsided and Pastor continued with his sermon. Granny was laughing even while we were on our way home.

"That will teach you to pay attention in church next time."

Chapter Eight

While having breakfast one morning, we heard a man calling, "Delivery!"

Grandpa looked outside. "It's a telegram," he said.

The man handed him a beige piece of paper. Grandpa signed a book and came inside while unfolding the paper.

Granny picked up her apron as if wiping her hands while gazing at Grandpa's reaction.

Grandpa was pale in the face when he said, "It's Henningston."

Henningston was Aunt Edna's eldest son. He was eighteen years old and Granny's favorite grandson. Granny wanted him to move to Corn Island, but she said he had a better opportunity for his education in León. My mind went back to the last time he visited.

I recalled him saying to Granny, "Granny, when are you going to make some good crab soup?"

"When you bring the crab," she said, smiling.

"Okay, I am going to get some crab. Grandpa, can we go crabbing?"

"Sure, son, whenever you're ready."

That night, each had a crocus bag and flashlight in hand. Grandpa put on his black rubber boots, which he had fashioned to his liking by cutting off the top part of the boots, following the curve of the original design. Now it looked more like a shoe with a curved standing tongue than a boot.

"Can I come with you?" I asked.

"No. You will get in the way," Grandpa said.

"No, I won't. I can hold the flashlight."

"No, we don't need anyone holding the flashlight. Besides, we will be walking close to the rocks, and it will be too dangerous. You stay home with your grandmother. She needs the company."

They faded into the darkness behind a small spot of light that led them through the narrow path, and my envy trailed behind. My consolation came in the realization of Granny's desperate need for company and her requirement for me to step in. She needed me.

On the porch, fully engaged in my new role, we watched the passersby way into the night.

"Come on, let's get to bed."

"But they are not here yet. We have to wait for them."

"It's past your bedtime, and we don't know how long it will be before they get back."

"But I am not sleepy."

"You may not be, but I am. Come on."

Reluctantly, I dawdled along in my effort to extend the time before reaching my bed. Not long after resting my head on the pillow, the sound of voices in the dining room caught my ear and I sprang to my feet. Bursting with glee, delighted not to have fallen asleep, I dashed to the kitchen. The brown crocus bags rested in the galvanized metal wash basins.

"Can I see!? Can I see!?"

Henningston opened a bag and took out a live crab, being careful to avoid the claws. He held it up. The two eyes stuck up in the air like the tips of matchsticks, but shiny. I marveled at how different they were from the land crabs that roamed around in the yard. Land crabs were gray, dull, and ugly, but these were bright pink and vibrant. Their backs were flat, and their legs wiggled.

"You see, these are the two fins." He pointed to the two lower legs that looked like small paddles. "This is what they use to swim with," he said. He reached into the bag and took out a lobster. "Check this one out."

"Wow, that one is huge!" I said. It was a spiny rock lobster. He held it from the back and the pink creature flapped its tail under. His two long tentacles moved around as if inspecting the place. Grandpa was happy about their catch.

"We got some good whelks too," Grandpa said to Granny, who also came out to look. He showed her the whelks in the bag. They had dozens of them.

"Come on, you have seen enough. Get to bed, or you won't want to get up in the morning," Granny said.

Satisfied with having seen everything, I complied and hopped into bed.

The next day, Granny called Ms. Vanji to help her with the cooking. She balanced a huge pot on three big rocks in the backyard, started a fire then proceeded to make the soup with herbs and spices as the wind carried the smoke to the heavens. The aroma of crab soup filled the air and Henningston grabbed a big bowl. Granny sent soup to the neighbors and I cracked the crab's legs and claws and took my time eating the sweet, pink flesh. What a treat we had!

I was brought back to present day when Grandpa said, "It is not good. Henningston is gone."

Granny dropped to her seat as if she had no strength in her legs. "Oh no, what happened?" Granny asked.

"He was hit by a bus."

"But how?"

"I don't know much. I need to make arrangements to go to León. I don't think you would be able to come now. Beverly is in school."

"Yes, you go," Granny said.

My energy evaporated. The smile was erased from my face, and I felt a sudden heavy feeling in my chest. The tears rolled down Granny's face. Grandpa turned and looked through the window while wiping his eyes with his handkerchief. He left quietly. Through the window, I gazed as he faded away into the distance.

Granny went into the room and put a suitcase on the bed. She moved at a crawl, as if in a daze, slowly placing Grandpa's clothes into the suitcase. Grandpa came back a while later.

"The only flight to Managua leaves tomorrow at seven in the morning. I got a ticket. I sent a telegram back to Edna, telling her we got the message and I would be coming tomorrow."

Our existence was now coated in gray; we operated through a gloomy haze. Even the sounds of Granny and Grandpa's voices and words uttered were quiet and seemed to require great effort.

Grandpa left the next morning. Ms. Vanji came to help. Granny was quiet and cried often. A week went by before Grandpa got back. We listened attentively to his recount of the dreadful events on his return.

"I got there in time for the funeral," he said.

"What happened?" Granny asked.

Grandpa went on to explain, "Edna said he was in bed when he heard Ivania and Juanita saying they were going to the movies. He did not want them to go to the movies alone. He got up and got dressed and walked with them. Juanita and Ivania were in front of him when a guy came out of the bushes and grabbed Juanita. Henningston grabbed the guy and they fought. Another guy came out of the bushes and while one held his hands at his back, the other punched him under his chin and threw him. His head fell off the sidewalk just at the curve of the road. A bus was passing at that moment and crushed his head. Everything happened so fast. There was nothing anyone could do.

The lighting was dim in that area and the two guys had a motorbike hidden in the bush. They ran off before anyone could stop them. There is an investigation going on, but God knows if they will ever find out who did this."

Granny and I listened quietly; the image of the dreadful event rolled through my mind like in a horror movie.

"The next time we go to León, you will be able to visit the grave," Grandpa said. Granny nodded.

"The girls are devastated," he continued. "They feel it was their fault because if they didn't want to go to the movies that night, he would be here. He was just a loving and caring brother and wanted to protect his sisters. I told them it was not their fault. The ones to blame are those criminals who wanted to harm them. There are such unexpected turns in life. A life cut so short for no reason."

Granny gazed in silence at Grandpa as he spoke. The corners of her mouth and shoulders drooped as she listened.

Draped in sadness, I watched as if the whole event was unreal. I never heard of someone so young dying before, let alone someone as close as my own cousin. It was like watching my emotions floating down into a deep, dark pit.

Outside, the chickens cackled and the clouds drifted across the sky as if nothing had happened. Life went on as usual, but inside, it was as if the lights had gone out and the household mourned in darkness.

Chapter Nine

Climate-wise, there were two seasons on Corn Island; hot, and rainy. But fruit-wise, we had as many seasons as there were fruits.

I loved these seasons, but there was a downfall. Every year, just before mango season and pear season—we called avocados pears, as we did not have the traditional American pear—Granny said it was important for me to take a laxative, to be cleaned out, in order to prevent boils or sores from partaking excessively of these delicacies.

One morning, she prepared my favorite breakfast—ripe banana fritters. As she mashed the ripe bananas and added the flour, I asked, "Can I lick the bowl when you are finished?"

"No, eating this raw flour is not good for you."

"But you let me lick the bowl when you make cakes."

"Yes, but I don't want you eating this raw flour."

I could not understand her logic, but I decided not to take the argument any further and wait for the golden-brown fritters and sunny-side-up eggs, which proved to be a great delight.

After breakfast, about to dash outside for one of my

morning explorations, she called. Turning around brought me to a not-so-welcome sight. There she stood with a dreaded cup of senna tea. She came closer; too close for comfort. The cup was almost at my lips. The thought of the bitter, repulsive taste and the awful smell caused my face to grimace and my shoulders to tense.

"Come on, drink it."

My fingers twisted in a ball as I looked on sheepishly.

"Come on. I don't have the whole morning," she said, handing me the dreaded red cup. "This is mango and pear season; you have to get your clean-out."

"But . . ."

She helped my hand to my face and at the first sip, I gagged.

"Tit Ive!" someone called. It was the sound of deliverance. I was relieved when Granny rested the cup on the table, took off her apron, and went through the door.

Reaching for the cup, I dashed its contents out the window and made my way to the kitchen. The room was starved for sunlight, but through the dimness, the bowl with remnants of batter was visible. I brought the spoon to my mouth for a good lick. Instantly, I felt a sting, which caused the spoon to drop as I covered my mouth while spotting a swarm of biting ants.

I sprinted to my room, making distance between me and the scene of the crime. My lip throbbed and grew bigger and bigger, but I kept quiet in my hiding place.

Shortly after the lady left, Granny called, "Beverly!"

"Yes, ma'am?"

"Come here."

My glance followed the wooden planks on the floor as I approached wearily at what I believed was my certain demise.

"What happened to your lip?"

"An ant bit me."

"How could an ant bite you on your lip?"

I glanced down at my hand and twisted my fingers again, in search of an answer.

"You went at that batter, didn't you? I saw the biting ants there. You see what happens when you don't listen? When you can't hear, you will feel. What happened to the senna?"

"I drank it," I said, glancing around to avoid looking at her.

Her eyebrows raised. "Okay," she said.

I scurried out of harm's way, relieved the matter wasn't dire and delighted to have gotten away with my little trick.

The next morning, after breakfast, she approached with a little brown bottle and a big spoon in her hand. My heart skipped a beat, a lump came to my throat, and I gulped.

"I noticed that senna didn't work on you yesterday, because I didn't see you going to the bathroom."

My eyes opened wide and my jaw dropped.

"I think you need something stronger," she said. "That's why I am giving you this castor oil today."

"Ah! No, I don't need that," I said, taking a step back. My skin crawled at the bare mention of the name. Oh, how I wished to have drunk the senna the day before!

She poured the awful contents of the bottle into a big spoon as I squirmed in anguish. My blood left my face and went cold.

"I am not walking away today," she said calmly as she poured.

The awful smell permeated the place. Oh, how I wished for a visitor; anyone! But there was complete silence. My eyes slightly crossed and my lips curled down as the spoon drifted closer to my face. The awful smell of the pale-yellow oil reached closer and closer to my mouth.

"The longer you take, the longer we'll be here."

A queasy feeling washed over me as I scratched my head. "Can I have a candy after?" I asked.

"Fine."

Candy in hand, I squeezed tight, took a big gulp, and gagged.

"Don't you dare, or we will have to do this again."

Fumbling, I tried to get the wrapper off my candy, eager to take away the taste and help my dilemma. Later that evening, I was on the run. Granny was satisfied.

Even though we had a hairy mango tree in the yard loaded with fruits, and another mango tree up the lane across the road also loaded with mangoes, Granny decided it was a good day to go and collect mangoes elsewhere.

"We will go and get some mangoes at the mango walk," she said.

"Mango walk? Where is that?"

"You will see when we get there."

Up the road we went, swinging our buckets. The morning breeze was cool on our skin. The golden rays of sunlight glistened under the clear blue sky. Granny hailed at the neighbors as we went off the road onto a narrow lane, trailing behind Grandpa.

We got to the most beautiful meadow my eyes had ever seen. A true depiction of the Garden of Eden. The grass meandered between the trees like an oversized carpet perfectly tailored to fit the space. Almost as if it had been mowed by a team of garden specialists—the handiwork of nature itself. Bunches of golden-yellow mangoes embellished the branches amidst the luscious, green leaves. The whole scene looked as if it had been drawn by an expert artist.

The mist of the morning dew rested on the blades of grass, softly grazing my mint-green rubber slippers and the exposed sides of my now-damp feet. The birds sang to each other as I stared in awe at the countless mangoes lying under the trees.

"Well, there are enough mangoes here to stone dogs," Grandpa said.

"You can say that again," Granny responded, smiling.

The variety was vast.

"Take your buckets and find your favorites. I am going under the number eleven," Granny said.

"I am going under the bull nut," Grandpa said.

I chuckled at the name of Grandpa's favorite as he turned and walked away.

I hesitated, not knowing which to choose. A yellow one caught my eye. Ripe to perfection, with just a hint of pink at the top. I brought it to my nose and took a long sniff. The fresh, sweet aroma took my breath away. One after the other, I added to my bucket. Then Grandpa said, "Look, there is a sugar mango over there."

My head went up right away and I heard myself say, "Sugar mangoes? Yum!"

Sugar mangoes are small, and their seeds are tiny and flat. But they are oh so sweet and were my favorites. Shuffling with my heavy bucket in the direction of the sugar mangoes, I continued my collection. Wobbling along the way, my bucket was so heavy.

Granny looked at me and said, "Child, you better put in that bucket only what you can carry because everyone is going to carry their own load."

My glance went to my bucket and then back under the trees. The temptation was strong and my resistance weak. A more perfect one always appeared. It was such a waste to leave all those golden beauties scattered about. It was as if we hadn't taken any, and my struggle to resist one more was getting the better of me.

Granny and Grandpa were heading back, and keeping up was proving to be a challenge. I hoped they would encounter some friends along the way; a few chitchat stops would conveniently slow their pace a little, because I was beginning to wonder if, just maybe, I had accidentally picked up more than I could carry. But no, this bucket would get home, at all costs.

I switched hands often, and put my bucket down a few times, but kept going. The closer we got to home, the better I felt. At home, we had a mango feast. They were so juicy and sweet. Granny said we had to send some to my aunts and to my father.

Grandpa got three medium-size boxes and started packing. In went coconuts, mameys, avocados, and some green mangoes. Granny said we had to put the fruits in green so that by the time the package arrived, they would just be ripe.

Granny had baked some buns and soda cakes, and she added those as well.

Grandpa wrote letters for each. Then, on the side of Aunt Edna's box, he made a slice with his pen knife, folded some money, and put it in the slice. He marked it with a red marker and put a piece of clear tape over it.

"How are they going to know you put money there, Grandpa?"

"I told Edna to look for her surprise. She knows what I mean by that. She will know what to look for," he said.

At breakfast a few days later, Grandpa said, "Well, Ivania will be here in a few days."

I almost choked. "What? Ivania is coming? Is she coming alone?"

"Yes, she will be spending a few days with us."

"Ooh!"

I looked forward to Ivania's visit. We had a good time together when she visited alone, but when her siblings came with her, not so much.

The day she arrived, we greeted each other with hugs and

laughter. She went to the room and came back with letters. Granny was elated.

One morning during her visit, Granny said we should get the dusting stick and clear all the cobwebs in the guest room. The dusting stick reached almost to the ceiling. It had a soft pink duster brush at the end, and even though we could hardly see any cobwebs in the corners, we had to clean it anyway.

In the room, at the very top, was an area like a small attic. Grandpa kept boxes stored away up there. From the ground, the sails of a boat peeked from the surface.

"Look," I showed Ivania. "There must be toys in those boxes. Let's get up there and see."

"How we goin' get up there? We don't have a ladder."

On the other side of the wall above the bed was a window. I decided to climb it to get a better look. At the top of the window, my hand landed on something heavy, which I took down for a closer inspection. My eyebrows went up and my eyes widened.

"Ivania, look, it's a toy gun, but it's really heavy." Pressing the point of the gun to Ivania's forehead, I said, "Don't make a funny move, or I will shoot you."

Ivania moved the gun away from her forehead and said, "No, I don't want to play with that."

I proceeded to open the barrel. "Look," I said. I could not believe it. The barrel was full of real bullets. I headed straight to the kitchen. "Granny, look what we found in the guest room. It's a real gun, and I almost shot Ivania with it. I thought it was a toy."

"Oh, my God. Put that thing down! I don't know why your grandfather would have a gun in this house. Thank God you did not pull that trigger!"

I rested the gun on the table and went back to clean the room. As soon as Grandpa came home, Granny went into a rant.

"Malcolm, do you see what those children found in that room? Beverly almost shot Ivania with that thing."

"I had that gun high above the window. What were they doing all the way up there?"

"I sent them to dust that room. The best thing is not to have those things in the house, period," Granny said.

Ivania and I looked at each other, but neither one uttered a word. Our gaze was towards the kitchen, trying to capture their every word. When the rant subsided, Ivania said, "You would have been in so much trouble if you had shot me."

"Yeah, but you would have been dead."

We stayed in the room long after, not wanting to face Grandpa. A few days later, Ivania left unscathed.

Chapter Ten

At the beginning of the year, a collection for Mother's Day was started. It was the teacher's idea, and we were elated at the prospect. The teacher said Mother's Day would be on the 30th of May, a grand event in Nicaragua. We all brought a jar with our name taped across the middle and were promised a field trip to the store. Eagerly, we awaited the magical event. The day before our outing, the teacher called, "Come on, kids, get your saving banks."

"Yes!"

We jumped to our feet and dashed to the table. Back at our seats, following the teacher's instructions, we emptied our jars and tallied our collection on a sheet of paper. The teacher turned the event into our math project.

The following day was our long-awaited outing. Excitement filled the air amidst giggles and laughter. Everyone wanted their total savings to be a secret.

"What are you going to buy?" Miriam asked.

"I don't know, I have to see what they have," I said.

"Listen up, kids. I want you all on your best behavior; no running. I want you to walk to the side of the road, and if you misbehave, you will be in trouble. Is that clear?"

"Yes, ma'am," everyone answered in unison.

The store was a mile away. We went to the two main stores on the island and the only ones in the area that sold items suitable for gifts. The bigger store sold everything, from groceries, vegetables, and meat, to tools and home supplies.

We ran from one end of the store to the other; the room was dim due to lack of electricity. The only sources of light were a big double door, two small windows at the front of the building, and one to the side.

And there, at the back of the store in a display case, was the perfect gift. After a long wait to gain the shopkeeper's attention, I showed her my choice and hoped for it to be affordable.

It was a lovely Chinese folding fan, adorned with crimson roses, a tassel at the base of the handle, and black lace adorning the outer edge. It was exactly what I wanted for Granny.

"Miss, what is the price for that fan over there?"

Holding my breath, I waited to hear the price. Relieved it was affordable, I decided to purchase it. The lady put the fan in a little box, and I grinned from ear to ear.

My thoughts drifted to Granny at church, happily fanning away; dignified, regal, distinguished. She would not be using that old piece of cardboard anymore.

She is going to be so happy! It did not matter what anyone else bought, my gift was the best. The lady at the store did us a favor by wrapping our gifts and off we went.

On our way back to school, amidst whispers, giggles, and laughter, we eagerly anticipated the day of our Mother's Day program. The event took place that Saturday.

Dressed in my Sunday finest, I wore a light pink dress adorned with dainty white lace on the chest, white shoes, and white socks. Granny found a seat, as did the rest of the parents. The program started, and we sang a couple of choruses. After reciting my poem, Miss Pearl called me and handed me a piece of paper.

"Someone was supposed to say this poem, but now I need you to go up and read it."

Suppressing my desire to say, "Well, let her read it," I bit my tongue when a voice rang out.

"And now a poem entitled . . ."

"Go," said Miss Pearl.

I dashed off to the stage and promptly read the poem:

A Mother's Love

"A mother's love is like a dove
So pure, so white, so true
Her warm embrace
her gentle touch
of fragrance oh so true
a love that lifts, that guides, that soars
sincere, serene, sublime
No other love can rise above
A spotless mother's love."

Back in my seat, I thought of the beautiful poems, real to others, perhaps, but to me were mere rhyming words.

One by one, names were called, and smiling faces rose to collect their gifts and hand them to their mothers. In return, a big hug and a kiss. At the sound of my name I sprang to my feet, floated towards my grandmother with pride and glee, and extended to her my gift.

"I can't take that gift from you. You know I am not your mother. You need to hold that gift until you meet your mother one day. Then you can give it to her."

My world crumbled at the sound of those words as if a bucket of ice-cold water had been thrown in my face. My punishment for not having a mother. Not even my gift would be accepted.

"But I didn't buy this for her, I bought it for you. I don't even know who she is."

"Matters not."

Awkwardly, I glanced around, hoping no one noticed. All my energy evaporated from my body. I blinked through my tears, trying to clear the haze, bowing my head while swiftly wiping my eyes. Grateful that amidst the scene of hugs and laughter, my plight and I paled in the background. I could not let my friends see me cry. Some drifted hand in hand with their mothers while others sat in their laps.

"I am so proud of you," one lady said to her daughter, while another said, "I love you, baby."

These were all words that were foreign to me. A display of affection I had never experienced. The lump in my throat was hard to swallow. My chest was tight, suppressing my breathing. The gift in my hand, once a source of exhilaration, joy, and excitement, now induced sadness, dejection, and misery. Yet, I forced a smile. A smile visible only on the surface; a difficult outward expression devoid of a genuine twinkle in my eyes.

The walk home was silent, my emotions crushed, broken, shattered. In the room, I sat on my bed with the gift in my hand and sobbed, finally able to let it all out, allowing my tears to now run freely. I threw the gift under the bed, not ever wanting to see that stupid thing again.

On Monday in the classroom there was much chatter, pacing back and forth, big smiles painted on everyone's faces, and comments about how excited or happy their mothers were and how much they liked their gifts. I listened quietly and forced a smile, but I kept my distance to avoid questions. Miss Pearl told the class how happy she was that everything went so well and was proud of the class for a job well done.

My eyes fixed on the notebook on my desk, wishing I

could be anywhere but there; longing for class to be over as if a stroll up the road would somehow erase my sadness.

At home around the table, I examined the dainty pink, red, and yellow roses embroidered on the pristine white tablecloth, protected from any accidental spill by clear plastic. They were a reminder of the roses on the fan I bought, but I tried to take my mind off the fan and focused on the delicate placement of every row of thread instead. It must have taken someone a very long time to place each and every one of those stitches to create the beautiful masterpiece. The green leaves perched on the vines drifted softly between the flowers. Granny sat at the head of the table, peeling some potatoes.

"Granny, did you make this tablecloth?"

"No, I wish I could embroider like that. I bought it in Managua."

"I like the flowers on it. They are very pretty."

"Yes, one of these days, you will learn to embroider like that, and then you will be able to make pillowcases, sheets, and even pretty tablecloths like this one."

Granny finished peeling the potatoes and picked up an alapine—mamey apple—one of my favorite fruits. She cut a piece and handed it to me. The thick, peach-colored flesh crunched, and the sweet flavor exploded in my mouth. Granny never mentioned anything about my gift again, and neither did I.

Ms. Vanji came by often because she helped Granny with the cooking sometimes. She swayed from side to side as she walked. Her skin was black and smooth, and her stomach jiggled when she laughed. She had been with us for as long as I could remember and was a part of the family.

Grandpa said I was never to frighten her, though, 'cause

she suffered from the fits. I learned later that meant some sort of seizure.

One day, Granny said she would be making some Nachtmaals. She asked that I call Ms. Vanji. I liked her. She was very nice to me.

I skipped across the road along the narrow winding lane shaded by trees and shrubs. The tiny wooden hut was dwarfed beneath the heavy thatched roof at the end of a narrow winding trail. At the door, seated on a stool deep in conversation with Ms. Vanji was Don Juan, an old Spaniard. While not originally from Spain, the locals called anyone who was of Spanish or Native American descent a Spaniard.

He passed by or stopped every now and again to say hi to Grandpa. His yellowing gray hair ruffled like loose feathers, his paper-thin T-shirt, once white, was now a dingy beige, and his wrinkled khaki pants seemed taken from the wash bundle. His back faced the lane and I sneaked by, hoping he wouldn't see me.

Grandpa's words were fresh in my mind. "Whenever you see Don Juan around, I want you to avoid him. I don't want you around that fresh old man."

I sneaked around the back to wait for Don Juan to leave.

"There is someone at your back window. I saw a head or something," Don Juan said.

They saw me, I thought.

"No, it must be a pig or something," Ms. Vanji said.

I rose to my feet the very moment Ms. Vanji put her head to the window and quickly disappeared from my view.

"Oh no. Vanji," Don Juan said, his tone sounding alarmed.

I ran to the door to see what he was alarmed about. Ms. Vanji was on the floor, twitching. She had gone straight into a fit.

"Go! Go and call your grandpa," Don Juan said.

I dashed through the narrow lane.

"Grandpa! Grandpa, come quick! Ms. Vanji got the fits, and you need to come!" I shouted, almost out of breath.

Grandpa rushed out of the house and up the lane. "You stay outside and wait."

Wondering what was going on inside, I paced. After what seemed an eternity, Grandpa surfaced. Ms. Vanji was conscious, but still not all with it. He and Don Juan took her to our house to continue looking after her. Don Juan explained what happened. I guess Grandpa thought my actions were a severe infraction, deserving of more than a punishment. Grandpa's tyrannical presence was made known in more ways than one as he stood tall with his black-and-blue belt in hand and beckoned my presence.

I approached at a crawl. There was no way out. Each time his hand came down, I skipped, hoping to ease the effect, but it didn't seem to help. One thing I knew for sure; Grandpa could never be accused of saving the rod and spoiling the child.

I had discovered in previous offenses that if I yelled often enough, "I want to pee! I want to pee!" I could save myself some lashes as Grandpa would let go and I could take a quick retreat to the outhouse and away from my predicament.

Ms. Vanji was okay in a few days and life went on as if nothing happened. I made sure not to frighten her again.

Chapter Eleven

My school only reached the second grade. It would be my last year, and comments about graduation buzzed in the air.

"Those of you who are given parts for the graduation, make sure and learn them well," Teacher Pearl instructed as she handed us the sheets of paper bearing the poems.

On the evening of graduation, the halls bustled with children showing off their best outfits. Pastel colors, frills and laces, white shirts, and dark pants filled the hall. Students escorted parents to their seats. The Nicaraguan national flag of blue and white adorned the stage, and voices echoed the National Anthem. All the males saluted the flag with their hands on their foreheads while the ladies held their hands over their hearts.

After the singing of the anthem, students sat next to their parents in a hall filled to capacity. After reciting our parts, I went back to my seat next to Granny.

The teacher handed out awards and spoke of the student who had obtained the Student of the Year award for high academic achievements. My name was called, and my mouth dropped. Smiling from ear to ear, I made my way to the stage under the sound of thunderous applause. A gift wrapped in colorful paper was handed to me. It was the most beautiful paper I had ever seen and the first gift I had ever received. I had never gotten a gift, even at Christmas.

The smile on Granny's face, the look of pride and joy, was pleasing. The notion that through my achievements they experienced joy was an indication I was good at something and not just a burden. I glanced around at the people clapping. They were happy for me too. With my head and chest held high and glowing with pride, I made my way back to my seat.

After graduation, we went upstairs to the church for a special service. Hymnal in hand, I sang proudly, wanting to impress Granny and show off my ability to read the hymnal. She noticed I was lost after singing the first line and smiled.

"You need to sing the first line of each chapter, then the second line of each chapter until the song is finished," she explained.

This seemed strange, but I went on singing.

After the church service, we walked home under the bright moonlight and twinkling stars.

"Can I open my gift now?" I asked as we stepped into the door.

"Go ahead."

I removed the tape at a crawl to avoid tearing the wrapping. The smile on my face morphed into a frown as a large, black rubber tarantula surfaced in its transparent plastic packaging, which I carefully ripped off, releasing the awful-looking creature. A long, clear tube attached to a red rubber ball dangled at the end of the tube. On the floor, I tried to figure out how the contraption worked. With a good squeeze of the ball, the tarantula leaped. After a bit of entertainment, an idea came to mind. I could play a trick on my friends.

The next morning, our neighbor, Ms. Ortiz, was seated in her doorway. She was deep in conversation with someone in her house. Tarantula in hand, I dashed across the road and stood next to the wall. Ms. Ortiz's back leaned against the doorframe and her leg was on the step.

I tiptoed towards her and placed the tarantula next to her foot, then took a few steps back and squeezed the ball. The tarantula leaped off the floor and Ms. Ortiz screamed as she slammed a piece of two-by-four wood she had next to her hand. My tarantula was flattened like a pancake by the sudden blow. My mouth fell open and I gasped as I stared in shock at my now motionless tarantula.

"Ms. Ortiz, you broke my tarantula!"

"You almost gave me a heart attack. You know better than to go around frightening people with that ugly thing."

I gazed at the flattened creature and squeezed the ball. There was a squishing sound of air, but no movement. My tarantula was dead. I picked up the fragments and went home pouting, hoping Granny would be sympathetic to my plight.

"You should have known better than to scare people with that thing. Serves you right. That will teach you a lesson," she said.

Pouting, I stormed away to the small dining room and sat at the table. The sail I had seen before came to mind. A quick glance up revealed its presence next to a brown cardboard box. Surely there must be some other toys in that box. Just below was a shelf tucked in the corner of the wall, tailored to fit the triangular shape of the corner. Above that along the wall were two rows of smaller shelves displaying some small bottles of medicines and oils.

Placing a chair next to the stand, I made my way up, but my efforts were futile. I was still too short. Perhaps if I held onto one of the shelves, I could climb a bit further. But in my attempt to achieve this feat, I accidentally hit the top shelf, causing it to tilt, and down came the bottles with a sudden crash. With that, everything on the bottom shelf was knocked down in a disastrous domino effect, breaking the silence with the tumbling sound followed by Granny's blood-curdling yell coming from the kitchen.

"Beverleeey!"

Trying to avoid the bottles, I scurried in dreadful expectation of my demise and froze when Granny stepped in.

"What are you doing?"

"I, I, I was just trying to get the sailboat."

"You pick up every one of those bottles this minute. You have the devil in you today. If you can't hear, you will feel."

Thankful the bottles were not broken, I gathered them at lightning speed.

Granny stood over me akimbo, her lips squeezed tight and her brows knit. After I finished gathering the bottles, she grabbed my ear and led me into the dining room to kneel in my usual spot.

"You will kneel there, and you better not move."

In silence I knelt, gazing at the seams on the wall and the restricted view through the door, hoping that Grandpa would not come and find me there since that could result in an even more disastrous outcome. I shuffled from one knee to the other to distribute the discomfort, at times even sneaking a quick rest on my calves. After a while, she surfaced from the kitchen.

"Get back up on your knees and face that wall." My knees and back ached, and now I wished Grandpa would hurry up and come home because a beating would be quicker than to continue kneeling, but he was taking forever to get home.

"Get up from there and go and fill these buckets with water," she said.

These words were music to my ears. Up to my feet I rose and reached for the buckets, happy that my punishment was finally over.

At times like those, I longed for the day I could go and visit my father. I wondered what it would be like to spend some time with him. Would he punish me as well? Surely not—or at least I hoped not.

Chapter Twelve

In the yard, Grandpa was busy at work. Long pieces of two-by-four lay on the ground. A wide piece of lumber sat perched on two stands next to him. A sea of golden shavings swirled at his feet.

In his hand, he had a steel tool resembling an iron, with a wooden curved handle at the back and a wooden nub at the front. He held the curved handle in his right hand and the wooden nub in his left as he pressed down hard and pushed forward on the wood. The shavings curled at the top and floated to the ground like autumn leaves.

"What's that?" I asked, pointing at the tool.

"This is a hand plane."

"What you makin'?"

"I'm makin' a coffin."

"A what?"

"A coffin."

My eyes widened and my mouth dropped as I stared.

"Why you makin' a coffin? Who died?"

"I'm making this for a man. He is old and very sick, and his family wants to make sure it is ready for when they need it."

"Beverly, leave your grandfather alone! Go by Ms. Diney. She needs you to do something for her!" Granny shouted from the kitchen.

Grandpa's mom, Ms. Diney, was very old. She had to be the oldest person alive. She lived across the road from us. Her wooden house with a tiny porch was hidden behind shrubs and trees.

I ran across the road and there she was, under a tree, sitting on a wooden stool, a small broom in her hand. Her yard was spotless. The shadows of leaves danced and swayed with the motion of the wind and the chirping of birds overhead.

"Hi, Ms. Diney. Granny sent me."

"Hi, baby. I was just sweeping up some leaves. Let me put down me broom."

Her pale-white skin sagged on her arms. Her curved back and tiny frame trudged to the back of the yard.

My glance trailed up in the trees in search of her chickens. Unlike us, she did not have a coop. Her chickens slept on the tree branches, but they were still roaming around.

"Come, baby," she said, breaking my train of thought.

She went through the back door and onto the dark, uneven wooden floor. The room was bare but for a table pushed against the wall under a window. "Wait a moment." She stepped up and went through another door leading to her dining room, then to her bedroom. I stood in the kitchen waiting for her return.

She returned with a piece of brown paper and a bag with some threads and a small container of needles.

"I need you to thread these for me. These needle holes are so small, I can't see to thread them," she said as she escorted me to the living room. "Sit here." She pointed to a chair next to a small round table.

I threaded the needles with different color threads and inserted them into the brown paper, then wrapped the thread around the two exposed edges, as she had shown me. When finished, they looked like a bouquet of flowers on the brown paper background.

She sat up straight in her rocking chair and took the brown paper to inspect my finished work. Her gray curls were swept softly into a bun at the base of her neck, and a sweet, soft smile lit up her face.

"It makes it easy for me to mend whatever I need without having to worry about threading the needle. Thank you, baby," she said.

As I was about to go through the door, a movement in the corner drew my attention. Squinting to focus my vision on the dark corner, I drew closer for a better inspection. My eyes adapted a bit better to the dark and zoomed in on the slight shimmer of a black snake crawling along the floor next to the wall. Frozen in fear, I stared, hoping it would not try to come my way.

"Ms. Diney," I whispered, as if not wanting the snake to hear me. "There is a snake right there."

"A what?" she asked.

"A black snake."

She leaned back in her rocking chair and lifted her legs off the floor. "Call your grandfather," she said.

"But if I leave, I might not know where it goes," I continued to whisper. "Where is your broom?" I asked.

"It's right there behind the door."

Tiptoeing towards the door, I peeped behind it and in slow motion, reached for the broom. Clutching my weapon, I tiptoed back towards the creature, holding my weapon above my head, hoping it would not head in my direction while trying hard to control my fear. With force, I slammed the broom at it and jumped back with caution as it scurried along the wall.

"Be careful," she said as the unwelcome guest slithered out of the door.

"It's gone," I said.

"Thank God. You wait a while before you go out there."

I waited a little while longer. "Okay, Ms. Diney. I am leaving now."

"Let me close the door behind you, darling. I don't want that thing coming back in here."

When I got back, Grandpa had nailed the sides of the coffin together, and it was now taking shape. Frowning, I shrugged my shoulders as I stepped past him, not wanting to get too close.

I told Granny of the incident at Ms. Diney's house.

"It is good that you were there to help poor Ms. Diney. You must always remember to do good, and good will follow you. It will follow you, your children, and your children's children. But if you do evil, evil will follow you, your children, and your children's children down to the seventh generation. So always choose to do good."

Attentively, I soaked in her words; words that have seen me grow and have moved along with me wherever I go. I repeat them to my siblings, my children, and my friends, for I truly believe evil follows those who do evil and good follows those who do good.

Later that evening, I went to Ms. Mary's house. Quecha, Nando, and Marvin, her younger brother, were in the living room.

"You know what? Guess what Grandpa is building."

"I don't know," said Quecha, raising her shoulders.

"A coffin," I said, waiting for their reaction of dread.

"Who died?" asked Nando.

"Nobody, but Grandpa said it is for an old man who is really sick, and he may die."

"Well, my granny already has a coffin," said Quecha.

"Yeah, right. Where is it then?"

"It is in a room upstairs. It's right up there," Nando said, pointing to a doorway. My eyes trailed fearfully in the direction he was pointing.

Their granny was a dark lady with very white hair. She didn't come out much. Most of her time was spent in her room.

My curiosity grew stronger than my fear, and so I drew closer to the stairway. The wood beneath my feet creaked in my approach to the entrance. I squinted my eyes to adjust my vision up the dark, creepy staircase. A tall, white, wooden panel reached the ceiling, barely visible through the darkness. At the top, a faint wall faced a corner leading up to even more stairs.

"Do you go up there?"

"No, we are not allowed up there. It's been up there from a long time ago," Quecha whispered.

"My mamá says that one time our granny was very sick, and they thought she was going to die. That's why they had the casket built. But she got better, and they put it up there for when she dies," Quecha explained, staring at me and shaking her head to the tune of every word.

"Let's go up there and look at it then."

"No, we are not allowed up there, I told you," said Quecha.

"If you go up there and look at it, the ghosts are going to haunt you when you go to bed," said Nando.

"No, they won't."

"Yes, they will. The duppies (ghosts) will pinch you in the night, and you will wake up with a bunch of black-and-blue spots all over you," he said.

I looked skeptically at him. "Yeah, right."

"You don't believe me, ask my mamá. That's why they tell you not to trouble the dead."

"Yeah, but she's not dead."

They went into the kitchen and Marvin said to me, "Come, I'll show you. I go up there all the time."

"Let's go," I said.

He grabbed a flashlight and we crept up the dark, narrow staircase. Step by step, the wooden stairs squeaked under our feet, forcing us to move slowly with each gentle step.

At the top around the dark corner, a stuffy smell lingered in the air. We leaned against the wall and Marvin pointed at a door straight ahead. My heart raced in anticipation.

"I hope there are no rat bats in there," I whispered, hoping he would confirm in the negative.

"Shhh," Marvin said.

We took another step up, stepping as softly as we could to avoid the squeaking sound. But all I could imagine were the ugly rat bats with piercing red eyes, pointed ears, sharp Dracula teeth, and black, devilish capes flapping at us as we opened the door.

"Wait," I said. "You sure there are no bats in there?"

"Shhh!"

We moved up one step while resting against the wall. With his finger over his lips, he signaled to be quiet and turned the knob on the door as he slowly pushed it open. The hinges screeched, and my breathing stopped. He signaled for me to come closer. I tiptoed forward and peeped in. He turned on the flashlight. The large circle of light floated over the dust-filled mahogany coffin, resting on the floor against the wall.

I gasped. "Let's go!"

He pulled the door shut and I rushed back down the stairs, panting.

It was time to leave, but at the door, the view up the road was pitch-black and eerie. Previously, racing through the darkness had been a breeze, but tonight, my get up and go got up and left me standing. Somehow, the route got way too spooky. The thought of asking someone to go with me was strong, but the voice in my head won the argument. *If I do, they will say I am scared. I'm no scaredy-cat.*

Mustering courage, I surveyed the path once again; it was now or never. My hand slid sluggishly down the doorframe, one foot dangled in the air moving ever so slowly towards the step, and reluctantly, my hand let go of the doorframe.

In a flash, I made a dash for it into the pitch-dark, running full speed ahead. Over a trench and into our yard, up the stairs, and onto the porch, I swiftly grabbed the front door and closed it behind me, panting as I tried to catch my breath.

The living room was dark but after another dash to the bedroom, I scrambled out of my clothes and into my pajamas while skeptically scanning the room, hoping there was nothing or no one lurking around. Into my bed and under the covers I slid, reciting my prayers at full speed.

"This night when I lay down to sleep
I pray the Lord my soul to keep
if I should die before I wake,
I pray the Lord, my soul, to take."

Barely giving my nose some breathing room, I hoped to quickly fall asleep.

The next day, Grandpa continued to build the coffin. The top lid was now sustained by hidden hinges. Wood molding adorned the edges, and a coat of dark wood varnish gave it a sheen. From the window, I watched as he took a thick, white lining and stapled it all around the inside and on the inside of the lid. The coffin was finished.

Normally I would be there working with him, but not this time. Working on a coffin was too spooky.

A man came to pick the coffin up. Grandpa and the man lifted the coffin and put it in the back of the truck. It was a relief to see that dreaded coffin fade into the distance.

Chapter Thirteen

The dark of night lingered outside at the crack of dawn when I awoke. My internal clock was ticking, announcing my favorite Sunday morning routine. Instinctively, I surged out of bed, grabbed my ugly, moss-green bathing suit, and rushed off to grab Grandpa's navy-blue bathing trunks. The roosters crowed while a hint of sunlight peeked through the branches.

We had to put a move on it. We had to be back before 9:00 a.m. for Sunday school, and going to the beach after church was a no-no.

I could hear Granny now. "Do you see the time? You are not going anywhere in that scorching sun. That broiling-hot sun can give you a stroke!"

Grandpa was still sound asleep when I got back to his cot. I put my hand on his shoulder and whispered, "Grandpa, Grandpa, wake up. It is getting late. We have to go now."

He let out a soft groan. "Wait, I'll get up soon."

"No! You have to get up now. See, I have your bathing trunks right here. You have to get up."

"Fine. Go and get my slippers."

Not long after, we headed across the street and down the

narrow lane. Blackie, our black Border Collie mix, and Popita, our brown Corgi mix, led the way. Popita wagged her hips. She had no tail to wag, but her beautiful brown hair was all she needed. She knew she was gorgeous. The dogs were just as excited as I was. The path along the winding trail took us under a huge mango tree. The trunk was so big, Grandpa said it must have been there for hundreds of years. A patch of shrubs loaded with white and purple coco plums caught my attention. The sweet, cotton-like flesh melted in my mouth, and my hands filled with extras.

As we approached our favorite spot, the sound of the waves rolled in the distance. Grandpa picked up some dried coconuts on our way. The cool white sand felt soft under our feet, and Popita and Blackie ran and played. In the distance, the clouds bowed and kissed the ocean as the sea breeze caressed my face. It was heavenly. I moved closer, allowing the bubbles on the swells to wash over my feet. Grandpa took aim and threw a coconut into the sea.

"Go fetch," he said.

Popita and Blackie threw themselves into the water, and I followed.

"Let's see which one of you is the fastest!" he yelled.

We paddled back, the coconut now pushed in front of me as a float, with Popita and Blackie on either side. On the beach, they took the coconuts and tore the husks to pieces, playfully running along the beach.

Grandpa got into the water. "Come and dive under my legs," he said.

"Okay, but no tricks this time, promise?"

"Promise," Grandpa replied.

I distanced myself to get ready for the dive. The pearl-white sand peeked through the crystal-clear water. After taking a big breath, down I went, eyes wide open, as I had no goggles. I could see his legs moving back each time I tried to get closer. I jumped up and said, "Grandpa, you are moving."

"No, I am not."

"Yes, you are. I can see your legs moving, no cheating."

"No, it is the waves you are seeing," he replied with a grin. Down I went again.

"No, it is not the waves. I see your legs moving."

He laughed.

"You promised! Stay still!"

"Okay."

I knew he was up to his tricks as usual. Down I went again and this time, I was able to dive right through his legs. I pushed up to the surface.

"There! I did it." I said, gleaming with pride, waiting for Grandpa's confirmation of a job well done.

"Yeah, but you touched my leg when you went under."

I frowned, "No, I did not. Grandpa, you promised. No cheating."

"Okay, come and hop on my shoulders." I glimpsed the twinkle of a smile as he dove under and I thought, *He knows I did well but doesn't want to say it.* I smiled, grabbed his hands, and hopped on his shoulders.

He stood up and counted, "One, two, three!"

Off I went, trying my best to go in headfirst, but I made a big splash.

"That was a belly flop," he laughed. "Time to go."

"Already? We just got here!"

"Time to head home, or your grandmother will throw a fit," he said as he walked out of the water.

At home, Granny was making Duff, my favorite dessert. She stirred in the vanilla and grated the nutmeg.

"Mmm," I said. She sliced the dough and placed it in the delicious punch. The fluffy, white slices of bread floated in the punch like clouds in the sky. I could not wait to get back from church.

Back at the table, I wished I could skip lunch and go straight to dessert, but Granny was not having it. She had prepared beef soup for lunch.

"Don't you dare slurp around this table! Only pigs slurp, and I am not sharing my table with no pigs," Grandpa said.

The soup was mouthwatering, but I made sure to leave space for my Duff. On my knees on the chair, I watched as Granny took out the Duff. One bowl for Grandpa, one bowl for her, and one bowl for me.

Quickly, I scooped up a spoonful and started eating it. The burst of sweet dough drenched in vanilla, cinnamon, and nutmeg lifted me to Lalaland.

"Papá don't know what he is missing," I said after I took my first bite.

Granny smiled and said, "Yes, you got that right."

"More for me," Grandpa said. And we all laughed.

Chapter Fourteen

Granny handed me a crisp, red ten-córdoba bill and sent me on my way to buy tomatoes.

"Oooh, tomatoes," I whispered, then rushed to tear off a piece of brown paper, added some salt, and raced up the road. Before reaching the Chinaman's shop, while surveying the open field of what seemed like an endless amount of coconut trees, I noticed several men scattered about, gathering coconuts. Some were on mules, their legs sprawled forward, giving room for the large wire baskets on each side. The baskets were loaded with coconuts heading to the Copra factory, a few steps away. Mounds of coconuts were dispersed among the trees like small volcanoes.

At the shop, my chin barely reaching the wooden counter, I asked, "Can I have one pound of tomatoes, please? And Granny said to add a small one," I added.

The Chinaman weighed the tomatoes and put them in a bag. I reached in for my small, red, juicy tomato and bit the tip, then unfolded my little brown piece of paper and dipped it in the salt. My steps slowed to a crawl as I took my time to savor every bite. "Mmm!"

A man passed by on his mule, towards the factory, a few steps away, and I followed.

The constant noise floating out of the wooden walls of the factory drew my attention. The *chip, chip, chip* of the coconuts being shelled and the squishing sound of the dagger piercing and splitting the husk away from the coconut held my attention. The unpainted pieces of scrap wood nailed haphazardly together formed a makeshift fence to keep people out, but could not detain the curious eyes of a seven-year-old.

In between the wide cracks in the wood, I peeped. At a far corner, a young man stood in front of a pole planted in the ground that reached his waist. A sharp dagger, like an oversized spear implanted at the top of the pole, pointed to the sky. A coconut, still in the husk, went over his head.

Next to him was another young man, like his twin. Their hands went up in one accord, as in a synchronized dance; up in unison, then suddenly down. As the coconut hit the dagger, they twisted it forward, breaking the husk. Three strikes and off came the husk with absolute precision as if in a dance routine. The coconut devoid of its husks went onto one heap, and the husks on another.

Two other young men held coconuts already out of the husk. Each had a coconut in one hand and a machete in the other. One wore a dirty white shirt tied to his waist and a straw hat that shaded his brow. His exposed chest glistened with sweat. The other young man, with his pants rolled up below his knees, chipped at a coconut with a speed not even Grandpa could compete with.

They raced each other as the harmonious *chip, chip, chip* filled the air. The coconut lost its shell in no time. It was a wonder they still had fingers. They emptied the water into a big bucket, split the coconuts, and tossed them into long trays lined up to their left. They glistened in the sun as if in an oven. The fresher batches were white, but the older batches were various tones of golden brown.

A big door led to an enclosed area. I wondered what was happening inside as my view was blocked. The smell of the naturally roasted coconuts dispersed a delectable aroma like coconut candy. The entertainment was good, but I knew I had to hurry home. A few steps ahead, the blue of the sky met the ocean, calm and still, while a big boat leaned on the pier.

As soon as I entered the door, I asked, "Granny, what do they do with all that coconut at the Copra factory?"

"Oooh, they do a lot of things," she answered. "With the husk, they make rope."

"What? I didn't know they use the husk. I thought they just threw the husk away."

"No, they have a big machine at the back of the factory that they use to make the rope from the husk, and they ship it out on the boats. With the dried coconuts, they make oil, and the trash is in the bran we buy to feed the pigs . . . which reminds me. You better go and soak the bran now."

Out of a barrel Grandpa kept just under the floor, I filled two five-gallon buckets half full of the bran and topped them up with water from the well. The bran soaked up the water and became a delicious-smelling slush.

It wasn't long before Grandpa was home.

"Malcolm, I need some coconuts, when you get the chance."

"Okay," he said. He got his long machete. "Let's get some coconuts for your grandmother," he said to me.

Granny peeped through the window and shouted as we walked off, "Malcolm, make sure to not let that child play with that machete before she cuts her finger off."

"Okay," he said in slow motion as we crossed the road.

When we left Granny's sight, Grandpa surprised me by removing his short machete from his waist. He had it hidden on the inside of his pants hip all along.

"Here," he said. "And you better not let your grandmother know that I brought this for you to use, or she will have a fit."

Wide-eyed and with a sly giggle, I grabbed the machete and proceeded to collect coconuts along with Grandpa. We made a heap next to an old tree trunk.

"Let's get these husked," he said. He slapped the trunk with the machete before he sat on it.

"What did you do that for?" I asked. "Why did you slap the trunk?"

"I got to make sure this trunk is not a snake. You always have to be careful, you know."

"That tree trunk is too big to be a snake, Grandpa."

"No, there are snakes even bigger than this. They could swallow you whole. One time I sat on one to tie my shoes. I was never more frightened in my life."

Fixed on his every word, I asked, "But how did you know it was a snake?"

"I knew when the thing moved. Dead stumps don't move, you know."

I stared, eager to hear more. "And what did you do?"

"I took off running. That's what I did."

I threw my head back and laughed so hard that Grandpa laughed too.

"People say you are supposed to run in a zigzag to get away from a snake. Well, I think what you have to do is run as fast as you can. So, I ran full speed straight ahead to get away from that thing."

We laughed as he husked one coconut after the other. He made it look so easy, while I struggled to get just one done. We proceeded to chip the coconuts. He chipped three perfectly, while I worked on one.

He looked at my coconut and said, "Bev, there is no way we could take that one home. You chipped all the oil off."

"How can you chip the oil off a coconut?" I asked, chuckling. My coconut was in fact covered with white gaps, while the one in his hand was brown all over.

"See, the oil is in the brown part, and you chipped most of it off," he chuckled. "You'll get it next time."

He cut a triangle at the top of a coconut and handed it to me. I turned it up to my head and had a good drink, then wiped away the drops off my chin. I was delighted with my reward, and thought of what a good team we made. We gathered the coconuts and headed home.

A lady came by that evening looking to buy a pig. I listened to the conversation as she negotiated with Grandpa.

"I will give you three hundred córdobas for the boar, and two hundred and fifty córdobas for the sow."

"Okay," Grandpa agreed. After the lady left, we went to the pigpen and Grandpa emptied the buckets of sweet-smelling bran into the feeding bins. Watching them slurp the liquid mush and gulp it down was a pleasure. I wondered about the transaction. As I saw it, the two pigs were both the same size, yet the lady paid a different price for each.

"Grandpa, why did the lady pay you more for the boar than she did for the sow when they were the same size?"

Grandpa looked at me, his brow joined ever so slightly, and while waiting for his response, I wondered, *Is he thinking of what to answer me? Or is he puzzled because I asked?*

"Well, the boar is heavier than the sow, and that's why the boar is more expensive."

"Oh."

We leaned on the fence and watched the pigs. There was a sow with several piglets suckling at her teats.

"You know, you deserve a little pig. You see those over there?" He pointed to the little pigs that were suckling. "Choose one. I am going to give you one."

My eyes widened and a big smile came over my face. I looked at the pigs and quickly pointed out my choice.

"I want that female one over there, with the white spot and the two bells."

"But why don't you take the boar? Remember, the lady

paid more money for the boar than she did for the sow because the boars are heavier."

"Yes, but if I take the boar, then I will only have one. But if I take the female one, then she will have a lot of boars. That's why I want the female one."

He leaned his head and squinted ever so slightly as a smile surfaced. "Okay," he said. "It's yours."

I was now the proud owner of a pig and was bursting with glee at the notion. With my head held high I marched into the house floating on air, and what was even better was that Grandpa said I deserved it. It was my reward for hard work.

A few days later, three guys came strolling into the yard, sitting high on their mules with their empty wire baskets on both sides.

"Tit Ive!" the first one called.

"Oy!" answered Granny as she peeped through the window. "You all are a sight for sore eyes."

"Yes, we have been keeping busy these days. We are just wondering if we could get some coconuts."

"Go right ahead. It is good timing because I am running low on coconut oil."

"Okay," they said as the mules continued one by one behind the house, heading through the bushes.

Later that evening, they headed back out with their baskets full to overflowing with their freshly husked coconuts.

"Tit Ive!" they called. Granny went out to them, and they paid her for the coconuts and said, "We leave you with a sixty."

"Thank you, man, I needed that. I will get some coconut oil made tomorrow."

The next morning, Grandpa was up early and chipped a lot of coconuts before he left. After breakfast, Ms. Vanji came and she and Granny continued chipping until all the coconuts were chipped. They were placed in a big, round aluminum dish pan. They cut a triangle at the top of the coconut and drained the water in a glass. The water was so nice and sweet.

In another big dishpan, perched on a wooden stool, Granny placed her big grater. She leaned over and rested her hand on one side, and with the other, she held the coconut and grated away. Sometimes she grated the coconut whole, leaving a thin layer of white flesh inside, which we called the tongue. I liked to eat the coconut tongue because it was soft and juicy.

Granny and Ms. Vanji took turns grating.

"Can I get a turn to grate too?" I asked.

"No, you will grate your finger," said Ms. Vanji.

"No, I won't."

"Well, I don't know that for sure, and we better not take any chances," she said.

Every now and again, Granny took the grated coconut from under the grater and put it to the sides of the pan to give herself more room to grate. Ms. Vanji put the trash in yet another pan and poured water on it. She squeezed and squeezed the coconut trash to get all the milk out, placed a strainer on a bucket, and made a big ball of trash in her hands. Then she squeezed the milk through the strainer and into the bucket. She emptied the bucket into a big pot and put it on the fire hearth to boil.

As the milk boiled, they skimmed the froth off and let it boil for a long time. The sweet aroma filled the air. If I didn't know they were making oil, I would have thought they were making coconut candy. The smoke seeped through the big seams at the back and sides of the fireplace and floated up into the sky. They boiled and skimmed until all that was left was the oil. It took a long time, but in the end, Granny poured the oil into bottles, and she had fresh coconut oil for cooking.

Chapter Fifteen

It was late December, and the sweet sound of Christmas carols played on the radio. Cheerfully, I sang and bopped to the tunes. Each morning, I marked one day off the calendar as Christmas drew nearer. Santa had never found my house before, but I made a list for him anyway and hoped this time, he would. I daydreamed about meeting him, or even just catching a glance at him.

"Granny, would you wake me up when Santa comes this Christmas?"

"Why do you want me to wake you up?"

"So I can see him, and thank him for my gift."

"And how do you know Santa is going to give you a gift?"

"Because I made a list, and I was good all year."

"Oh, okay. We'll see."

The week before Christmas, Granny said we would go to the store. She wanted to see what they had. I perked up, eager to tag along, and couldn't remember the last time we went to a store together. I always went to the store by myself, and Grandpa went to the store on the weekends, but Granny never came along.

Dressed in her allamanda yellow dress and her beige

shoes, me in my baby-blue dress and my black shoes, we stepped out onto the road. The hot, blinding sun beamed mercilessly overhead. Granny opened her big black umbrella, which she took with her everywhere she went. It was to shade her from the sun or shield her from the rain. I held onto her left arm to take refuge under the shade of the umbrella, gleaming like the sunshine as we sauntered along. We passed Ms. Flora's shop, but no one was on the porch, so we went on by.

A bit further up the road, someone yelled, "Hi, Tit Ive!"

"Hi, Marie, how you doing?"

"Good, thank God."

"It's strange seeing you on the road. You takin' a little outin'?"

"Yes, just going up the road."

"Okay, you have a good day."

Someone else passed by and she said, "Good morning."

Then another person passed by. "Good morning."

As the person passed, she said, "You must always say good morning or good evening to people. Never pass people without greeting them and giving them a smile. It does not take anything away from you. And it costs you nothing."

We passed the Chinaman's shop and continued across the road to another store. A glass counter divided the store straight down the middle, and overhead toys hung by clothes-pins on a rope above the counter. Mesmerized by the display of toys in their boxes lined up on shelves behind the counter, I stared in awe. There were dolls in pretty dresses of diverse colors and cute hairstyles, in different lengths and colors. Their eyes twinkled behind their long lashes. Boxes of fine-looking porcelain dishes with dainty flowers, teapots, cups and saucers, spoons and forks, and oh! A pink dining room table and chairs with folding legs. It was the most beautiful sight any eyes could behold.

"Granny, are you going to buy something?" I asked.

"I am not going to buy anything, but maybe Santa might bring you something if you behave yourself. Which one you like?" Gleefully I pointed to a doll and to a set of dishes with cups and saucers and the table set. Oooh, they were the prettiest.

"Go over to the Chinaman's shop and let me know if they have toys over there also."

"No, they don't," I said, still in a daze.

"You don't know because you haven't been. Just go," Granny said.

Reluctantly, I eased away. About to cross the road, I glanced back. Granny was pointing to a toy with her umbrella. Could that be a good sign? Was she telling the shop-keeper she would buy one for me? Walking around the China-man's shop to satisfy Granny's request, I confirmed they had no toys. I went back over to join Granny but she was already saying goodbye to the lady.

"The Chinaman's store doesn't have any toys," I said as we left the store, disappointed she was not carrying any bags.

"Those toys were so pretty," I said, glancing back.

"Yes, they were," she said. "Come on, let's go."

I held onto Granny's arm to share the shelter under her umbrella, daydreaming of all the beautiful toys and wondering whether I would be lucky enough for Santa to bring me one. I prayed he would not miss our house again.

On Christmas Eve, Grandpa bought me two packs of fire-works wrapped in red tissue paper and a small box of sparkles. Mario, Julio, Rudolph, Ligia, Quecha, and Nando came over to fire the rockets. Granny and Grandpa sat on the porch. The night was cool and dark, but the light from the veranda illumi-nated the space. Grandpa gave me a cigarette and a lighter.

"Light the wick right here," Mario said, pointing to the wick protruding from the top of a pack.

"No, they will go off all at once, and be finished. I am going to open the pack so I can light them one at a time."

After carefully removing the red paper wrap and unraveling the cord, the rockets fell on the step, one by one. I gave them each a few to add to what they brought with them and lit the cigarette.

"Let me hold it, let me hold it," Mario said.

We took turns with the cigarette, quickly tossing the firework once lit. Some were tossed far into the darkness, others high over our heads. The loud pop along with the sound of laughter echoed, and the small pieces of paper floated down like confetti, covering the yard. The smoke and the smell of sulfur filled the air.

"That one didn't pop. Get it, Rudolf!" Quecha shouted. Rudolf ran to pick it up. His hand was almost on it when the loud pop went off. Quickly he jumped back, stumbling in his attempt to get away, and we roared with laughter.

"Be careful, you all. You don't want to burn yourselves with those rockets," Granny said.

Cigarette in hand, I lit one and tossed it as far as possible. All eyes were on the red dot in the grass as we waited for it to pop, but to everyone's surprise, the pop went off in my hand. The sound rang out in my ears and I almost jumped out of my skin. My fingers tingled and burned, and the palm of my hand was black with soot.

I had accidentally thrown the cigarette and kept the rocket in my hand. Everyone roared with laughter. Ligia held her belly, she was laughing so hard. The smell of sulfur lingered in my nostrils. My eyes watered as I rushed inside to cool my aching hand by pouring water over it, followed by a dab of Vaseline to soothe the pain. On my return, everyone seemed to have been waiting.

"Let's see, let's see," they said.

"It will be fine," I said, still nursing the burn, but trying to make light of the whole thing.

They laughed even more.

"See, I told you to be careful with those things," Granny said.

We held the tip of our sparkler rod over the flame from the lighter until it burst into a bright golden glow. Stars shot through in the darkness.

Rudolph and Mario ran to the road, where it was even darker, the twinkles vivid through the darkness.

"Granny, Grandpa, look, look!" I shouted, pointing to the golden flicker above their heads lighting up the night. When we were done, the yard was a mess. My work was cut out for me, but it was all worth it.

"Get to bed, young lady," Granny said.

"Can I stay up until Santa comes?" I asked.

"No, how you know what time Santa is going to come? You don't even know if he will come," Granny said. "Get to bed."

"Will you wake me when he comes?" I asked.

"Yes, go to bed."

At daybreak on Christmas morning, a light in the small living room pierced the darkness. It was coming from a flashlight. As I was about to investigate, Granny called: "Bev, come and see what Santa brought you."

I hopped out of bed and ran to see. We didn't have a Christmas tree, but Granny held the gift.

I looked at it and asked, "Where is he? Did you see him?"

"Yes, but he was in a hurry. He had so many gifts to deliver. He left in a hurry."

"But where did he go?"

"He went up the road towards Ms. Mary's house. I think he went to leave their gifts. Come and see what he left you."

"No, Granny, wait. I will look at it later. I'm going to catch him!" I shouted as I ran through the door and up the road. It was before daybreak and visibility was poor. Into Ms. Mary's yard I ran, the grass wet from the morning dew. On the front door, I pounded.

Knock, knock, knock.

Ms. Mary came out. "My God, Bev, what happened?" she asked.

"Have you seen Santa? Did he stop here?"

"Bev," she sighed. "Yes, he came here, but he left already. He was in a hurry."

"Where did he go?"

"He went up the road."

I took off running up the graveled road, still barely seeing my steps, swerving as I ran, trying to avoid the potholes in the road. I arrived at Ms. Melinda's house. Again, I knocked loudly at Ms. Melinda's door.

Knock, knock, knock.

Ms. Melinda opened the door and asked, "Bev, what you doing here this hour of the morning?"

"Ms. Melinda, I am trying to catch Santa. Did he stop here?"

A smile came over her face. "Ai, Bev," she sighed. "Yes, but he left a long time ago, and he was really going fast. He went up in the air with his reindeer. There is no way you are going to catch up with him. It is best you go back home."

I inhaled deeply. I was so close and yet so far. It would be a whole year before I would get the opportunity to see him again. But Ms. Melinda was right. I headed back home downcast, barely dragging my feet, saddened that I missed Santa. The journey back now seemed twice as long.

Back home, Granny asked, "Did you see Santa?"

"No, ma'am," I replied, dragging my words. "He was gone already."

"Never mind, you will get to see him next year."

The next year seemed so far away. My eyes went to my two gifts sitting on the table. "Can I open them?"

"Yes."

Excited to see the contents of my gifts, but wanting to preserve the pretty Christmas paper also, I slowly lifted the tape and opened the paper to reveal the beautiful, bright-pink foldable chairs and table I had seen in the store.

"It's the table and chair set!" I shouted.

Next, the set of white plates and cups with their dainty pink flowers surfaced on the bottom.

"I got plates and cups too!"

I moved on quickly to open the next gift, also being careful not to tear the paper. My jaw dropped. Laying in a perfect box, smiling at me from behind a clear plastic cover, was the most charming doll my eyes ever beheld. She was a true beauty. Her light-blue dress matched her twinkling eyes, and white socks and shoes adorned her feet. Her golden curls caressed her forehead, and the blush of her chubby cheeks matched her bright-pink lips.

My fingers traced her face through the clear plastic, not wanting to take her out of the box so she would never get dirty or destroyed. She was fit to be seen, but not touched. Every detail of her was perfect; the intricate design and embellishments of her beautiful dress, the tiny collar under her neck, her puffed sleeves, and the white laces and dainty bows. Was I really awake? Or was I dreaming? These were my very first toys, and they were all mine.

On the table, I placed the unfolded table and chairs and set the chairs under the table neatly. They were too small for my doll to sit on and too small even to hold a plate from my dining set, but it was so cute. Pretending I had a host of guests sitting at my table, I escorted my doll for her to take a look. Next to the table, I placed my plates and cups, holding the dainty handle of my cup between my finger and thumb to sip my tea; all the while wearing a fixed smile on my face. I took a deep breath and exhaled. It was a dream, and the best day ever.

The day after Christmas, Granny got busy in the kitchen baking her Christmas cakes. The ingredients were spread out on the table.

"I need you to rub the sugar and the butter," she said.

With the large pudding pan on my lap containing the butter and sugar, I rubbed and rubbed to melt and incorporate the sugar. Granny then added the eggs and I rubbed some more. Once done, it was time to grease the pans and Granny filled them with the creamy yellow batter.

The aroma filled the house as the cakes baked, and when finished, she set the cakes on the table to cool. Shortly afterward, she proceeded to take the warm cakes out of the pans and rested them on the small dining room table out of harm's way.

Later that evening, Granny took a cake to Ms. Diney. I was home alone. On the living room floor, I sat with my new toys. The sheer white curtains billowed in the wind next to my table and chairs. My cups and saucers were set nicely in a circle, and my knives and forks rested next to the plates on the floor. I glanced at my doll in her box, pleading to get out.

"Ok, Tania, I will take you out today because we are having a party, but you have to be careful and not get dirty, okay?"

I took her out of the box and sat her on the floor across from me. Her arms reached out to me and her dress spread out nicely around her.

"I will pull the chairs out for our guests to sit. You stay here, as I need to go and get some tea."

I went out, filled a cup with water, and on my way back, I glanced at the cakes on the table.

"Okay, we will move the party to the dining room. I am sorry, can I offer you a piece of cake?" I asked.

I ran to the kitchen and fetched the knife. I took the plate in front of Tania and asked, "May I take your plate, miss?" I cut a nice slice of cake and placed it on the plate.

"I am pleased to serve you, ma'am. If you would like some more, please let me know, as there is a whole cake there just for you."

I took another plate. "Excuse me, ma'am, I will serve you now. There is enough cake for you to all have your own personal cake."

And so, I took a nice slice from every cake to properly entertain my lovely guests. I served tea, and we had a wonderful time of chatter and laughter. I had a bite.

"Hmm! It's delicious! It's the best cake ever." The party moved back to the living room, and we waltzed. In the middle of our dance, I heard a shout.

"Beverly!!" I jolted clean out of my waltz. By the tone of her voice, I knew it was not good.

"Yes, ma'am?" I ambled nervously to my demise. I guess I moved too slowly because Granny met me halfway. She grabbed my hand and dragged me to the table.

"What did you do?!" she shouted. "Why did you cut all the cakes? I baked these cakes to give to my friends, and how do you expect me to give these cakes to them now? You didn't even cut one cake, you cut them all!" she shouted.

I stood frozen and stared at the cakes and the crumbs on the table next to each cake. I stared motionless at the transformed creature standing before me. The raised brow and wrinkled nose, her open hands framing her face, her fingers stiff by sheer rage.

She grabbed my hand and led me to her room, where she grabbed her belt and I got it. Tears flowed down my face; disappointment enveloped me as a dark shadow, evidence of my wrongdoing. I wished I could take my actions back, but it was not possible. I was escorted to my usual spot in the corner of the dining room, where I was ordered to kneel. Definitely not a good way to end a beautiful party.

Chapter Sixteen

Every once in a while, on a weekend, Grandpa would take out his favorite records and listen to music on a small turntable in the living room. This was one of those weekends. Four varnished rocking chairs with rattan weaves on the back and seats faced each other. Granny's and Grandpa's arms followed the curve of the wooden handles. Next to them in a child-size matching rocking chair, I mimicked their stance as we listened attentively to the music.

"Grandpa, I am sitting in my chair just like you."

"It's not your chair, it's your aunt Edna's chair," Granny said.

"Grandpa, would you put on 'La Parranda?'"

He took the record out and I gazed at the cover. There was a guy at the corner with his leg in the air, dancing with all his might. He looked so funny!

"Grandpa, look, that's me, I am the girl with the high boots," I said, laughing. "Put it on! Put it on!"

"Wait, be patient. Let me finish listening to my song." The soft music played, and the record spun and spun. The player was disguised as a briefcase with a handle and all. The top was held open by a shiny metal brace, and inside the cover, the bright-red velvet was pristine. The little lever with the tiny needle lifted up and landed perfectly on the side of the player like magic.

Grandpa took the small record and the centerpiece off the turntable and put on "La Parranda," a long play. Granny sat quietly. The music started and I took to the floor. Grandpa sat down and they both watched as I danced away with my hand on my hip. I wiggled, my feet stepping to the beat, my hands in the air as I turned around and wiggled some more. Granny and Grandpa laughed and laughed.

"Look at this damn fool," Grandpa said.

I didn't care. I sang along and danced the night away.

Granny was laughing so hard. She held her stomach, and as she leaned back laughing, her chair rocked back and forth. She laughed until she had to wipe tears from her eyes. "Now for your father to see what a clown he has for a daughter," she said.

I continued dancing all over the living room. When the music stopped, Grandpa turned off the record player while Granny and I dragged our chairs to the veranda next to his. We watched the passersby through the dark of the night. A man passed by on a motorbike with a girl seated behind him. Her legs hugged his hips.

"Look at that. Don't ever let me see you sitting on a motorbike like that. A lady should have both her legs on one side of the motorbike, not sprawled open to the world. When riding a motorbike or a horse, a lady should have both her legs on one side," Granny said.

I listened attentively.

Shortly afterward, a lady and a man strolled by. The tiny fire from her cigarette followed the movement of her hand as she walked.

Granny commented again. "Now look at that. Don't ever let me see you with a cigarette in your hand like that. A lady should never be seen smoking a cigarette," Granny said.

I listened attentively to her words. They were an indication, to me, of right and wrong, cementing in my mind the desire to live up to these teachings in order to not disappoint or bring shame to Granny and Grandpa—a notion I carried with me through the years.

I glanced at the person coming up the road with a familiar hop. It was Nando. Ligia and Quecha strolled behind him.

"Hey, Kequenk," Grandpa said.

Granny looked at Grandpa and said, "Malcolm, stop that. Call that child by her name."

"Old lady, she needs to learn. She needs to be ready for what will come her way in life. People will call her even worse things than that. She can't be sheltered. She needs to be tough."

Grandpa called Ligia "Kequenk" because she had a speech impediment.

"Let's catch lighties," Nando said.

We called click beetles lighties.

"There are tons out tonight."

"Wait," I said, and ran to get a glass jar.

"Look over there," Quecha said, pointing to the back of the house.

The lighties shone green through the darkness. We went in the direction she pointed. They were scattered under the mango and star apple trees and into the bushes. I gasped at the spectacular sight. The whole backyard was illuminated by the magnificent creatures. The fluorescent green lights blinked and flickered, lighting up the whole area. The view was breathtaking.

"I got one!" "I got one!" "Me too!" echoed the voices throughout the bushes.

"Bring them. Let's put them in the jar," I said.

I held onto one and felt it click in between my fingers. *Click, click, click,* came the sound out of the jar each time they flicked their body and propelled themselves in a high jump.

"Quick, put the cover on! They goin' jump out," said Quecha, grabbing the bottle. "Let me hold it," she said.

"No, wait," I said.

"Open the jar," said Nando. "I got two."

Transfixed, I gazed in awe at the incredible sight. *How was this possible? How could these little bugs, the shape and size of a roach, create such a spectacular show? What made them light up like that?* I asked myself.

I lifted my eyes to the sky and gazed at the stars spread out across the dark-blue sky, but in between the trees and shrubs, the lighties flickered bright green. The chirps of crickets accompanied the show, and the voices in the shrubs faded in the distance.

"Bev!" someone shouted. "You not catching anything."

"Wait," I said, not really wanting to be interrupted.

"Come on. You just standing there doing nothing."

"Let's go in the front and see how much we got," said Nando.

We gathered at the step and stared into the jar, which irradiated with our catch.

"Look at how many we caught!" I showed Granny and Grandpa.

"Don't leave those lighties in that jar, you know, because they will die. What will you feed them?"

"We will let them go afterward," I said. "We just wanted to see how many we could catch."

"You guys have fun. Your free paper will soon burn when you get back to school next week," Granny said.

It was a new school year, and my first day at my new school. The school was adjacent to the church we attended. Compared to my previous school, this one was way bigger. The two rectangular concrete structures stood parallel to each other and were clearly visible through the aluminum and glass louvered window. The light-beige finish had an almost peachy aura from the rays of the sunlight illuminating the wall.

The atmosphere was daunting at first. I had difficulty finding my way from classroom to classroom, not knowing exactly where to go, plus unfamiliar faces, meeting new teachers, and adjusting to my new surroundings.

In my new classroom, I took a seat in the second row as the teacher shuffled paper at her desk.

A girl entered and said, "Good morning," as she passed by the teacher's desk.

"Beverly," the teacher said. I looked up, about to respond, when the girl said, "Yes, ma'am."

"You need to sign in."

I was awestruck. I had never heard of another person having my name before. It was a true novelty.

She took the paper and as she held her pencil, I saw she had two thumbs. I stared in awe. *How can someone have two thumbs?* I thought. Then I glanced at the hand holding the paper and realized there were two thumbs on that hand as well. *How was this possible?* She held the pencil just fine. Her thumbs moved together simultaneously as if they were one, and didn't seem to bother her in the least. But to me, it was another novelty.

Then, it dawned on me. She has twelve fingers and her name is Beverly. How awesome is that? She seemed to be a bit older than me. We had the same complexion, but her hair was shorter and of a coarser texture than mine, and she was tall and skinny.

At recess, I introduced myself. "Hi, I am Beverly too," I said.

She smiled. "I heard when the teacher called you Beverly, and I thought, what? There are two Beverlys in the class."

"I am new here, and you?" I asked.

"No, I attended this school before. I live next door," she said.

"Oh. Do they have a library at this school?"

"No, I don't think there is a library anywhere on the island."

I enjoyed reading the stories in my textbook. Books opened a world of fantasy to me. A library filled with books would surely be heavenly. The notion of being able to borrow books to take home and sit around and read to my heart's content would be priceless. Even if I could get only one, that would be a dream come true.

My heart sank. I was hoping there would be a library at this new school because it was so much bigger than my previous school, but instead, my hopes were shattered. My dream of reading was just that, a dream.

Each week, we memorized lessons in social studies and science or were called upon to recite our multiplication tables. Failure to do so resulted in two whops with a ruler in the palm of the hand as punishment for the infraction.

At recess, I asked a classmate who often received whips, "Does it hurt when the teacher whips you with that ruler?"

"No, I know what to do not to feel it."

"What do you do?"

"I rub garlic in my hand and when she whips me, it does nothing to me. I don't feel it. She could even break her ruler in my hand, and I wouldn't feel it."

Thoughts of the garlic trick swirled in my head and that evening when Grandpa asked if I had any homework, I said no.

The next morning, I got a clove of garlic and wrapped it in a piece of paper. I went to class, hoping not to be called to recite my assignment, but prepared if I was. Before class, I rubbed my hand with the garlic. "P.U.," I said to myself as I turned my nose up at the smell.

Everyone stared and unfortunately, I was called. I stood at

the front of the class and the teacher said, "Let's hear the passage."

"I don't remember it."

"Extend your hand."

Hesitantly, I extended my palm, conscious of the pungent garlic smell, and waited for the blow. The first whop landed with a painful sting. I drew my hand back swiftly. Right away, I knew this garlic thing didn't work. I glanced at my peers looking on in complete silence while I tried my best to keep my composure and not frown or cry.

"Come on, give your hand," she repeated.

Reluctantly, I extended my hand again and *wham!* The slap of the ruler against my hand echoed in my ears. My face flushed with embarrassment and my palm burned red from the sting, but I tried hard to suppress my pain with a shy grin.

Shortly afterward, I asked to be excused and went to the restroom to wash away the remnants of the useless remedy, along with its awful smell. Even after washing with soap a couple of times, the smell lingered. This garlic trick was definitely not for me. This was a lesson learned.

It was mid-morning, and on my way to the living room to sweep the floors, as I passed the bedrooms, I felt a strange sensation of being followed. I stopped, and somehow, it felt as though whoever was following me had stopped too.

I walked slowly again, then swiftly turned around. My eyes caught sight of a man who hid quickly behind the door. He wore a well-tailored black jacket, black pants, well-polished black shoes, and a snow-white ruffled shirt with a collar up to his neck. He quickly took off his low black top hat and pulled it over his face as he hid behind the door. I ran towards the door and peeked behind it. There was no one.

Just then, I heard Granny call, "Bev!"

I looked up and saw her looking at me with a puzzled look on her face.

"Did you see him?"

"See who?" she asked.

"The man. He hid behind the door when I turned around. Did you see him?"

"Come here." I went to her and she said, "That must have been your guardian angel. I want you to learn a prayer and I want you to say this prayer anytime anything like this happens to you again, and don't be afraid. The prayer is Psalm 23."

The Lord is my Shepherd I shall not want, he maketh me to lie down in green pastures, he leadeth me beside the still waters, he restoreth my soul, he leadeth me in the path of righteousness for his name's sake. Yea, though I walk through the valley of the shadow of death, I will fear no evil, for thou art with me, thy rod and thy staff they comfort me, thou preparest the table before me in the presence of mine enemies, thou anointest my head with oil, my cup runneth over. Surely goodness and mercy shall follow me all the days of my life and I will dwell in the house of the Lord forever.

I repeated the prayer over and over until I learned it.

At the gate, while enjoying the evening sun, my eyes caught a glimpse of a young, brown-skinned man strolling barefoot toward me. Threads hung from the uneven, cut-off legs of his shorts. The sides of his slit T-shirt blew in the wind. Where once there were sleeves, now there were only jagged armholes. His slanted eyes squinted even more as he said, "Hi, sis."

It was my older brother, Rockwell. I had met him a long time ago, but rarely saw him. He stopped by every now and again. Most of his time was spent fishing and diving.

"Hi."

"What you up to, sis?" he asked.

"Nothing," I said.

"I bring something for you."

"For me?"

"Yes." He put his hand in his pocket and pulled out the prettiest pink shells I had ever seen. I gasped at their beauty. They were the biggest and shiniest shells I had ever seen. Their unique designs and speckles reminded me of the speckles on a fawn.

"Wow," I said.

"I found these when I was diving."

"How did you get them so shiny?"

"There is a trick."

"What's the trick?"

"Put them in powder, and they'll keep their shine."

"Oh, I am going to keep my shells in powder too. I am going to keep them always shiny."

Then he put his hand in his pocket again and brought out a handful more. "I got these on the beach," he said, smiling.

"What! Thank you!" I said. There were several kinds, and they were all shiny and pretty. "I will keep them in a bottle."

"Okay, I will bring you some more next time. See you later," he said as he went up the road.

"Okay," I said, and ran inside.

"Granny, can I have a bottle please?"

"A bottle? What do you need a bottle for?"

"Rockwell brought me the prettiest shells and I want to put them in a bottle."

"When did Rockwell bring you shells?"

"Just now, he was walking up the road and stopped to give me some shells."

"And why didn't he come in and say hi?"

"I don't know."

Granny gave me a small bottle. I ran inside and got some powder and put my shells inside. I could not wait to go to the beach and look for more. This became my favorite pastime—to walk the beach and look for shells.

It was the end of December, and I was happy to be on vacation, as was every other eight-year-old on the island. Granny went to visit a friend of hers who lived across from the airport. We walked across the airport runway, a paved area slightly wider than the road, and got to their house.

While she chatted with her friend, I stayed outside and leaned on the fence post. The children raced up and down on their bicycles. Pebbles and rocks littered the narrow, winding dirt lane that cut through high grass on both sides. One boy fell off his bicycle and into the bushes, and another tried to help him up.

"Buay, you see? Ah tell you, you can't ride."

"It's the rocks, man."

"Yeah, man, the rocks," they all laughed.

Soon they were all back on their bicycles and racing again. *It must be so much fun to have a bicycle,* I thought.

My mind drifted to the big bicycle Grandpa once had reclined against the window in the bedroom. My hands had moved softly over the soft cushioned seat, unable to sit on it as it was too high. *One day I will be big enough to reach the seat,* I said to myself while I gripped the soft rubber on the tip of the shiny handlebars and admired the slender wheels.

The hollow feeling in my gut came to mind the day I walked into the room and saw the empty space. My shoulders sagged and drooped; my hands hung limp when Granny said that Grandpa had given it away. I had been so eager to grow up to be big enough to be able to reach the seat and ride that bicycle. That dream was taken away in an instant.

Up and down the road the children went, swaying back and forth. *I know I could learn to ride very quickly,* I said to myself.

"Come on, let's go," Granny said as she pulled me out of my thoughts. We walked across the runway as they faded in the distance.

Will I ever be able to get a bicycle of my own? I wondered. *Perhaps if I write to Santa, I might be lucky.*

We strolled home, my eyes drifting through the tall coconut trees, and below, the vibrant green accordion-shaped cups of the unopened new leaves on the young palms swayed in the wind. On the oceanfront, I gazed at the boats tied to the dock. Others were anchored out on their own, with names like *Island Princess* and *Blue Diamond.*

Men busied themselves on the pier, and Granny greeted random people along the way. The sun, warm, bright, and inviting, shimmered over the clear blue water. The vast ocean extended to the horizon. The clouds moved ever so slowly across the clear blue sky.

We took our time as we strolled along, as most islanders did. There was no need to rush. It was one of those rare times I strolled with Granny on an outing other than going to church, and I felt special and privileged to share in such pleasure.

Chapter Seventeen

The *tweet, tweet* of a yellow warbler drew my eyes between the branches of the mango tree, and the gentle sway of the leaves brought me to a place of sweet serenity amidst the pleasant coolness of the peaceful morning. The crow of a rooster brought me back to earth. I had work to do.

The coconut broom in my hand was well-tested to ensure it met the high standard required for the job. A firm grip on the handle and strong bristles on the bottom indicated it was well suited to accomplish the task. The clean sweep of some dry leaves in a small area confirmed the broom was good to go. Next to the step, I rested my well-tested apparatus and looked around the yard as I examined the turf.

It was seven o'clock—a good time to start. The earlier, the better.

"The early bird gets the early worm," Granny always said.

Work was always more pleasant in the cool air, as later in the day the sun blazed hot like fire on Corn Island.

"Where should I start?" I asked myself aloud.

The barbwire fence at the side of the house was weighed down in a thick layer of bright-green vines and gave the area the look of an abandoned place. It beckoned for attention. The pillow-sized bulk that ran along the full length of the fence was in serious need of cleaning.

"Yes, this is a good place to start," I told myself.

After a good pull at some vines and the realization that this was not a job for small, bare hands, I reached for the machete. The task seemed overwhelming, but not impossible. I could do this.

Being careful not to hit the barbwire and blunt Grandpa's machete, the chore went on. Little by little, bit by bit, the cuttings on the heap grew larger and larger. With extended arms, gripping as much as my small arms could carry, I trekked to the heap at the back of the house. The wad of wilted leaves impaired my visibility. With my head looking over my shoulders, I guessed each and every step along the way to drop my first load on the top of the mound. *Granny and Grandpa are going to be so proud of me when they see how clean I am going to leave this fence,* I thought.

In my attempt to attain a sense of belonging, I strived to impress my grandparents through my chores. It was a way to catch their attention and make them proud of me, a way to earn their acceptance.

Several trips later, the bundles of wilted leaves were piled high on top of the heap. Sweat rolled down my face and into my eyes, making them sting and burn. I wiped my eyes and forehead with the back of my grimy arm, my efforts futile. The under part of my dress tail proved most effective.

I looked at my dirt-caked nails and smiled at what I thought Grandpa would say. *"You better clean those nails because I could plant cassava in them."*

On the other side of the house, I continued to sweep under the mango tree and the star apple tree, moving slowly as the pile of dry leaves grew higher and higher. Steadily, I dropped my loads on top of the heap. My throat burned with thirst. After fetching a quick drink of water in the kitchen, I plodded out again to continue my task.

Around the cluster of palm-like supa trees—pejibay—I swept. Their trunks were covered in sharp, two-inch-long, jet-black prickles. In between the needle-length spikes I reached in an attempt to extract one, but this was next to impossible. After a couple of painful strikes, I gave up on the idea.

My eyes climbed the prickly trunks to the top. The clear blue sky peeked through the leaves as they swayed in the wind. Four large bunches of bright orange-red supas dangled at the top like bunches of miniature coconuts.

How is Grandpa going to get those bunches of supa? I wondered. *No one can climb this tree, that's for sure. The stick we use for picking fruits is way too short and the bag way too small.*

Hours later, I was finally finished. The chickens cackled and the roosters crowed as they flapped their wings and went along, picking the freshly exposed earth. Even the breeze seemed cooler as it flowed softly under the trees. Ms. Mary stood at the window speaking to Granny.

"Wow, Tit Ive, your yard looks spick and span. Bev did a good job."

"Yeah, she can do a good job when she put her mind to it," she replied.

I smiled, pleased with the comment, and continued on to the cacao tree to get my treat.

A bright-orange cacao hung from the trunk, ripe and ready. With both hands, I gripped and twisted it until it was free. A few taps of the fruit on the tree trunk while gently turning the fruit round and round, just as Grandpa showed me, caused it to break into two halves. Removing the top exposed a cluster of cotton-white seeds heaped high, resembling a huge ice cream cone. The soft, cotton-like flesh over the seed melted in my mouth, mmm! Tangy and sweet.

On the concrete ledge of the house post, I sat in the shade and ate my cacao, removing the delicious seeds one by one from the vine in the middle of the cluster. Next to the semi-dried collection of seeds drying on the well's concrete ledge, I added my contribution. Once completely dried, Granny would parch them to make cacao tea.

Saturday evenings were the best. It was when Grandpa went to the store to do the grocery shopping. On his return, he always brought me a treat. A Cuban Piruli, a lollipop, or peppermint candies in a bag. Sometimes even a twin-stick popsicle.

What will he bring me this evening? I pondered. As he entered the yard, I ran to greet him. I looked up at the small box he carried on his shoulder like a puppy waiting for a treat.

"Grandpa, did you get me a treat?"

"I don't know. You have to wait and see."

"Yes, you know."

"No, I don't. You have to wait and see."

He put the box on the table and proceeded to take out the groceries. I knelt on the chair, waiting patiently. One by one, the items surfaced: two cans of Carnation milk, a bag of flour, a bag of sugar, rice, and coffee, then finally, a newspaper package wrapped like a big cone.

"Roasted peanuts! Oooh, thank you, Grandpa!" I chuckled, hugging the parcel to my chest as I hopped out of the chair. "You see, I told you, you knew!"

It was already dark. Granny packed away the groceries, and we went on the porch. On the stairs, beneath the light of a single bulb, unfolding the top of my newspaper cone, I reached in for my peanuts. Firmly squeezing and cracking the shell, I emptied the contents into my palm, and a gentle pinch of the kernels removed their delicate burgundy-red covering. A soft blow in my hand sent the burgundy-red skins into the air. I then handed some to Granny and Grandpa because it is always good to share.

A few days later, Grandpa got an impressively long stick from a friend of his and with a large bag attached to it, picked a bunch of supa. Granny put them to a boil, then I waited patiently for them to cool. Granny placed some plump ones into a bowl and handed them to me. I gripped the top with my teeth and slowly peeled the skin away, exposing the bright-orange flesh. Savory and delicious, a tiny mini coconut was in the middle. Sometimes I cracked the shell with my teeth, the flesh in the center like a miniature coconut, but nah, it was not as delicious as the orange flesh. That was the best.

December popped around. It was time to start the Christmas cleaning: time to remove cobwebs from around the ceiling and corners of the house. Down came the curtains, piled high for Ms. Zena to wash. The wiping of the walls followed. I got the bucket with soapy suds, dipped a rag inside, then tackled the beadboard panels and wainscoting trim. On my knees, coconut husks in hand, I tackled the floors. The smell of Pine-Sol floated through the air, leaving behind a clean, fresh scent.

The calendar on the wall drew my attention each morning. Eagerly, I counted down the days left until Christmas.

Christmas was that special time of the year when even the weather changed. The climate became cooler, and we got an extended vacation from school. There were special programs, both at school and church, and excitement was in the air as people rallied around in anticipation. And yes, I would have another opportunity to meet Santa.

Chapter Eighteen

Eagerly, I marked another day off the calendar. Only a few more days remained before Christmas.

"Take this bowl and go and get me some mimbros. I want to make some pepper sauce today. When you get back, I have something to tell you," Granny said.

"Tell me? What?"

"I said to go first. I will tell you when you get back."

Bowl in hand, I headed to the mimbro tree, puzzled by her comment.

What does she want to tell me? In front of the mimbro tree, I picked a couple of mimbros off the tree trunk and put them in the bowl. Then I said to myself, *She always tells me what she wants to tell me right away, so why didn't she tell me now? I better hurry up so I can find out. The quicker I get back, the quicker I will know.*

I filled the bowl, then took a small one and took a bite. The sour taste gripped the tendons in my neck and wrapped them over my ears. At least that's how it felt as my mouth watered. *I should have brought some salt,* I thought, and quickly made my way back to the kitchen.

"Granny, here are the mimbros. What are you going to tell me?"

She took the bowl and smiled as she looked at me.

"Tomorrow, we are going away." She put the bowl on the table.

"We are going away? Where we going?"

"We are going to visit your father in Managua, and we will also visit your aunt Edna and aunt Delcy."

Mesmerized, I gasped. "What? Tomorrow?"

"Yes, we did not tell you anything before because you would not have known what to do with yourself."

My jaw dropped and my eyes widened as I danced in excitement.

"And we are going to stop in Bluefields so that you can meet your mother."

Her words stopped me in my tracks. Not convinced or even wanting to believe what I heard, I questioned myself. *Did I really hear right?*

"I am going to see my mother tomorrow?" I asked, staring into Granny's face, wanting to make sure I understood correctly; attempting to read the expression on her face, making sure it was not a joke.

"Yes, you are going to meet your mother tomorrow."

Not knowing whether I should jump up or sit down, I froze and gazed through the window, lost in thought as if transported to that faraway land I often dreamed of. Bluefields was a place known to me only in my thoughts.

My mother . . . the notion of finally seeing her face . . . an image that always eluded me. *What will it be like to see her for the first time? Will she like me?* Butterflies flickered in my stomach. I wasn't sure if my nerves were for the thought of getting on a plane or the notion of meeting my mother. *Is this really going to happen?* The idea of seeing my father again was also unnerving. *Would he evade me as he did before?* I wondered. In addition to all this, it would be my first time flying because being a toddler on my arrival, travel escaped my memory, and I had no recollection of going anywhere since.

Granny broke my thoughts as she spoke. "We have to pack our things this evening, as we are going on the plane early in the morning."

The excitement was overwhelming, resulting in a desire to jump and prance, but at the same time, I was reflective. My heart raced and my fists clenched as I took deep breaths in an attempt to calm down, as if by clenching my fists I was holding my heart to reduce the racing thump.

That evening we packed, and for the first time, I was eager to go to bed to fall asleep, wake up, and find it was time to go. Instead, I tossed and turned. I lay wide awake, counting sheep. At the crack of dawn, I shot off to the dining room. "Granny, we are going today, right?"

"Good morning, Beverly, did I sleep with you? How many times do I have to tell you to always remember your manners?"

"Good morning. We are going today, right?"

"Yes, Beverly. Come and have your breakfast, then go and take your bath and get ready. We need to get to the airport early. Your grandfather is bathing now."

"Yes, ma'am."

Ms. Vanji came over. She would take care of the house.

I raced through breakfast faster than ever before. It was as if my jaw didn't want to keep up with my brain and chew faster. Overtaken by jitters, I made a dash to the bathroom, took my bath, wrapped myself with the towel, and ran out. Granny and Grandpa were already dressed.

"Your dress is on the bed. Go and get ready, and don't waste time, as we don't want to be late," Granny said.

Shortly afterward, I was out of the bedroom, dressed in my Sunday finest and ready to go. Grandpa went ahead to have the luggage checked in. "I'll see you there," he said as he left.

Along the road, wild yellow daisies swayed softly in the wind as I hurried along in front of Granny, keeping close to the edge and away from the traffic, even though there was not much traffic to evade. In the distance, the familiar airport was in sight when I felt something sliding loose under my dress and down my legs.

Making a swift maneuver to grab the mysterious object, it dawned on me that it was the towel. In my rush, I pulled my dress over my head and forgot to take off the towel. Wide-eyed, I glanced back at Granny and said, "It's the towel. I forgot to take it off."

Granny frowned and shook her head. "Give it to me. I will put it in my hand luggage," she said.

Embarrassed, I glanced around, hoping no one was close enough to see me pull off the towel from under my dress in the middle of the road. Granny pushed it down in her bag and we continued.

At the airport, I spotted a huge propeller plane on the runway. A blue horizontal stripe was painted across the middle. The vibrant blue stemmed from the cockpit straight across to the tail, encasing the windows. Above the line, the words "LA NICA" were depicted in big, bold letters in the same blue as the stripe.

In front of the engines, the three-prong blades of the propellers curved majestically, one blade almost touching the ground. The blue-and-white flag with its triangular shield perched high on the tail as if flying in the wind.

A tall ladder guided our steps up to the open door as we boarded. My hand glided along the metal rail as I climbed the stairs.

My emotions went around in loops as if on a roller-coaster ride. One minute, I was thrilled about the new adventure of going on a plane ride; on the other hand, I was excited about spending time with my father for the first time. But the thought of meeting my mother was nerve-racking. *What is she like? Will she be happy to meet me?*

Granny and Grandpa walked ahead as we went down the

corridor. Grandpa showed me my seat at the window and took his seat across the aisle. Granny sat down next to me and we fastened our seat belts.

Shortly afterward, the noise of the engine replaced the murmurs of the passengers and the plane started to move. The aircraft marshal signaled to the pilot with his orange baton, and the plane rolled onto the runway. The flight attendant opened a pamphlet and instructed, then took her seat and the engine revved, speeding past the coconut trees as they waved their palms in farewell.

Up and up we went. My back pressed into the back of the seat and my fingers gripped the handle as my heart raced in my chest. Trying to clear my ears, I yawned and then gasped as the plane did a sudden drop. The unexpected turn to the side, the rapid ascent, the constant motion, and the noise from the engine were more than I could bear. *This must be what they talk about when they refer to a roller-coaster ride,* I thought. *Now I know that I don't like roller-coaster rides.* My stomach churned.

"I'm not feeling well," I whispered.

Granny handed me an airbag just in time for me to discard all my breakfast. The sour taste in my mouth and the putrid smell in the bag made me want to be sick even more.

"We will soon be there. The flight isn't long," Granny said.

But this was the longest 'soon' I had ever experienced. Time seemed to stand still; 'soon' never seemed to come. When the wheels finally touched the runway, I sighed in relief and wished they would hurry up and open the door so I could get my feet on firm ground and breathe in some fresh air.

Granny and Grandpa's friend, Miss Julia, came to the airport to fetch us. We all climbed into a taxi. The bright-red soil on the road was so different from the pale, sand-mingled soil on Corn Island. The evidence of rain was clearly visible through the large puddles of mud that lined the street.

The taxi rambled from one side of the road to the other, trying unsuccessfully to avoid the puddles. Up and down, the car dipped in and out of the puddles thick as paint. Copious amounts of red paste painted the path. The colorful shades of umbrellas floated along the road. Children in torn shorts and tattered shirts ambled along. A boy walked backward as he shouted at another, laughing as he went.

This is Bluefields, I thought. I was finally here. I had heard of this place so many times, the place where my mother lived; a town on the Atlantic side of Nicaragua. The population is composed mainly of people of African descent who came to the country from Jamaica or the Cayman Islands, but they also have various indigenous ethnicities native to the land such as the Spaniards, the Miskito Indians, the Ramas, and the Garifuna. Each group speaks its own language. The Blacks speak English, the Spaniards speak Spanish, the Miskito their Miskito dialect, the Ramas their Rama dialect, and of course, the Garifuna speak Garifuna. But as the national language is Spanish, education, radio, and TV are all conducted in Spanish, and therefore, most of the population is bilingual.

We disembarked at Ms. Julia's house. A beautiful, white, cottage-style structure with a wraparound porch and a concrete walkway leading up to the steps invited us in. Parallel panels of dark wood finished the floor. A large bench leaned against the wall at the entrance. To the left, a white wooden swing hung by chains from the ceiling. Ms. Julia's sister, Ta Jane, greeted us warmly as we arrived. Her name was Jane, but they called her Ta Jane—short for Sister Jane.

"Welcome, stranger," she said as she wrapped her arms around Granny.

We settled into their guest bedroom. Shortly afterward, we were invited to lunch, which was not very appealing as my stomach was still queasy from my roller-coaster ride. Granny and Grandpa chatted with Ms. Julia and Ms. Ta Jane.

"We will have to rise tomorrow at the crack ah dawn to catch the Express," Granny said.

The Express, I gathered, was the boat that would take us

to Rama. "We want to be in Managua for Christmas. Today is the twentieth already. We have a whole day of traveling, so we'll get there on the twenty-first, just in time for Christmas."

I went onto the porch and held onto the swing. Up the road, the glossy gray hue of a lake caught my eye, and the soft breeze off the lake blew coolly on the porch. Shortly afterward, Ms. Julia and Granny came out as well.

Ms. Julia called to a boy passing by. She went out and spoke to the boy and he left. Then Grandpa and Ms. Ta Jane came out too. They talked and laughed for a while. Ms. Julia pointed to the boy she had spoken to earlier. He approached the house along with a lady.

Granny said to me, "Bev, do you see the lady coming with that boy over there?"

I got up from the swing and stared up the road. "Yes, ma'am," I replied, dragging my words ever so slightly.

"That lady is your mother."

I could not believe it. There she was, just a few steps away. We made eye contact, yet there was still a distance between us. Her features were not yet visible, and my legs froze as I stared.

Then, as if propelled by sheer emotion, I dashed off as though seeing the finish line in a one-hundred-meter race, stopping only as my arms wrapped around her in a big embrace. In my mind, this was the appropriate way to meet and greet your mother for the first time.

"Hi," I said awkwardly, not knowing what else to say or how to address her. I was feeling bashful and apprehensive, skeptical of her reaction, wondering what Granny and Grandpa must be thinking as they looked on. I glanced back to take in their feedback, but they were now too far away.

"Hi," she said.

She was an attractive lady with a dark-brown complexion, dressed in brown pants and a pink blouse. Wefts of her dark-brown hair graced her neck. She bent down and returned the hug. I was taken aback to see her with a cigarette in her hand.

Oftentimes, Granny had said it was awful to see a woman smoking a cigarette. It was an abomination; an undignified look.

"Don't you ever let me see you with a cigarette in your mouth," Granny once said. I wondered what Granny would say now.

My mother took a long haul on her cigarette and gave a slow puff of smoke in the air as she approached the porch. They greeted each other and after a short introduction she asked, "Is it okay if I take her home to introduce her to the family?"

"Sure," Granny said.

We walked in silence as I tried to keep up with her. Feeling uneasy, curious, and apprehensive, anticipating the moment I would meet my people; the ones I had been told didn't want me. I wondered what was going through her mind. An expanse of soft, green, low-cut lawn widened before us, proving an opportunity for comment.

"This field is pretty," I said, trying to make small talk.

"Yes, it's called Big Field," she said.

On the fringes, a white house high on stilts drew my attention. Straight ahead, another smaller house with green wooden walls and a pink-railed porch invited us into the neighborhood. We continued awkwardly across the field and entered a yard.

"This is where I live," she said.

To the right, a boy in tattered, navy-blue shorts pulled on a rope from a pulley that dangled from a stick. This was held by two posts stretched over and across a well, and he leaned in to reach for the bucket that surfaced out of the crater. The ends of his unbuttoned yellow shirt flopped in the wind. Into the pail next to his feet, he poured the contents of the bucket.

"That's your brother, Charles," she said in passing.

Trailing behind her, I tried to keep up, but my gaze was fixed on the boy. I was awestruck at seeing my brother for the first time. His stare was also fixed on me. The grass stopped at the edge of a patch of red soil, facing an unpainted wooden house perched high on stilts. The wood walls were aged dark gray; the windows opened wide, sustained by two hinges hanging crookedly against the wall.

A flock of pigeons pacing back and forth on the bare red soil took my breath away. Their tiny pink feet marched swiftly, following the forward movements of their heads bopping back and forth as they pecked on their feed. Some lifted in short flights and back down again. The flop of their wings and the muffled cooing floated above the flock. There were white ones, brown ones, and black ones, but most of all there were gray ones. Their necks wore a shimmer of green that rested perfectly on a clean gray. I had never seen real live pigeons before, and there they were, as tame as the chickens back home.

An old woman with a chocolate complexion and a short silver Afro watched us from the kitchen window as we approached. She held a sky-blue pipe to her mouth as she blew smoke into the air like an active volcano. We stopped just at the foot of the stairs. She came to the door and my mother said, "This is Gangan, my grandmother."

Expecting a warm greeting and a hug, I stepped forward, about to make a closer approach, and barely said hi when she took her pipe out of her mouth, puffed some smoke in the air and said, "Oh, so this is that spoiled brat that old lady is raising."

My eyebrows reached for my hairline; my eyes widened, puzzled by her comment. My mind raced in defiance. Why would she call Granny an old lady? She is older than Granny. And how would she know if I was spoiled or not? She doesn't know me, and I'm not a spoiled brat.

My mother beckoned. "Come on," she said, jolting me out of my thoughts.

Happy to comply, we went to my mother's house on the

right, facing the other house. My mother took a seat in a chair made of wrought iron wrapped with a light-blue plastic string, her back to me. Quietly seated on a green wooden bench behind her, I waited for a conversation to start. Instead, she gazed through the window in complete silence.

Awkwardly glancing around, not knowing what to say or do, I waited. A little girl came into the room and pulled a door to what seemed to be a bedroom. Holding onto the handle, she stared at me, and I returned a puzzled look at this intrusion. Granny always said that when company came to visit, they stayed in the living room or in the dining room, but never in the bedroom.

Turning to my mother I said, "That little girl is going into your bedroom."

She glanced at the little girl and said, "That's your sister Lisa."

"Oh," I said, awestruck at this new revelation. At a loss for words, unaware I even had a sister, my glance went back to the little girl. She approached my mother and propped herself between her legs. She continued to stare at me.

"Go and call Katherine and Delrin," my mother told Lisa.

Lisa went running out the door. Shortly after, another girl, a bit older, came into the living room. With her came another little boy, smaller than Lisa. They scanned me up and down as they entered the room, dawdling close to the partition and as far away from me as they could. I wondered who they were.

"This is Katherine, your sister, and that's Delrincito, your brother," my mother said.

Slowly, my chin went down as I stared intently, trying to get my brain to digest what I heard. *Yes, she said they were my brother and sisters. Wow, I had no idea I had so many siblings!*

My sister Lisa took her position back between my mother's legs and continued to stare. I'm also her daughter and should be able to lean on her lap as she was doing, but somehow, I knew that liberty was not afforded me.

My eyes lifted to Katherine and Delrin, who inspected me as they would an alien from outer space. They glanced at each other, communicating through their eyes. My mother broke the silence. "This is your sister, Beverly."

If only I had a camera to capture the gape on their faces as they glared. I would have won an outstanding best picture award for sure.

Delrincito answered, "No, she is not."

Katherine elbowed him. No one else muttered a sound. If tension was cheese and I had a knife, I could raise my hand in the air and cut a slice. Trailing the wall, they eased themselves through the door.

"Am I the eldest?" I asked, just to have something to say.

"Yes," she said, rising to her feet. "It's time to head back."

The sun was dim as we crossed Big Field, once again in silence. At the house, she knocked on the door and Ms. Ta Jane opened it.

"I bring her back," she said.

"Would you like to come in?"

"No, thanks, I am just dropping her off." She hugged me. "Okay, have a safe trip," she said.

"Okay, thank you," I said, and she left.

Granny and Grandpa asked, "How did it go?"

Still trying to figure it out myself, I said, "Okay. I have two brothers and two sisters."

"Oh, okay," Granny said.

"Man. I forgot to ask her when is my birthday."

"You can ask your father when we get to Managua," Granny said.

"You came just in time. We are about to sit down for supper," Ms. Julia said.

After supper, a muffle of conversations drifted around me, but I was lost in my thoughts. Trying to decipher the events of the evening, I asked myself if I have so many brothers and sisters, why am I not there, living with them?

"Time for bed, young lady. We have to be at the dock at four a.m. tomorrow," Granny said, interrupting my thoughts.

It was at daybreak when we arrived at the wharf. Silhouettes of the passengers paced back and forth in the dark, like shadow people. Wedged at its side, sandwiched against the pier, the tiers squished and the water lapped rhythmically as the vessel swayed. We stepped onboard and fumbled across the empty hall, trying to keep our balance as we reached for our seats, our eyes straining to adjust to the darkness.

The noise of the engines was deafening, the awful smell of burnt diesel nauseating, and my heart raced. I got close to Granny and leaned on her nervously, fearing I may be sick again. The noise got louder as the boat moved slowly forward.

Into the darkness I stared, wanting desperately to be able to lie down and sleep and not wake up until we were already there. That was wishful thinking. The roar of the engine was constant, as was the bumping sound as the bow went up and then slammed back down on the water. After a while, the glimpse of daybreak peeped on the horizon, and visibility became clearer and clearer.

The boat meandered through the river path, breaking the reflection of the trees and shrubs as it undulated forward. Golden rays of sunlight pierced through the branches. A tinge of dusky pink brushed the horizon while overhead, the clouds moved slowly on. The vivid green and yellow appeared brighter in the distance, and the coconut trees seemed to curtsy at our approach.

Small canoes carrying natives glided along the riverside as tiny huts seemed to float by along the riverbanks, becoming more frequent as we approached Rama. Women stood waist-deep in the murky water washing clothes while the children swam and played. We approached a large pier and the people onboard busied themselves collecting their possessions as they got ready to disembark.

On shore, we approached a tiny hut with a big open

window. Plastic bags full of loaves of bread and pastries hung from the frame and sill, and adjacent tables shaded by overhead branches provided a place to sit.

"You sit and watch the bags. I will see what they have for breakfast," Grandpa said. Granny went with him. The aroma of freshly brewed coffee filled the air. In the distance, a row of buses lined the street. People lined up to buy tickets, and others were getting their luggage onto the buses. It wasn't long before Granny and Grandpa came back with bread, cheese, and coffee, and a cup of chocolate for me.

Grandpa ate quickly. "I'll get the tickets."

A short while later, he came back with a young man to assist with the luggage, tickets in hand. We made our way onto a blue bus. Once again, I smelled the awful smell of burned fuel. The *psst* sound of the buses seemed to spread the fumes that permeated the air, filling me with dread. I got a handkerchief from Granny and covered my nose. Oh, I couldn't wait for this trip to be over!

"How long before we reach Managua?" I asked.

"The ride will take over eight hours," Granny said. My heart sank. I wished I had not asked the question.

After what seemed an eternity on the road, I tried to calm my nerves, my anxiety, and the feeling of nausea by gazing at the scenery. Some areas were so beautiful, they took my breath away. The early morning sun enhanced the colors of the meadow. The hills, valleys, and luscious greens of grass were kept low by the grazing of the cattle or perhaps nature itself. The trees in the distance mirrored the creation of carefully crafted bonsai. Cattle scattered, grazing in the distance, creating a view so beautiful only the hand of a painter could capture it. How I wished I had such talent.

My thoughts were interrupted by the slowing down of the bus. People walked towards the bus with big baskets on their heads, others with plastic bags carrying peeled oranges and green mangoes cut up in slices, pastries, and loaves of bread. Children chanted, "Rosquiiillas, churros, galletas, heladooos."

"We can get off here and rest our legs a bit," Grandpa said.

"We can use the restroom and get something to eat," Granny added.

They bought a bag of peeled oranges. Granny said they would help to settle my stomach. They also bought some rosquillas and some churros to eat along the way. I especially liked the finger-size churros. They were crunchy and covered in sweet molasses.

Soon afterward, we were on the road again. My thoughts drifted as I bit into my churros, excited about the proximity to our final destination and the anticipation of finally being able to spend a lot of time with my father. *I am going to spend Christmas with him. Wow.* I smiled at the thought.

Chapter Nineteen

We arrived at my father's house late in the afternoon and had supper together that evening. Granny and Grandpa entertained themselves with small talk and prepared for their next day's early departure. They were going to Chinandega to spend Christmas with my aunt Delcy and her family.

"You'll stay here and spend Christmas with your father," Granny said.

The prospect was unnerving and uncomfortable, and I cringed at the thought. Having not spent time with him before produced an uneasy feeling. He was alien to me, but for him to love me, he would have to know me. It was now the time for me to get to know him as well, and this was the time to achieve that. This was my chance to embrace the moment and overcome the discomfort.

The next morning was Friday, the 22nd of December 1972. It was 4:00 a.m. and still dark outside. We were up early to take Granny and Grandpa to the bus stop.

"Have some breakfast," Papá said, but Grandpa declined.

"Have some bread and butter at least. Here, you have a glass of milk," Papá said, putting the glass in front of me.

"No, thank you. I don't like milk."

"You need to drink it. Milk is good for you."

Not being accustomed to having plain milk before, the taste was awful. After the first sip, I quickly rested the glass back on the table with a frown. It had no sugar and tasted like medicine.

"Have some more," Granny said. "You heard your father. It is good for you."

Not agreeing with his opinion, I glanced around in search of a cat who could help me out of my predicament, but my efforts were futile.

"Come on, drink some more. Hurry up, we have to leave soon," Granny said.

After another forced sip, I pushed the glass away and was happy when Granny and Grandpa got up to leave.

We dropped Granny and Grandpa at the bus stop and my father took me for a stroll in the city. The morning sun, bright and warm, illuminated our path, and the cool morning breeze caressed our skin as we strolled along. His presence next to me was a novel experience. I was pleased to be escorted by him and mesmerized by the sights of the city. The well-paved streets and high-rise buildings had clean, straight lines and shiny glass windows. Cars lined the street and were parked next to the pavement and walkways. Folks busied themselves as they crossed the streets going about their daily routines.

I was awestruck by the never-before-seen traffic lights. They changed from yellow to red and then green. Store signs with big letters and bright colors protruding from the front of buildings captured my attention. I marveled at the sights while impressing myself with my ability to be quiet. Was it the novelty of it all? Or the mere fact that the man next to me, even though he was my father, was a complete stranger?

While I was born in Managua, to my knowledge, this was my first time visiting. The place was so different from Corn Island. Not only structurally so, but also the tooting of the horns, the cars, buses, and the men pushing mini white freezers on wheels with cones and popsicles painted on the sides, ringing bells on the handles as they chanted, "Helaaaados! Helaaados! Helados!!" It was all so different from back home.

While taking in all the novelties of the city in which I was born, it dawned on me that I still didn't know my birth date. This was the time to find out.

"Do you know what day I was born?" I asked eagerly.

"Yes," he said. "Your birthday is on the nineteenth of April."

I gasped in relief at finally getting the information that meant so much to me. The idea of being able to stand in class and finally give a date brought a smile to my face. We window-shopped for a while, which was a new experience for me. Back home, the stores had no window displays to look at.

My eye caught a glimpse of a pink tricycle with dainty pink-and-white tassels hanging from its handles. Quite aware it was too small, it nevertheless brought the bicycle I wanted to mind. Christmas was in a couple of days, and I wished for Santa to bring me a bicycle. *Maybe I could ask my father to buy it for me,* I thought. But no, I could not do that.

Granny's words came to mind. "You never beg anyone for anything. If you have, you have, and if you don't have, you do without, but you never beg."

This is not begging; he is my father. Surely this is not considered begging. It is more like asking. Besides, I had never asked him for anything before. But this was a tricycle, and what I wanted was a bicycle. He would know it was too small for me and, as such, he would buy me the bicycle instead. If I don't ask, I will never know.

After my long internal deliberation, I cleared my throat.

"Ahem, would you buy me that tricycle for Christmas, please?"

The words were so hard to utter, not only because it was against what I was taught, but because I was making every effort to hide my shame and pride. He peeked at the object in the window and walked away. His response took what seemed like forever, then finally he uttered, "We'll see."

His words seemed ironic, and just another way of saying no, resulting in mixed emotions. I felt sorry and downhearted for having asked, but I gave myself credit for at least trying. I resigned myself to the outcome.

In the meantime, we meandered around, arriving at a small wooden house with a strange structure. The wood was placed vertically as opposed to horizontally as seen on the houses back home, and the unpainted panels were aged and decaying. We entered the house and my father introduced me to Ms. Cristina. Her skin was a light shade of brown and her long, black hair was draped in a big bun that sat at the top of her head.

"Hi, Beverly, come, let me show you your sister," she said in her distinct Spanish accent. Puzzled by her remark, I questioned myself. *Did I hear right? Did she say, your sister?* I followed her lead and she took me to a crib, and there, fast asleep, was my new five-month-old little sister, completely unaware that she had a visitor.

"Her name is Carolina. I just put her down to sleep," Ms. Cristina whispered as she eased me away from the crib and toward the backyard. In between a tall, rain-rotted wooden fence stood a huge mango tree. The width of its trunk exposed its age, and its branches sheltered the clean-swept patio from the beaming sun. A gentle breeze floated over the dark compact soil as I sat around an aluminum table and waited patiently for my father and Ms. Cristina to finish their talk.

"We will visit again some other time before you leave," my father said, escorting me out.

The stroll back was uneventful, and just before reaching home, I noticed snacks hanging from the walls at a little store adjacent to the apartment. Two doors led the way to the Spanish-style interior courtyard, encased by high concrete walls. Straight ahead was the door to my father's apartment and, on the side, another door. Both faced the paved patio at the center of the complex. He stopped at the door next to his and introduced me to a lady.

"This is your aunt Orcilia," he said. She was plump and short in stature, of light-brown complexion, and her black hair was cut as short as that of a man but for the soft waves at the top.

"Hi," she said with a bright smile.

"Bev is here to spend Christmas with me. Where is Violeta?"

"She is still at work," answered my aunt Orcilia.

"Violeta is also your aunt. I will introduce you to her when she gets home," he said.

Eager to spend the three córdobas Grandpa had given me, I asked if I could go next door to buy a snack.

The store was situated on the ground floor of a very big house. A well-varnished row of rocking chairs lined the wall on the porch. Overhead, a red-striped hammock peaked between the balustrade railings. In the store, a young lady, as beautiful as a doll, stood at the counter. Her long, black hair caressed her shoulders, her unblemished light-brown skin radiant.

"Hi," she said with a smile as I walked in.

"Hi," I replied.

I glanced around in awe; I was in snack heaven. There

were so many options to choose from. Most were different from what I had seen before, but I decided on a box of Cracker Jacks, mainly for the surprise hidden in the box. I took my time opening it as I strolled back home.

That night, my father's friend, Ms. Lynn, and her son, Tony, came to visit. He said they would be staying for the holidays too. They were all laughing and talking around the table when, suddenly, the ground shook. Having not experienced anything like this before, I watched everyone's reaction. I was certain it was not my imagination. They felt it too.

"Wow! You felt that?" my father asked.

"Sure did," Ms. Lynn replied.

"That was an earthquake," my father said.

"Earthquake!? That was just a little tremor. Nothing compared to the earthquake I felt a couple of years ago when we had to run out of the house it was so bad. Now that was something! Man, I was cutting buttons, I was so frightened," Ms. Lynn said.

They laughed and continued with their previous conversation.

Around 9:30 p.m., my father said, "Lynn, girl, it is time for me to hit the sack. I am tired."

"Me too. We better go in too."

Wondering what Granny and Grandpa were doing and feeling uncomfortable and uneasy about going to bed in a strange house surrounded by unfamiliar people, I took my time walking to the room.

Around 12:30 a.m., we were awakened by one of the worst tremors I had ever felt in my entire life. The building shook furiously.

"Get up! Get up!" My father jolted me off the bed just before the inner concrete partition crumbled on top of me.

Feeling my way around in the pitch-black, trying to get to the door, my father's voice sounded.

"Come on, let's get out!"

"Aaah, I think my head is burst," said Tony. "A brick or something hit me."

Finally reaching the door, desperate to get it open, my father said, "It is stuck." There was only one window in the front, which unfortunately was framed by a burglar bar that obstructed our exit.

"Let's try to go through the back door," Ms. Lynn said.

"No, we can't make it out through the back. There is a tall, solid concrete wall there with broken glass bottles at the top. We can't make it over that wall."

"I think I have a cut on my back too," my father said. "The only way out is this front door, come on, push. I think it is blocked by concrete. A wall must have fallen in front of it. Let's all push at the same time. Come on, everybody, push."

With all hands on deck, we pushed and pushed and managed to open the door about eight inches wide. It was just enough to squeeze through. Broken concrete blocks obstructed the way.

"My head is bleeding a lot," Tony said.

"Wait," my father said. He took his shirt off and tied it around Tony's head.

Startled by a distant scream for help, we turned toward the sound.

"Help! Help! We are in here. We are trapped! We can't get out!" came the muffled voices through the barricaded door.

Blocks had fallen in front of Ms. Orcilia's doorway as well.

"We have to try and help Orcilia and Violeta," my father said.

Rambling through the darkness, balancing on the broken blocks in the direction of Ms. Orcilia's door, we placed our focus on getting her out.

"We are coming! We will get you out!" my father shouted.

The rubble was piled high, almost to the top of the door, trapping them in the building. Without help, they had no way out. The earth shook violently again, making our balancing act on top of the pile of debris almost impossible.

My father pushed me and said, "Go! Go! Run to an open space!"

Over the broken blocks I trudged, in search of the street through the darkness. My feet hit the level pavement and I continued on, my heart racing, not knowing where to go. Ms. Lynn, Tony, and my father stayed back to help get Ms. Orcilia and Violeta out of the house.

Up the street, I continued in search of open space, having no idea where to look. Everything was unfamiliar. I was surrounded by remnants of buildings, some so badly damaged that holes gaped in the walls and heaps of cement lay in the streets and walkways. Instinctively, I drifted to an illuminated area caused by radiance from a fire in the distance. Even the moon withheld its light. The screams and wailing permeated the air like the smoke in the expanse.

"Oh, my God!"

"Oh, my God!" The words emanated like an echo from all directions.

The earth groaned and trembled in anger once again. I tried to run but stumbled as if trying to keep my balance on a rocking boat. People, shaken to their knees, cried in fear. Anxiety crept through me, like venom through my veins, slowing my movements almost to a crawl. My eyes rose in time to see a tall building collapsing on itself as if it were a stack of matchboxes piled high, one on top of the other, having the bottom knocked from under it.

Thick smoke mingled with dust and filled my nostrils. The dryness of the dust dried my throat. Like ants from a disturbed nest, people scattered and ran in all directions. I stumbled over broken blocks and other debris.

Folks kneeled in the middle of the streets with their hands in the air, crying out, "God, have mercy. God, have mercy!"

Others pointed to the moon. "Oh, God, look, look!

I glanced up at the moon. It was a full moon, but there was an unusually bright ring of light around it. I had never seen such a circle of light around the moon before.

"Oh, my God, oh, my God. It's judgment day!"

"It's judgment day!"

"The Lord will appear soon! He will come right through there!" A lady pointed toward the moon. Some scrambled in panic, and others screamed. I kept looking back and forth. To the moon, then to the people. Not wanting to miss the Lord's coming, nor the people's reaction to his coming.

"Oh, God, forgive me, forgive my sins, Lord!" a lady on her knees cried out.

Paralyzed, not knowing where to turn or what to do, looking in the direction of the screams, my mind drifted to a story I heard at Sunday school. People will hide behind the rocks at the coming of the Lord, and the earth will shake. Will it be too late? Will God hear their cries and forgive their sins? Was it really judgment day?

Gazing at the individuals, many on their knees, my eyes glanced through the darkness, penetrating deep as if wanting to float through, to drift over the expanse, and to know what was happening beyond the reach of my eyes. A loud bang echoed through the air. A gas station some distance away exploded in flames. The massive ball of light pierced through the darkness, the bright orange glow imposing as if seeing a city in the distance in your approach through the night. Folks crawled on their knees, screaming even louder.

"Lord forgive me!" they shouted.

A struggle went on within me. My eyes wanted to see what was happening, while my mind questioned, *Where do I go?* My legs refused to move, and my heart raced. Knowing I had to get to safety, I wondered, *But where is that?* Safety seemed fleeting. Crossing the street seemed a good option.

While I hurried to reach the street, there was another tremor. A huge, gaping crack formed before my eyes, going across the road from one side to the other. A white Toyota pickup truck fell into the crater and was trapped in its grip. The earth shook violently again. The crater swallowed the front of the truck like a snake swallowing its prey. My breathing was short and fast. The grip of my fingers was in a tight fist, and the sound of my racing heart echoed in my ears. Around my feet, I looked down to examine the ground for signs of opening, not wanting my feet to be on the ground. Oh, how I wished I could fly!

A white concrete fence glinted through the dim light in the distance, capturing my attention. The height below my hip, I climbed on top, trying to avoid the ground for fear the earth might open up and swallow me as it did the truck. While standing on the concrete fence, I surveyed the area. I scanned left and right, then up at the moon, then down on the ground. *Is the ground going to open?* I wondered.

To my right, through the darkness, a big spark raced toward me, like a meteorite. It zoomed overhead. *How could this be?* I thought, but then realized it was running along an electrical wire. It whizzed past me as it flickered like Christmas sparkles, straight along the wire and toward the gas station.

I stared in the direction of the gas station and suddenly, a huge explosion resounded. The small white building went up in red and orange flames. The loud bang urged me to run, but fear gripped my feet, keeping them from touching the ground. Motionless, I stood.

The earth shook and the buildings crumbled. A puff of dust and smoke went up, covering the space above where the building once stood. The people continued to run aimlessly. I glared through the dim moonlight, peeping through the choking smoke as it spread through the wreckage as if searching for something lost, then seeped up to the skies and vanished. *How could this be happening?* How I wished I had someone to cling to, someone to tell me it would all be okay, but there I was, alone, a few days before Christmas. It was the year 1972.

At daybreak, I could not believe my eyes. This was not the place I walked through the day before. I recalled standing outside the apartment as I surveyed the street, admiring the nice buildings and folks walking up and down with parcels in their hands with laughter on their faces. The city smiled in preparation and anticipation of the Christmas events.

But now, all that was left was debris, open space, and a gruesome sight. The only familiar view was the blue sky. Even the roads were damaged. There were big piles of rubble, skeletons of buildings, bent steel and twisted zinc, shattered bricks, and broken glass. Remnants of what was.

Smoldering heaps were everywhere, capturing the gazes and sighs of onlookers avoiding the proximity for fear of being crushed at the least provocation. Light poles leaned in all directions. Wires sagged in the air, and others lay flat on the ground or mixed between the ruins.

Now the city mourned. Smiles turned to frowns, and tears flowed like water in a trench on a rainy day. The gripping devastation, the looks of despair, and the traumatic expressions painted their faces. People roamed about in a daze. Some yelled at other relatives or friends, asking, "Have you seen Maria?" "Have you seen Javier?"

Names; just names that meant nothing to me, but so much to them.

"Do you know if the hospital is standing?"

"No, all the hospitals are gone."

Others yelled statements to whoever would listen.

"The fire station is completely destroyed!"

"The nightclub collapsed. They say no one survived!"

The fire raged in many places, drawing the gazes of motionless onlookers, the sense of urgency snuffed out.

The sun peeped over the horizon, announcing a new day. People crawled over the heaps in search of loved ones.

Some warned, "Be careful, there are live wires over there."

Some showed their blistered, bleeding fingers, raw almost to the bones from digging through the debris with their bare hands, trying desperately to rescue loved ones. Having no way to tend to their injuries; no Band-Aids, no gauze, no medicine.

The sun blazed overhead. The place was now deserted. *What should I do? Should I leave? Should I stay? Will I ever see my father again? Were they able to help Ms. Orcilia and Ms. Violeta? Did they survive?*

Even though I came on my own two feet from the house, I had no idea if I would be able to find the place again. Looking to the right and left, everything seemed the same to me. I thought someone would have come looking for me by now, but no one had. *Where is my father? Does he not care? Should I try to get back? No, maybe I should stay in the same place, just in case they come looking for me.*

Time went by for what seemed an eternity, then finally a familiar voice. "Bev!"

Quickly, I turned to see my father walking toward me. I sprang to my feet. "Hi!" I exclaimed, smiling as I dashed to hug him, relieved and grateful he actually came to look for me.

"Come on, we need to go where the rest are," he said.

Walking along, I wondered where they found their open space. The clouds brushed softly across the baby-blue sky on that bright sunny day. It was a deep contrast to the surrounding scene. If only we could keep our eyes fixed on the sky, escape reality, or snap our fingers and bring the buildings back as they were the day before.

I glanced up at him. The look on his face was a picture of anguish. I wondered if he knew the way because for me, coupled with not knowing the place, the familiar areas the day before were no longer, and all sense of direction had vanished. Where was up the road or down the road? Our view traveled freely along, unrestricted from obstruction. The day before we had strolled happily, taking in the view. Today, we drifted along aimlessly, numb, awestruck, and gloomy.

My father pulled me out of my thoughts as he said, "See what's left of the apartment."

I didn't even realize we were walking in front of what was once the apartment.

All that was left was the roof lying on top of a pile of broken blocks. I didn't even recognize the place.

A few steps away, the figure of a girl caught my attention. It was the girl that sold me the box of Cracker Jacks the day before. She wore a pink nightdress but was acting strange. She was going round and round in the same spot, continually spinning around. I looked at my father and asked, "What happened to her? Why is she spinning around like that?"

"Her parents died. The house fell on them. She has lost her mind."

I gazed at her, thinking; *This could not happen to someone as beautiful as her. Yesterday, she had everything; a lovely home and a family. How could she be left with nothing today? Will she ever get better?* My face sagged in sadness. I wanted to go and hold her, take her with me. *What will become of her?* I thought. Helplessness had a grip on me. My father sighed and beckoned me to go on.

We walked a little further and came upon a broken concrete wall, the remnants of what seemed to have been a bedroom. Now, only a single broken wall surrounded by broken bricks remained. Next to the wall, a lady in a white cotton nightdress sat on a small wooden stool. A little girl around eight years old, naked but for red silk panties, was lying across her lap. Tears rolled down the mother's face as she smeared talcum powder all over her child's lifeless body.

Motionless, I stared, startled at the sight. *Am I seeing right? Is she really dead? That could have been me,* I thought. *I am her age.* I had never associated death with someone as young as me before. In my mind, only old folks died, not children. I squeezed my fingers tightly into a ball as if by doing this, somehow, I could soothe her pain.

My father went to the lady and said, "You need to move from here. It is too dangerous for you to be here next to this wall. It can fall on you at any time."

"I cannot leave. I cannot leave my children," she wept, not taking her eyes off the little girl. Next to her was a white crib. I walked to the crib and peeked in. To my shock, there was a baby boy in the crib. Big pieces of concrete blocks were still on top of his mangled body.

"There is a baby in here," I said. My father took a glimpse but said nothing. My eyes were fixed on the tiny body sticking out from under the huge block resting on his head, his blue plaid shirt with dainty red stripes. There was a baby-blue duck at the top of the safety pin holding his white diaper, and deep creases in each of his chubby legs, with pale-yellow socks on his tiny feet.

I turned to the lady as she spoke. "You know, all she wanted for Christmas was a chain. I bought it for her, but she didn't even get to see it. I was going to give it to her as her Christmas gift," she said painfully.

"Yes, this is very hard, but you have to move. You have to get to safety," my father said.

"No! I have to bury my children," the lady sobbed.

My father removed the sliding front of the crib and laid it on the ground. Then he took a sheet from the crib and placed it on top of the piece of crib lying on the ground. He lifted the child from her mother's arms and placed her on top of the sheet. Then he picked up the baby boy and placed him next to the little girl.

The lady observed in silence as the tears ran down her face.

He covered the children with the sheet, grabbed a handful of dirt, and sprinkled it over the bodies. He said, "Ashes to ashes, dust to dust." He turned to the lady and said, "Miss, come on now, your children are buried."

She got up and moved the stool from the wall and we continued on. I was so thankful for being alive. It was as if God had held me in the palm of his hand.

A group of people inspected a small wooden structure, and I stopped to see what they were looking at.

"It is incredible," one man said.

"How could this still be standing?" asked another.

"It is the only thing standing in this whole area."

"The next house I build will have to be built from wood, just like this."

"Yes, it remained standing because it was able to sway with the movement. It didn't crack or crumble, because it is flexible," said another.

I caught up with my father, and shortly afterward, I spotted the rest of the familiar faces under a tree. They looked at each other in complete silence.

Tony had his head bandaged with the shirt. My father wore a T-shirt. I had no idea where he got it from. There was no medicine to put on the wound and no way to get to a hospital. There was talk that the hospitals had all been destroyed.

"We need to look around and see if we can find some pieces of cardboard or plastic or anything we could use as shelter. Thank God we have this tree at least," my father said.

People walked from one direction to another, surveying anything they could use for shelter. Everything was valuable, even a piece of newspaper. Even finding a secluded spot, a place to hide, where they could take care of their basic needs.

A man walked past a short distance away with a sack on his back. It was rumored he had been going around removing limbs from exposed bodies in order to get the watches, bracelets, and rings. If he could not easily remove the jewelry, he removed the finger, the hand, or the whole arm to get it.

We were told there was a house nearby that had a working pipe with running water. My father and I went over there to see. A man came out carrying a load of clothes on hangers and piled them in the back of a light green Volkswagen minivan parked in front of the beige concrete house. The walls covered in large, gaping cracks resembled a puzzle, some dangerously deep, as if fashioned by a flash of lightning. The living room was almost empty.

On the outside wall, water dripped from a pipe. People gathered, waiting to get permission to get some water. A lady came out with yet more clothes and put them in the van.

Someone asked, "Can we get some water from your pipe?"

"No, this is my water and I don't have any to give to anyone."

My jaw dropped. *Did I really hear right? Was she really denying water to some desperate people? She is leaving anyway.* I gazed in awe, frowning. I thought of how many people came to our house on Corn Island to draw water every day. Not one person had ever been turned away. *God will surely punish this lady for being so mean,* I thought.

Not believing there were people in this world who were so heartless and cruel, we turned away.

"Let her stay with her water. She is packing her van and leaving. She certainly can't take it with her. How can someone be so selfish? May the Lord forgive her," someone mumbled.

Back under the tree, there was not much shade from the blistering sun overhead. Seated on a piece of a cardboard box, which was more than most had, time drifted by. My throat burned with thirst and my stomach growled.

The sound of an aircraft caught our attention. Glancing up in search of the sound, I exclaimed, "It's a helicopter."

"I hope they are bringing some help," Tony said.

The aircraft circled around as it dropped some small parcels everywhere. Running to pick up a package, eager to find out its contents, I discovered it contained powdered milk and sugar. My face lit up, smiling from ear to ear as I emptied the contents into my mouth. It was a delicious treat. The milk stuck to my palate, but that was no problem. I stuck my dirty finger in my mouth and dislodge the caked milk. I smiled happily and kept on sucking.

After one of their rounds, the helicopter circled again, but this time it came much lower. The continuous buzz and chopping sound of the blades against the wind got louder as it tilted toward us and landed in an open field. The propeller still spinning, I ran through the high grass on the gravel-filled terrain. It was the first time I had seen a helicopter this close and I was mesmerized by its close resemblance to a dragonfly. It was as if I was watching a giant needle case. That's what we called a dragonfly back home. Even the color was the same. The front was shiny and shaped just like the big eyes on the needle case. How I wished my friends could see it!

The pilot stepped out, capturing my gaze and admiration.

His cheeks were pink under the hard, green aviator helmet with a glass covering over his eyes. Green, long-sleeved overalls and black army boots completed his attire.

"Do you want to see inside?" he asked.

Spellbound, I could not believe he had actually spoken to me. I sprang to attention. "Yes, sir," I replied eagerly.

"Come on," he said, smiling.

In glee, lifting my legs over the high grass, I drew closer, instinctively stooping my head and cautiously approaching the extended blades. I was intrigued by the Cayuse glass, which allowed me to see right through to the seat. A peek through the open door gave me a good view of the cockpit. I was mesmerized by the many buttons and clock-like meters on the dashboard. How I wished my friends were there to see it!

The pilot walked around a little, stretching his legs, then came back to the helicopter and sat in the smooth, black leather seat. The propeller slowly picked up speed. In no time, it was spinning so fast I could barely see the blades, then up and up it went back in the air and quickly out of sight. After a deep breath, I sighed and made my way back to the tree.

People stood around talking about their horrific experiences. One lady spoke. "I am so sorry for that man over there. He had to shoot his daughter."

"What do you mean he had to shoot his daughter?" another lady asked.

"She was trapped under a concrete wall and could not move. She begged him to shoot her because half her body was crushed, and she was in so much pain. She knew she could not survive without medical attention. The girl begged him, 'Please, Dad, take me out of this pain.' He had to do it. He pointed the gun and turned his head as he pulled the trigger.

Can you imagine that man's pain? It was his only daughter, you know," the lady continued.

As I sat listening, a feeling of helplessness, impotence, gloom, and sadness came over me like a wet blanket on a cold and dreary night. My glance roamed from one person to another. Some sat with their heads in their hands, others were silent, their gaze fixed in the distance. A lady sat motionless as her tears opened a clear path down her cheeks. I wondered what was going through their minds.

Others spoke freely, sometimes as if speaking to themselves. Even though they were strangers, no one introduced themselves anymore. They simply talked to anyone who would listen. The comments flowed around me.

"We have been set back over one hundred years," a man said mournfully.

"It will take the country many years to recover from this one," said another.

"Even people who had insurance lost everything. It is as if they had no insurance. There is no way to claim anything." It was as if people were speaking to hear themselves. Not really expecting a reply.

"There is no money either. All the money you had in the bank is gone. There is no bank left standing," one woman said.

"Where do we go from here?"

"There are fires burning all over the place. There are no fire trucks to put out anything either," another said.

A man came towards us. "They are asking for help to pull out bodies. They are hoping to bring equipment to build trenches, but we can start piling the bodies in one spot. There are bodies everywhere."

He was heard, but no one moved, and no one answered. It was as if the tremors had taken away all the mental and physical energy, the life, the vitality. The bodies walking around were like zombies. Strangers walked to a group, spoke their minds, and then walked away aimlessly. Like in a twilight zone.

"This is going to get really bad in a hurry with all this heat. Soon we will not be able to stand the stench," someone said.

"There is fear that cholera is going to break out soon. The government has also ordered that people leave the city," he added.

"There are buses leaving the city, but you have to get to the highway."

"And go where?" a lady asked.

"I don't know. Anywhere but here," the man said.

"Come on," said my father. "We need to see if we can get on a bus to Chinandega."

Along the way, people rambled on heaps of rubble, digging through the debris searching for relatives. Mangled bodies held from their arms and legs were tossed one on top of the other like rag dolls. I stared and asked myself, *Are they really people? They look more like mannequins, like the ones I saw in the display windows, lifeless.* One by one, they made human heaps.

"They are getting a backhoe to dig some trenches. There are lots of bodies to bury," one of the men stated.

A backhoe rolled in with its long arm extended. The continuous sound of the engine rumbled while the heavy bucket at the end of the arm clapped and dug its teeth in, grinding against the concrete blocks and tunneling its way through the wreckage.

The thought of Christmas now seemed something of the past.

The highway glistened yellow in the distance under the bright sunlight. It was our only way out of the city.

Chapter Twenty

Hot, hungry, thirsty, and tired, we journeyed towards the bus, feeling as though we were crossing a desert. The line of buses on the side of the road was a welcome sight.

Bus after bus, door after door, we asked, "Where is this bus going? Is this bus going to Chinandega?"

"Yes," one of the bus drivers finally replied.

Relieved by the few empty seats and for shelter from the blazing sun, we boarded. My throat burned with thirst. People continued hopping on, and soon, all the seats were taken.

Unlike my earlier experience of a bus full of smiling faces, laughter, and chitchat, the mood on the bus was somber. Sadness was painted on each face, their stares distant, spaced out as if their minds searched for answers somewhere beyond their reach. Dust-filled, uncombed hair stood stiff on heads, clothes gray with grime, makeshift bandages stained with old blood. Heads leaned on windows, hands were folded in laps or holding up chins as if even the weight of their heads was too heavy.

Are they thinking the same of me? I questioned as I glanced down at myself. Slowly, I reached my hand over my head. My pajamas were dirty too, and my feet were ashy with dust, but surely, I did not look as bad as they did. Well, at least I hoped I didn't. *Did I?*

Did these people even know where they were going? Some folks probably got on the first bus they found; whichever bus would take them wherever. Maybe they were simply looking for empty space, as I did the night before. Searching for somewhere to be, somewhere safe, a place to start over, to go wherever the bus would take them. After all, the ride was free.

What's going through their minds? What was their story? Did they lose a loved one? A mother? A father? A sister? A child? Or perhaps all their earthly possessions? Where would they start over? And with what? Perhaps they were thinking of where they would get their next meal. Where would they sleep when they got off the bus? There were so many questions, so much uncertainty, and so much sadness.

It was a long, three-hour ride. My father said nothing. The bus was quiet except for the howling noise of the engine. Some folks napped, their heads bopping from the movement of the bus.

In Chinandega, we knocked on Aunt Delcy's door, but there was no answer. My father went over to the neighbor to find out if they knew of their whereabouts.

"Meridi!" the lady said excitedly. "We thought you were dead. I am so glad to see you alive! Thank God, you made it."

"Yes, I am glad I made it too. It is a sad situation there in Managua right now. I'm still in shock over the whole thing."

"I'm sure you are. The whole family went to León, to Edna's house. They wanted to all be together. They are going to be so glad to see you."

"Yes, I'm sure. We'll try to get there. Thank you."

"Have some water and something to eat before you head there."

Her words were music to my ears. She handed us each a glass of water, which disappeared in a quick gulp. Water had never tasted so sweet before. We sat at her table and were served white rice and mouthwatering stewed chicken with lots of gravy. It was the most scrumptious meal I'd ever had. We thanked her and shortly afterward, made our way back up the road to a bus stop.

After yet another forty-five-minute bus ride, we made it to León. This was the hometown of Ruben Dario, a renowned national poet. He grew up here as a child and traveled the world, but came back home to spend his last days. After learning about him at school, I could not believe I was walking the streets where he lived. It was as if I was stepping back in time.

The landscape was unusual, a display of long, conjoined buildings depicting a separation of ownership only by the color of the paint on the walls. A straight sidewalk ran parallel to each, and in front, the straight paved road narrowed in the distance.

The roofs were Spanish-style red terra-cotta with patches of gray or brown, a clear depiction of their advanced age. The top portion of the buildings boasted an array of vivid colors, while brown, burgundy red, or deep green skirted the bottom. The doors were trimmed in contrasting colors, but there were no windows. Just door after door straight down the building.

This is strange, I thought. There were no yards and no trees anywhere—only pavement, roads, walls, and doors. They were so unlike the houses back home, which were wooden and on stilts with a yard all around.

My father walked ahead. The idea of me finally having some time with him brought a smile to my face. He had nowhere else to go, and it was my time now. We were not able to spend much time in Managua, and with all that was going on, it was not really conducive to having father-daughter time. But now, here in León, it would be a good time for him to finally get to know me and for us to spend some quality time together.

Quickly, I tried to catch up with him. He stopped at one of the doors and knocked. The door opened. I was so happy to see Granny there in the living room, sitting in a high-back rocking chair, her hands resting on the handles of the varnished rails. She rose in surprise when she saw us. A big smile came over her face as I dashed to hug her. Grandpa came out to see what was going on, and so did everyone else. Excitement filled the place.

"Praise God, you all are okay," Granny said. "Malcolm and Mr. Peña went to Managua to look for you all. They came back and said they didn't think you survived because of how they saw the place. We feared the worst."

I was surprised to hear that Grandpa and my aunt Edna's husband had gone to Managua in search of us. Grandpa was not familiar with the place, and moving around in Managua must have been extremely difficult, as most of the roads were blocked by debris.

Tickled that they cared enough to go looking for me produced a warm feeling inside, but then I thought perhaps it was my father they wanted to find. Nevertheless, being in the same place as Granny and Grandpa was comforting. They continued with their chatter.

Then my father said, "I need to get back as soon as possible to see how I can help. Cristina's house is still standing. She and the baby are fine. I will stay with her when I get back. Lyn and Tony went back to Bluefields."

This revelation was shocking to hear, for more reasons than one. First, he went to look for them before he came looking for me. This was news to me. He hadn't mentioned anything. Second, I hoped he would spend a few days with me. But of course, that was wishful thinking. For a while, I listened, but soon their voices faded into the distance as the voice within me grew louder.

A sense of sadness and loss came over me, knowing my dream of spending time with him again would remain just that, a dream. It was clear now. I was not important to him. I was a mere object he came to discard to give him the freedom to go back to his life. A life void of me. He could be with those he cared about and clearly, I was not one of them.

From the distance, Grandpa's voice drifted in. "Thank God you all made it through. I heard they are saying that over ten thousand people are dead."

"People don't really know," said my father. "All I know is that the whole city is gone. Whatever buildings are left will soon go anyway because they are badly damaged."

My father left early the next morning.

I gathered from Ivania that Frank, Monica, and Cecilia had gone to spend time with other relatives.

Mr. Peña took us on a drive for a quick tour around the town. He pointed out the cathedral ahead of us, a landmark in Leon, and said it had been built around 1747 and the early nineteenth century. Its European Baroque architecture was an impressive structure with intricate design and majestic presence, now a part of the city's history.

If walls could talk, I wondered what they would say. What stories would they tell? Would they paint a portrait of the hands that built them? Would they tell of the people who walked in its corridors? Would they tell of the way they dressed, the colors they wore, or the languages and accents they heard? I envisioned the mysteries hidden in those walls. A tale that, if written on the pages of a book, would be an interesting read.

We continued on a highway. The fresh air bounced off the green trees and shrubs along the way.

"There is another volcano, and another one over there," I heard as my aunt pointed into the distance.

"They look like mountains," I said.

"That's the Momotombo," Aunt Edna announced.

Funny name, I thought. Its peak pointed to the heavens, hugged by the clouds under a marbled, gray-blue sky. On my left, we approached a cotton plantation. I sat up to get a better view. As far as my eyes could see, lanes and lanes of snow-white cotton merged in the distance. Each row lined up perfectly. I gasped at the sight. *How could they achieve such precision?* A true feat of perfection.

Mr. Peña stopped at the side of the road and we got out and stared, captivated. *That's what snow must look like,* I thought.

"That's what you call white gold," Mr. Peña said.

Cotton bulged through the straps on trucks with wooden rails built high up on the backs. Men held onto the rails as they passed, and one after another they went by.

"Why do they call the cotton white gold?" I asked. "It's not gold."

"They call it white gold because it makes a lot of money for the country. They grow so much of it that they have to bring people from other countries like Salvador and Honduras to pick it so that they can export it to other countries," Mr. Peña said.

After a little while, we got back into the car and he drove off. He stopped at a stall next to the road where a man was selling vegetables.

"Ooh, wait, I need some onions," Mr. Peña said.

Not a very exciting stop, I thought. I hated onions. I always fished them out of my food, whispering under my breath, why does Granny put onions in the food?

He went to the vendor and came back with a bag full. *What is he going to do with so many onions?* I questioned.

At home, Mr. Peña emptied the contents of his bag. The golden vegetables rolled onto the counter. They were the biggest onions my eyes had ever seen. They were as big as oranges. The crackling sound floated through his fingers as he squeezed and ripped off the skins. The knife sliced through the white ball, producing thin rings that fell to the right of his hand as he pushed them to the side, forming a small heap that grew and grew.

Standing at a distance to avoid the repugnant smell, my cheeks tensed in a frown. He separated the rings and the pile grew bigger and bigger. He placed them in a big bowl, then proceeded to sprinkle salt, then added vinegar, and then stirred.

If at home, I would dare my friends to eat it, but I wasn't at home, and he wasn't one of my friends. He was just weird. Lifting a wad of the white rings with his fork, he leaned his head back, opened his mouth wide, placed a wad in his mouth, and chewed. I gagged at the sight.

"How could he do that?" I asked. "Onions are awful. They taste bad and smell bad too," I said, holding my nose and arching my eyebrows. Ivania laughed.

"He eats onions like that all the time. Sometimes he takes them and bites them like apples."

"Yuck. He is goin' to have onion breath." We chuckled and ran away.

In the morning, the smell of freshly brewed coffee filled the air and drew me to the kitchen, curious to know what we were having for breakfast. In a clear plastic bag on the kitchen counter was a rack of golden brown, freshly baked rhombus-shaped bread stuck together at each angle. The smell was heavenly. Next to the bread, a butter dish held a rectangular prism of pale-yellow butter. My mouth watered. Next to the butter, fresh corn tortillas were held warm, wrapped in a blue kitchen towel, and on a platter were three rolls of oval-shaped, milky white *cuajada*.

I stared on, trying to decide what it would be; tortillas or bread. What a dilemma! At the table, I went for the bread, not being able to resist the delicious smell and the appealing look of the butter.

After breakfast, Ivania beckoned, "Come, let me show you something."

In the backyard, smack in the middle, was a vintage brick-and-mortar well. We drew close and peeped in. The perfectly circular structure reached almost to our chests.

"Can you see anything?" she asked.

"Girl, it's pitch-black in there. You get water from this?" I asked.

"No, we just throw garbage in there." She paused. "You want to hear something?" Before I could answer, she bellowed, "Heeeey!"

"Eeeey!" the sound roared back at us.

I yelled, "Helloooo!"

"Ooooh!" the echo answered back.

"They say that they used to use this well a long time ago to throw people in."

I arched my brow. "Yeah, right."

"No, for real," she said, wide-eyed.

"There must be a bunch of skeletons lying around down there, with their teeth like this." She rolled her eyes up and peeled her lips from her teeth. "And their hands like this." She pushed out her tongue to one side, held her arms to elbow height while dangling them, and jeered.

"Girl, you crazy," I said.

"You see how deep that is? I don't even think it has a bottom," she said.

"I know how we could see if it has. Let's light some newspapers and drop them inside," I said.

"Yeah, let's do it. Wait, I'll get some newspaper and matches," she said, and ran to the kitchen.

We leaned over the wall trying to avoid the yucky, wet, green moss on the unplastered bricks. I flicked the lighter and held it to the edge of the twisted newspaper in her hand. The flames climbed the edges and she let go. The red flames glided through the darkness, illuminating the inner walls, the depth abysmal. But before reaching the bottom, the flames were out, as if some giant being had been waiting to snuff out the flames before reaching the bottom.

"See, I told you it doesn't have a bottom," she said.

"No, I thought the skeletons were all seated at the bottom. They are the ones blowing out the fire," I said, laughing sarcastically.

"Ivania!" Aunt Edna called, interrupting our conversation.

Ivania ran off and shortly afterward she called, "Come, let's go!"

Off we went onto the sidewalk, passing door after door.

"Let's run," I said.

On the upwards slope of the pavement, I led the chase. Suddenly confronted by a steep drop-off and having no time for brakes, I gave a sudden leap off the ledge and landed flat on my stomach, with my arms and legs extended, while skidding on a patch of gravel below. I paused for a moment to catch my breath and let out a groan, then slowly got to my feet while bending over to inspect the stinging sensation emanating from my limbs.

My close inspection revealed some perfectly raw knees and palms covered with blood, dirt, and bits of gravel. My eyes slowly drifted toward Ivania, who was standing at the top of the sidewalk with her hand to her stomach, her head thrown back as if in pain while killing herself laughing.

"You think it's funny?" I growled, wearing a look of pain.

"Did you think you were a plane or something?" she

giggled. "I saw you take off. I thought you were goin' to fly," she chuckled as she threw her head back.

Feeling the burn, I continued to inspect my hands and knees. "Don't laugh. You think it's funny? You should have at least warned me there was a drop-off."

"Yeah! At what time? You were the one who went flying way ahead ah me."

"Man, Granny goin' kill me," I said as I examined my soiled dress.

Ivania bought what she came for at the store, and we left. Warily, I stepped into the house.

"What happened to you now?" Granny asked.

"She thought she could fly," Ivania swiftly replied with a giggle before I could utter a word.

"That will teach you to walk," Granny said with a serious growl. "Look at your dress and look at your knees."

"Her hands are all peeled up too," Ivania said with a sly smile.

I stared at the burnt-red tiles and back at my aching hands.

"Go and get out of that dirty dress," Granny said.

The next morning, I moved at a crawl, barely able to bend my knees as I cautiously made my way to the table.

"You see what happened to you yesterday. Maybe today you will slow down and walk for a change," Granny said.

Later that evening, we visited the graveyard to see where my cousin Henningston was buried. The cool evening breeze ruffled the leaves on the big mahogany tree overhanging his tombstone. A ray of sunlight peeked through the branches, draping a laced shadow on the ground. The somber look on everyone's faces, coupled with their silence as an expression of nostalgia, love, and longing; the artistic scene of the headstones and the monuments all drew my attention to the details of the sculptures, the silhouette of the images, the poetic messages, the lions, the crosses, and the angels with extended or folded wings guarding the sleep of those resting. It produced a sense of what it must be like to stroll in a museum. Reverently, we made our way out, leaving him behind.

The following day, we headed to Chinandega. Deep-gray asphalt invited us into the city. The trees and buildings cast a shadow along the wide streets. At the back of a pickup truck, a man bumped along on a blue rolled-up mattress. In the car's back seat, the wind blew and my hair stung my face. The place was pleasantly cooler than León.

Along the route, my eyes caught hold of two boys and a girl near my age standing next to a huge basket of ripe bananas. Their image drifted by quickly, and I pushed my head out the window to watch them fade in the distance. Along the road, huge baskets made of bamboo were ornately packed with pineapples, papayas, tomatoes, cabbages, and all sorts of colorful fruits and vegetables. Folks moved at a leisurely pace, up, down, and across the street.

At the door to Aunt Delcy's home, we stood on the walkway as Victor opened the door. I scanned the light-blue wall. Unlike Aunt Edna's house, this one had two windows. The living room was pristine with its light-beige walls and well-placed settee. A dark-brown center table held a porcelain floral arrangement at its center, and a lamp stood on top of each of the matching side tables. The place was immaculate.

Uncle Victor helped with the luggage and showed Granny and Grandpa to our room on the left side of the living room. The dining room was straight ahead and to the right. Six well-placed chairs varnished in high gloss glistened against the wall. Cupboards lined the kitchen walls, and in the middle was an island-style table. To the left was a patio, in a true colonial style, as it was in León, but this one was visible through a mesh that reached the ceiling, skirted by a concrete wall that reached my chest.

Peeping at the enclosed garden revealed an unexpected surprise. Hopping around out there were the most beautiful bunny rabbits I had ever seen.

"They are real!" I gasped, not having seen a real live bunny rabbit before. There, right before my eyes, were live, breathing bunny rabbits in an array of colors; gray, black, brown, white, and some with these colors combined. With their soft, sleek fur and bright marble eyes, my attention fixed on the white one with red eyes staring right back at me.

The sun reflected dainty pink through its long-cupped ears, perked straight up, listening to every sound. A brown one with its perfectly curved back munched on a carrot. Pale-green lettuce leaves were scattered around the yard, and they hopped around munching at their leisure. Their tiny tails, barely visible, peeped out from under them like little fur balls.

They stretched and stooped. Some were close together, head-to-head as if whispering secrets to one another, and others were far apart as if in their own world. Then suddenly, out of a hole under the building, a gray bunny dashed out followed by a brown-and-white variegated one. I watched in delight as they sailed across the yard.

In the kitchen, Aunt Delcy and Uncle Victor busied themselves making egg noodles. This was also a new phenomenon to me, being of the impression that noodles were only store-bought like rice or beans. But there they were, putting a thin layer of pasta into a machine as Uncle Victor turned the handle over and over, and out the other end came long stands of golden yellow pasta. What do you know? There was so much to see and learn in these towns, which were all different from back home on Corn Island.

Later that evening, we sat around the dining table for dinner.

"Take your elbows off the table," my aunt Delcy growled, giving me a stern look.

I dropped my hands quickly. Silence floated over us. My eyes traveled from one person to the next, waiting for someone else to speak, but no one did. Next to our plates were chopsticks instead of forks. Uncle Victor sat quietly with his jet-black hair spiked above his ears. His pale skin and slanted eyes were even more slanted as he smiled. Conversation resumed, but my attention was drawn to the chopsticks, staring at how the others held them. Eating with chopsticks was another novelty that was not working for me. I struggled to try to hold them between my fingers, let alone eat with them.

"Can I have a fork, please?" I asked.

"No," Aunt Delcy said. "Everyone is eating with chopsticks, and so will you."

"Give her a fork," Granny said to the helper.

"How you expect her to learn table manners this way?" Aunt Delcy asked.

"She will learn in due course," Granny replied.

The helper handed me the fork. Baby Edwin dangled from her hip; while my two-year-old cousin Richard peeped from behind her as he held onto her light-blue uniform.

After lunch, Richard rode around in his brand-new classic pedal car, which he got for Christmas. It was a beauty. The black tires trimmed with white rolled across the floor. The silver-rimmed windshield glistened against its comet-red body, and the round headlights stared ahead. Richard went up and down and round and round from the living room to the kitchen, to the dining room, and back again.

I followed him around, admiring how cute he looked. Uncle Victor sat in the chair next to a small side table. He was using a small brush. I came close and noticed he was painting some strange characters on the paper.

"What are you doing?"

"I am writing a letter."

"But those are not letters."

"Yes, they are. They are Chinese letters," he said as he continued to write the strange characters on the paper.

The days went by, and the time came to head back to Corn Island. On our way back, we stopped in Bluefields.

My mother lived in a district the English speakers called Cotton Tree, but the Spanish population called it Punta Fria.

The young man who was sent to call my mother the time before walked with me. I saw her near the well, and I greeted her with a hug.

"Glad you are okay," she said.

Somehow, her words did not match the expression on her face or her mannerism. I sensed she was not happy to see me. My enthusiasm quieted, and my mood became somber. I stepped back gently and withdrew like a tortoise retreating in its shell.

"We are going back home tomorrow morning."

"Okay," she said.

With that, we left.

The walk back to Ms. Julia's seemed long and the evening was dull and dreary, perhaps a reflection of my mood. My eyes followed the tips of my shoes, one step after the other, as they carried me along the grassy path. *Is this defeat? It sure feels like it.* I felt as if I set out to fight a battle and lost miserably. My mother did not even ask me into her home this time. Nor was the opportunity to say farewell to my siblings given.

About to step on the pavement, I took a quick glance back to see the yard fade into the distance. In my mind, two voices argued. One stated that I should have known better; that I was naïve to expect someone would embrace me and shower me with love when they don't even know me.

The other voice was more encouraging. *You are going home tomorrow. You should be happy. You will be back on familiar ground. You will be at home.* But what will Granny and Grandpa say? Would they agree that my cousins were right, that not even my family wanted me? My nose blushed and tears dampened my eyes. Blinking repeatedly, I ordered my mind to be quiet. It was time to compose myself and get it together since I was almost at Ms. Julia's house. Even though my arms felt weak, I had to reach deep down for strength and suck it up. I could not show my true feelings and let anyone see me defeated.

The next day I was back on Corn Island, delighted to be back home.

"Let's play a game of Monopoly," Grandpa said as he placed the box on the table.

"Okay, but no cheating."

"I never cheat. What you talkin' about?"

"Yeah, you always try to trick me."

"No, I don't," he said, grinning as I gave him a suspicious look. He unpacked the pieces and opened the board, placed the cards on top in their respective places, and handed out the money.

He took his lucky dog and gave me the shoes.

At the throw of the dice, he counted his spaces. Observing him closely, I mimicked his every move. He bought properties and collected the same colors at each purchase, then proceeded to buy houses, and so did I. He landed on one of my properties that had some houses and had to pay rent. I smiled and wiggled my head as he handed me the money while giving me a suspicious grin. Then he bought some hotels. A throw of the dice landed me on one of his properties with a hotel, and he asked for an astronomical amount of money.

"Why do I have to pay you so much?" I asked suspiciously.

"Well, renting a hotel costs more than renting a house," he replied with a crooked smile.

With my hands akimbo and a suspicious look, I said, "Okay, I want to buy a hotel then."

"Well, you don't have enough houses on your property to buy a hotel."

"Why not?"

"Because you need four houses, and you only have two."

Folding my arms, I frowned.

He watched me, smiling teasingly.

At the throw of the dice, I counted my steps cautiously around the board, hoping not to land on his property or, worse, land on "Go to Jail." *If I could only buy some hotels,* I thought.

He was adding more hotels, which meant I had to pay him even more, but my money was scant. Unfortunately, I landed at his hotel once again.

"Come on, pay up," he said with a big grin on his face.

"Okay, you win, but I am going to get you next time," I said.

These are joyful memories yet painful reflections of what was, and while thankful for the memories, they have a mournful effect, a monumental nostalgia, a sense of loss and bereavement. Cherished moments, precious memories never to return.

Chapter Twenty-One

On the porch, we waited for Grandpa to return. Folks strolled up and down the road, minding their own business. Beaming lights and the roar of the motorbikes pierced the darkness.

"You know, if you want to continue your education, you will have to consider leaving the island. The school only reaches sixth grade here."

Her words caught me by surprise. Lost for words and taken aback, I pondered. Now ten years old with two more years before reaching sixth grade, I wondered, *Why is Granny saying this?* Her words caused me to consider the familiar phrases heard so many times before:

"You don't belong here."

"You are only dragging down my mother."

"You are just a burden."

These words were as heavy as bricks on my small shoulders. After gathering my thoughts, I replied, "Where should I go to further my education, then?"

"You should consida Bluefields or Managua," Granny said.

I had not heard from my parents since the last time I saw

them two years ago. The thought of going to live with these two strangers was not appealing.

My thoughts raced. *But why? Why is Granny asking me this now? Is it because of my studies? Or because I am not wanted in the family anymore? Perhaps this is the simplest way to get rid of me in a polite way.*

My father came to mind. *Should I go and live with him? But would he really want me there?* During the two brief encounters with him, I got the impression of being in his way. He didn't have time for me.

Maybe I should go to my mother. My brothers and sisters are there. Perhaps that's where I belong. After a long pause, I asked, "If I have to go . . . maybe I should go from now then . . . I'm goin' to have to go anyway," I said, hoping Granny would say, "No, not now. When you finish sixth grade." Or something like that.

But to my surprise, she said, "Okay. I'll look into it."

My heart sank. Not expecting her to be so agreeable, I hoped she would say, "I don't mean now," or, "What's the rush?"

Something, anything to keep me there. But it did not happen. My blood settled to my feet, taking my energy, my joy, and my strength with it. My breathing stopped. It was true. I did not belong there. *Granny wants me to leave.* Something took hold of my chest and squeezed it tight. Blinking repeatedly, I swallowed my tears. The desire to wait for Grandpa now vanished.

"I'm sleepy. I goin' sleep," I said, dashing to my room.

The light shone dimly on the wall. The tears rolled over the bridge of my nose and onto the pillow. My newfound brothers and sisters came to mind. *Would they accept me? What would it be like being away from home?* A foreign place, with strange people. My cousin's words rang in my head again: *"Not even your family wants you."*

What if they are right? No, they are not right, I told myself, clutching my pillow and squeezing my eyes tight to silence my cousins' words from playing over and over in my head. *Once they get to know me, they will love me . . . an' besides, this is not happening anyway. Tomorrow I will wake up and Granny will say that I am not going anywhere.* Drowning my thoughts with my nightly prayers, I drifted to sleep.

The next day, the subject did not come up. What a relief! It was all in my head. *I won't say anything about it and will put this all to the back of my mind, not to be spoken of again.*

But a few weeks later, Granny said, "We made the arrangements. You goin' to Bluefields."

As if dunked in a bucket of ice water, I froze. *Is this really happening to me?* I swallowed hard, but the lump in my throat didn't move. Wanting to suppress the sound of those dreaded words, I took a deep breath, fighting the urge to run or to put my hands over my ears and scream, *Shut up, take it back!*

"Oh, okay," I said, and scooted away.

When were these arrangements made? How? I wondered. I had not been consulted. They really don't want me. It wasn't just a mere thought; it was a confirmation. This was my dreadful reality. A fear of the unknown gripped me like a choke hold, not wanting to know the details, not when, not how, but why? Yet I couldn't bring myself to ask, for fear of hearing the dreaded words, "Because you don't belong." Or, "Because you are not wanted here anymore."

I am not sure if audibly hearing those words would make a difference. The belief that those words were true rang louder in my soul and mind than the words themselves.

At the back of the house, I followed the narrow trail into the bushes in search of open space, a place to breathe. My world crumbled like the buildings in Managua, and my spirit was crushed. The thought of leaving home terrified me. Letting go of stability, leaving my world . . . but the worst part was the idea of not belonging, of being rejected by the two people closest to me.

Bereft, I wished I could somehow vanish in my tracks, or that the chirps of the blackbirds would drown my thoughts, or the breeze dry my tears, and somehow, somewhere, someone would greet me with open arms, hold me close and whisper softly, *"It is okay. Everything will be okay."* If only I could release the grip that took hold of my chest. The feeling of drowning, the sadness, the fear, the dread.

Crouching forward and hugging both elbows, I fought to control the urge to scream, to let it all out, but I could not have anyone hear my cries. Seated on a big rock under the bit an' sweet tree, I rested. Tears rolled freely down my cheeks. My energy oozed down my arms and out of my fingertips, carrying with it my hope, the remnants of my sense of belonging, my state of being. That love and acceptance I had so desperately fought for was now slipping through my fingers.

A few days later, while shopping at Ms. Flora's shop, she asked, "Why would you go and leave your grandparents now? They will miss you, you know."

"It was Granny who said that I have to leave to further my education," I said.

On other occasions, my modus operandi was to run home, but not this time. Now I trudged along as if carrying a heavy load. As if by slowing down, the time before my impending departure would be extended. Leaving Granny, Grandpa, Kitty, Blackie, Popita, and even my pigs; leaving my friends, my school, my church, my whole world behind broke my heart.

Life as I knew it may not have been a bed of roses, but it was *my* life. There was no other life known to me. The prospect of being uprooted to move to a foreign land, to live with a family I was not certain even wanted me, was overwhelming. It felt like I was losing control and falling deep down into a dark, bottomless pit.

The days were dull and gloomy. Maybe asking to stay would solve my dilemma, to implore not to be sent away. Perhaps this decision could then be reversed. But what would happen when I reached sixth grade? What then? I would have to relive this ordeal all over again, with the result being the same, having to leave anyway. Why delay the inevitable, then? *Besides, they are tired of having me around.*

Overshadowed by darkness, the evil whispers said to me, *This is not your place, see? You don't belong. If you belonged, you wouldn't have to go anywhere. Do you see any one of your friends in the position you are in? No, because they belong. Their parents want them around. Those are their people. These are not your people.*

Trying to quiet the voices, I tried to look for a solution. If they asked me to stay, the answer would gladly be yes. If only they would! Not caring if they were my people or not, they were all I had.

The dark of the nights became my refuge. No forced smile was required. No need to put one foot in front of the other. There was no need to speak. How ironic; though many times Grandpa said I talk too much, now even speaking took an extra effort.

In bed, shielded by the dark of night, my tears flowed while praying that God would help me to be strong. Yet, my stomach trembled with anxiety and fear. Everything stood still. Not even the curtains moved. The air was suffocating, and the pressure on my chest made my breathing difficult. My hope was to wake up and realize it was all a nightmare. This was not happening to me. I could not be so dispensable; so easily tossed aside.

"Ooh, stop this foolishness, I am a big girl now and must be brave," I said, wiping away my tears. The time to live with my mother was drawing near. The time for her to get to know me was steps away. *They are all going to get to know me and they will love me, and I am going to further my education, come back home, and make Granny and Grandpa proud. See, I am not going forever. Everything will be okay.* Pressing my head to my pillow and closing my eyes, I went to sleep.

Granny helped me pack my suitcase and in went my doll, still in her box, then my table set, my cups and saucers, and my collection of shells, all stored in a glass jar covered in powder.

"You are leaving, but we want you to know that any day you decide to come back home, you can just let us know. We will get your ticket to you right away," Granny said.

"Okay, thank you," I said, happy to hear those words from Granny, feeling a sense of relief that I was right. The possibility of coming back home was real.

In Bluefields, I hesitantly entered the house. Lisa and Katherine stood in the living room and stared. Katherine cupped her mouth as she whispered in Lisa's ear. They both looked at me and giggled. Charles and Delrin came in and took a glimpse at me on their way to the kitchen, minding their own business. Like an animal in a cage at the zoo, there to amuse the visitors, I waited. My arms and legs felt limp like a rag doll. My eyes were moist as I blinked my tears away, but forcing a smile, I muffled a, "Hi."

Night fell and I got ready for bed. The top bunk was assigned to me and I lay there and sobbed. I missed Granny and Grandpa dreadfully.

My mother heard my sniffles as we shared the same room. She came over and said, "You better stop that crying, 'cause this is not your grandparents'." Her tone was jarring, brusque, and piercing. There was not even a semblance of affection.

Shocked at the comment, I sank further under the covers and wished to somehow disappear. *What is this? What did I get into?* There was no warmth, no embrace. In fact, it was the opposite; cold and distant. Were my cousins right? Perhaps this family really didn't want me. Rejecting the thought, I told myself I needed time. Time to get to know them, time for them to get to know me, and time for them to accept me as part of their family. Yes, time.

Two days later, while in the kitchen, my mother approached.

"I have decided we are moving to Jinotega. We are leaving on Saturday. You need to get your things together," she said.

My mouth fell open. I was puzzled by this sudden decision. What a coincidence that I would arrive just when my mother was planning to move away. I just got here!

Why would my mother pack up my siblings and me to move to a place I haven't even heard of before? I wondered.

Keeping my thoughts to myself, I went with the flow. It was an adventure for my siblings. They were excited about the trip. Me, not so much. I was still trying to adjust, wondering what tomorrow would bring.

Chapter Twenty-Two

After almost two days of traveling through rough, winding roads, we arrived in Jinotega, a small town on the Pacific side of Nicaragua. It was late afternoon when we stepped off the bus, exhausted from the ordeal. My cheeks and nose were cold as ice, and my breath floated like a puff of smoke before my face.

"Look! Look! I am smoking," Lisa chuckled.

Shivering, I folded my arms, making my way through the dark, gloomy streets. My beige sweater wasn't warm enough in this cold town, damp from the mist and fog that permeated the place surrounded by luscious green mountains and steep valleys. Its mountain peaks pointed to the heavens like volcanoes in the distance and thick clouds feathered above its summits. The natives strolled around the town in a foggy haze, the Spanish rolling off their tongues. Their pale skin was the combination of a Sumo and Spanish heritage. Bright-red tribal ponchos with white indigenous designs draped their shoulders. The place was a deep contrast to Corn Island with its sandy beaches, warm weather, and abundant coconut trees, or even Bluefields with its red roads and rich Creole influence.

My mother's grand-uncle—Uncle Henry—lived in

Jinotega. He was the only person of dark complexion in the whole area and was the owner of a small restaurant/bar and casino. We stayed there for a few days while my mother got us enrolled in school.

After a week of being there, my mother said to me, "Well, I enrolled you at the Catholic school, but I decided not to stay here after all. So, since you're the only one enrolled, you'll be staying here. We are leaving."

"What?" I asked under my breath with a bewildered look.

A look she did not see because she left me standing there, staring at her back as she left. Surely, she was not serious. *She is joking,* I thought, even though she did not smile as she spoke. My brow frowned in confusion. A numbing sensation went through me, freezing me to the spot, and I went into denial. *No, I must have misunderstood what she said.*

The following day, as they got ready to leave, I realized she was serious. Off they went with not a care in the world. My siblings bopped their shoulders in excitement for their new adventure. Their bags swung to the beat of their swaying arms, and one by one, they boarded the bus.

My arms hung limp. The heavy pressure in my chest felt as if gripped by the coils of a boa constrictor, forcing me to gasp for air. I was paralyzed but for the movement of my eyes trailing the bus as it disappeared around the corner. My chest dropped as the air left my lungs, resulting in shallow breathing. A hollow frame devoid of hope and expectation stood motionless. *What next?* I thought.

This can't be right. What do I do now? Alone, in an unfamiliar place, surrounded by unfamiliar people and grief-stricken, my world grew dark, cold, and desperate. Maybe the time had come to write to Granny and Grandpa to ask for the ticket. But now it wasn't just a ticket or a flight away. I was in the middle of nowhere. Now it meant a journey back to Managua or Bluefields. *How long would it take for a letter to reach them? Or even to get a message to them, and how do I do that with no money? How could I travel back by myself? Navigate through unfamiliar roads in an unfamiliar place?* Overwhelmed and dizzy with anxiety, tears welled up in my eyes and slid down my cheeks, drowning in questions, but having no answers.

Yet again my famous cousins came to mind, but now the credit was theirs. They were right. There was no question about it. This trip was made for the sole purpose of getting rid of me, another way of getting me out of her life. *How could I be so stupid and naïve to believe in having a chance of gaining my mother's love?*

My emotions took center stage and went on a roller-coaster ride. Self-pity flexed its muscles and anger raged at my stupidity of ever having hope. Mad at myself for living in denial, not wanting to accept the fact that I was never wanted. Had it been to the contrary, would I not be living with her in the first place?

Now it was time to accept my predicament. There was no other choice but to make do. Take what I had, which was my enrollment, and make the best of it. Go to school, and see what happened next. Education was my self-imposed goal, and failing was not an option. Returning home after just a couple of weeks, downcast, broken, and defeated—that was out of the picture. That would mean letting myself down and I would not have that.

Wiping away my tears, I lifted my head and stared into the distance. Uncle Henry walked up behind me and startled me out of my thoughts.

"You'll go to live with Doña Coco up Barrio España," he said.

She was Uncle Henry's girlfriend. Her milky-white complexion seemed to have never seen the sun. A native of Jinotega, I met her daughter, Teresita. Her auburn hair brushed her forehead and ended in a loose ponytail at the back of her neck, leading to a bouncing wave of curls on her back. A sprinkle of freckles complemented her pale skin. I also met her son, David. His blue eyes were captivating. He smiled politely as they left. They lived in a nearby town with Doña Coco's parents. We climbed into Uncle Henry's light-green Ford and went to where I would now live.

The car went up a hill on an unpaved road and stopped at the very top, in front of a tiny, two-story, Spanish-style building. Its balustrade balcony on the second floor was an indication that it had been a nice home in its time and the best in the neighborhood. It was a pity that it had not been kept to its original standard.

The twisted white teardrop motif on the basil-green tiles greeted me as I entered the door. On the right, a door led to the living room, but instead of furniture, a heap of potatoes stacked in the corner reached almost to the ceiling. On the left, a steep twisted staircase lined the wall, and straight ahead was a tiny kitchen.

"Go upstairs and leave your things," Doña Coco said as she went into the kitchen.

At the top of the stairs, in front of the bedroom, the cold, damp air greeted me at the entrance. Rays of light from the first floor beamed through the gaping holes in the aged dark flooring. Pieces of wood lay on top of each other in what seemed an attempt to fix missing panels. The condition of the wood was such that even my gentle steps caused them to lift, causing me to gradually apply weight to carefully test for tolerance of my tiny, ten-year-old frame. The creepy sound of loose, rotten wood under my feet was unnerving. It was the first time I had to pay such close attention to my every step.

The sense of minuscule movements on my legs caused me to look down. Tiny black creatures covered my legs, urging me to stamp my feet, but the strong fear of falling through the rotten floor beneath caused me to pause. Swiftly, I made it back to the step and vigorously stamped my feet, but in a flash, my legs were covered again. My efforts were futile. Gripping one in between my thumb and index finger for a closer inspection revealed they were fleas, and trying to brush them off was pointless. It was an infestation, the likes of which I had never seen.

"It's a good thing I am not a dog," I said under my breath, trying to amuse myself. In between my fingers, I caught one and rolled and rolled so it would not jump, then cracked it between my thumbnails. "What a job I have—to kill all these fleas," I chuckled.

The full-sized bed was against the wall. Perhaps it was not as bad over there. There was plenty of light emanating from a door next to the foot of the bed. With each gentle step, I made it across the room. The door led to a balcony with a lovely view across the street and the green mountains in the distance. Its vintage, Spanish-style balustrade was beautiful, but the wooden floor was practically nonexistent. Looking down revealed the red earth and unkempt shrubs. "I better not try to wander out there, or I'll end up in the garden below," I giggled, resting my small bag next to the bed.

A couple of days after my arrival, Doña Coco announced she was leaving. Her relationship with Uncle Henry had come to an end. She took her bags and left. "What next?" I wondered.

Uncle Henry was living his life. He didn't visit. I was the least of his worries. I had the place all to myself.

Each morning I strolled to school, wearing my beige sweater, the only one I had. I was grateful that Granny had packed it for me. While on Corn Island, I had no need for it, as it was always hot, but now Granny's words came to mind, "Whenever you travel, you should always carry a sweater, just in case you need it."

She was so right. The weather was frigid, and how grateful I was for her insight. As luck would have it, the school was also Catholic, as was my first school back home, but this one was run by nuns. The uniform colors were the same as most school uniforms in Nicaragua, white blouse and blue pleated skirt, which luckily, I had brought with me.

At school, the nuns hurried along with their navy-blue veils and white crown bands. White wimples rested on their shoulders and chests. Below this, a large crucifix dangled from their necks. Their blue habits brushed their ankles as they drifted through the corridors.

A smile came over my face each morning as I strolled into the yard and glimpsed the big aluminum pot perched on three big rocks in the front of the classroom. The red flames shot up and out the sides, covering the pot in black soot while the porridge boiled, bubbled, and popped. A nun stood stirring with a long wooden paddle to keep a safe distance from the thick, boiling blend. The view produced a warm feeling inside. In the classroom, we waited patiently for the nuns.

Our class was the first stop. Two nuns lifted the huge pot, one on each side, gripping the ear handles wrapped in cloth. They placed the pot at the classroom door. This was our signal to rush to get in line with our plastic bowl or calabash in hand. Steam floated off the top and filled the room with a heavenly aroma, and one by one, the nuns filled our bowls. Oh, how I welcomed that warm bowl of porridge each morning! Their demeanor was gentle and kind, the closest expression of love and care I had experienced at the time. An act of kindness never to be forgotten.

One morning, as I walked next to a nun speaking to a teacher, I overheard her say to the teacher, "We have to make porridge for these children every morning because the place is too cold, and the children cannot concentrate or learn anything being cold and hungry." These thoughts were so true, and I was grateful for her way of thinking.

To a ten-year-old child living alone, with no one to provide me with a meal, their gesture of kindness meant everything. The only relative in the town was my grand-uncle, whom I rarely saw. He never asked whether I was in need of anything, nor did he offer, and I didn't ask, as Granny always said, "If you have, you have and if you don't, you do without, but you never beg." Well, I didn't beg.

Being in this situation filled me with a sense of despondency, hopelessness, shame, and sadness. Not wanting anyone to know I was alone and had nothing or no one, I kept to myself and put my best face forward. Some students found out Uncle Henry had a casino/restaurant and thought I must be well off.

"Your uncle has money," one girl said.

"Not really," I said.

"Why don't you bring us some potato chips?"

These were small pockets of thinly sliced and crisp potato chips rolled in wax paper in the shape of a cone. Seeing some in a big glass jar on the counter at the restaurant made me aware of what they referred to, and often I gazed at them as I walked by, but I had none.

"I don't have any." I shrugged and walked away. *If you only knew,* I thought.

The school was not far from Uncle Henry's restaurant. After school each evening, I went there to clean the place. I told myself it was a way to pay for my shelter, but it also offered me an opportunity to get some stale tortillas left over from the previous night.

The restaurant opened at night to entertain the customers from the casino and bar, but in the evenings, I was usually there alone. The tables and chairs were scattered around on the red tiles in the wide-open space. One by one, I hoisted the chairs onto the table with the legs sticking up in the air.

While I was sweeping the floor one evening, Ruth, my uncle's daughter, came in. I wondered if she was his biological daughter, as she was white and short, and my uncle was black and very tall. She looked nothing like him. Her auburn hair was held back in a low ponytail. Her hair was so thick, it made a huge ponytail. She was about a year or two my junior. Even though she lived with Uncle Henry, I rarely saw her.

"Hey, what are you doing here?" I asked.

"My dad is running some errands nearby, but I decided to stop here."

"Well, thanks for stopping by," I said, teasing, and we both chuckled.

"By the way, who is your mom?" I asked.

"I don't know," she replied. "My dad adopted me when I was a baby, and I never met my mom," she said as she sat down on a chair, putting her middle and ring finger in her mouth. Her fingers were calloused; her teeth distorted from years of the practice. "I am so out of breath, 'cause I ran here."

"Oh well, glad you came. Now I have some company."

She walked over to the Roconola, opened the coin dispenser, and took some quarters. "I'm going to buy some Kool Aid candies. Do you want one?"

"Sure," I said.

Off she went across the road. A short while later, she came back with four small plastic fruit-shaped bottles. The colors mimicked the fruits; a banana, a strawberry, an orange, and a pineapple.

"Two for you and two for me," she said. "Which one you want?"

"It doesn't matter. We can play eeny meeny miny moe," I said.

"Okay."

She put two fruit capsules in each hand and switched them around behind her back as she smiled at me. "Now choose a hand."

A tap at her right hand produced a strawberry and a pineapple. In my hand, I poured some of the strawberry-flavored powder and tasted it. The tendon in my jaw contracted and my mouth watered. "Man, these are sour."

She laughed at my reaction. "You want these?" she asked, handing me three quarters.

"Sure," I said, extending my hand. She dropped them in and scampered to the back.

I smiled and continued sweeping and mopping. While the floors dried, I stacked the coolers behind the bar counter with bottles of beer and soft drinks, and then moved to the kitchen to wash the dishes, clean the counters, and sweep and mop the floors.

About to leave for the day, it dawned on me that the fifty-pound sack of onions resting outside the kitchen door had to be cleaned. Letting out a deep breath and a sigh, I proceeded to untie the bag. Removing the rotten ones from the sack was gross. The horrible smell made me gag. One by one, I checked and cleaned off the excess dry skins from the good ones so they would not spoil.

It was almost dark when I finally finished. An inspection of the cupboard produced two leftover tortillas from the night before. At home, my spoils were crisply fried for supper. Some evenings I fried potatoes but could not get them fried crisp. They were always soggy, but edible.

As I look back now, many years later, I realize I was conditioned to believe that love and acceptance were something earned. That being a part of a family or belonging was something attained only through hard work, something you had to hustle for. It took me many years to come to the realization that no one can buy love, a family, or a place to belong. It is like the grace of God. It should be freely given.

Across the road, my neighbor grew chayote squash and gave me two, which I boiled, but they were awful. Boxes of beehives were strategically scattered around her yard, surrounded by high grass and shrubs. She gave me a piece of honeycomb and that was delicious. The pieces of wax had the texture of chewing gum, which I especially liked.

Every weekend was washing day, drawing from my memories from Corn Island, on the days when Granny and I pulled out the washboard and wash pans and placed them at the side of the house. The sun would hide behind the roof and the cool shadow floated overhead while the gentle breeze danced around us. Now I washed alone where the sun withheld its heat.

Doing laundry while standing outside in front of a pila—a concrete washing basin with a built-in scrubbing board—in the frigid cold was no fun. My fingers grew numb through lathering and scrubbing, the cold urging me to rush through the ordeal. The wet clothes were hung to dry upstairs in the room because outside, they took forever to dry. Hanging them in the room wasn't much different, but they dried better than being outside in the damp, cold air.

My communication with Granny and Grandpa came through letters, and the fact I was living alone was never mentioned, nor was my deep longing to return home ever conveyed. Instead, I wrote:

"This place is so beautiful and the people are friendly. It is a big city and the food is different but delicious. I attend a Catholic school, and I'm doing very well. I love it so much here."

The tears rolled down my cheeks through all my embellished lies. But it was my way to let them believe I was happy, and that everything was fine and dandy.

When handed my report card, Grandpa came to mind. I recalled the days I would take them to him and wait for his reaction. Now, my report card was for my eyes only. There was no one to hand it to. It was taken home for a few days and then returned to school when due. I came and went. No one to say go straight as a needle. There were no Sunday morning swims or Sunday school and no one questioned anything. I was functional on my own and no one was any the wiser.

I envisioned us at the table after one of Granny's delicious meals, a meal I wish now I had. Listening as Grandpa read my letter. Certain they would do the same, Grandpa reading aloud and Granny attentively listening. With my eyes closed, I recalled the smell of freshly baked bread and buns. The taste of a nice plate of rice and beans, potato salad, and the mouth-watering chicken leg I always got because it was my favorite. I journeyed in my imagination.

Eagerly, I waited to receive a letter from them. Time was set aside for the special occasion to get cozy in my bed and relish the moment. It was my form of entertainment, starting with my meticulous study of Grandpa's handwriting on the envelope. He had the most beautiful penmanship, an enviable talent. I wished for the ability to write with such flourish. The M in his name, Malcolm, had a graceful swerve at the beginning of the letter and ended with a flowing veer at the end. The Z in his surname, Zuñiga, was written with a similar swerve and veer.

In their greeting, they wished for me to be well. Their advice was to work hard and do well in school, and to behave and be a good girl. In itself, nothing truly exciting, but to me, it was a medium of connection with my source of belonging, producing a sense of joy. Yet my reading always ended with sadness and crying. I was cognizant of my reason for being there—to get my education—which I was diligently working on. The other was the ulterior motive of being with my mother, which I had no control over, but nevertheless, I read their letters over and over again, balancing my joy and pain.

I had gone in search of my mother, and when I found her, she took me as far away from her as she could, abandoning me there with not a care in the world. Even though I was supposedly left with my uncle Henry, it didn't seem to dawn on him I was a ten-year-old child with no one to turn to. He went on living his life, and who was I to complain? I was living in hope, telling myself that having a chance to be around family would produce love and acceptance. The search for a place in this world, a place to belong, a place to call my own, was *my* issue. This was no one's problem but my own.

Now, I could not let Granny and Grandpa know of my failure. They would tell my aunts and cousins. They would all gloat about how right they were. Going back would mean accepting defeat and result in an added burden to Granny and Grandpa. My family had, in fact, let me down, but the cross was mine to carry, and perhaps I deserved no better, or so I thought. Nevertheless, it was time to press on and succeed, pass my grade, and attain my goal. Doing well would be my ticket out. Finding the means to continue to take care of myself was paramount.

Aunt Delcy being a nurse was a reminder that I would be a doctor. I would have the nurses working for me. Granny and Grandpa would be proud.

One evening, weighed down by the heavy burdens of what was now my life, a whirlwind of thoughts went through my mind, wondering what tomorrow would bring. Questioning where I would get clothes and food, and fearing the outcome should it be discovered I was living alone, as if this was all a fault of my own doing. Would I still be able to attend class?

Thoughts of where I went wrong while trying to figure out how to fix my predicament flooded my mind. Answers for the means to gain the love of my family eluded me. What did I do to cause them to push me away? Would I ever be able to make things right and earn my space?

Ambling on the side of the road on a lonely highway, I searched for answers, as if by walking I could leave my loneliness, my despair, and my sense of abandonment behind, and as a snake shedding their skin, crawl out of sadness and worries, out of the darkness and into a glow of light. Tears rolled down my face as I sang.

Caminando por calles extrañas de la gran ciudad,
caminando muy triste y muy sola."
Walking on strange and lonely streets in the big city,
walking sad and lonely....

Huge trucks zoomed by loaded with large logs, and a firm male voice in my head said, *"Throw yourself in front of the truck. It will be so easy and quick. You won't feel a thing. No one would miss you anyway."*

Yet another male voice, this one more mellow, calm, and soothing, said, *"You know it is wrong to kill yourself. Who do you want to make happy, the devil or Jesus?"*

I snapped. Something burst forth from deep down and dragged me into consciousness, revealing that it was in my power to choose whom to listen to. It was an awareness of who meant good and who meant evil in my life, and I had the option to make a choice.

I will make Jesus happy. He is the only one who loves me, my thoughts responded with strong determination.

Glancing around at the unfamiliar area, void of buildings, the scenery was a blend of high grass and shrubs, capped by blue skies and scattered clouds as far as my eyes could see.

When did I get here? Where am I? How did I walk this far?

How strange it was that while the day smiled through a hue of clear blue skies, bright sunshine, and pleasantly cool temperatures, deep inside, my spirit wilted, limp and listless, like a frail plant without water, barely clinging to life. My emotions were dull and gloomy, a reflection that at times we don't see the world as it is, but as a mirror of our inner being. Our reality is created from within.

Having no idea how long it would take to get back home, I put one step in front of the other and kept on walking. My eyes traced a line of barbwire tacked to a row of posts along the way, as if indicating to me to hold on tight, to cling to hope, one post at a time.

Ahead, the black asphalt paved the highway, pointing to that lonely place, a place that would teach me resilience and endurance. A place to learn to stand on my own two feet. The grinding sound of the pebbles rustled under my feet while in my mind the whisper of a sound like that of the little train chanted, *I think I can, I think I can.*

A few days later, while in bed, my head throbbed. My body was hot to the touch and I shivered with cold. For the whole day, I was under the covers, getting up only to drink water. For about three days this routine remained constant as I roasted with a fever and had no food or medicine.

Slipping away in my sleep was my one desire. At least it would not be me taking my own life. Then things would be so much better. Each time I opened my eyes, hoping to wake up in heaven, there I was, staring at the same white walls, disappointment weighing heavy in my being, having to face yet another day. On the third day, my uncle came and peeped into the room.

"Oh, my God!" he said, and turned away. I closed my eyes. To my surprise, he came back shortly afterward with a parcel wrapped in a green cloth. Resting the small bundle next to me, he unwrapped the parcel, exposing a number of glass syringes and needles. Proceeding to inject the rubber sealing on a bottle, he extracted a clear fluid and injected me with it. *This is it; it could be poison for all I know,* my thoughts affirmed. He did not say a word, and there was no protest from me either.

He left, leaving me to doze off once again. The next day, I was still in the confines of my lonely room. Then a semblance of energy peeped into my body, along with the realization that the medicine was not poison after all. I was somewhat disappointed at the notion nonetheless, as this meant life as I knew it was about to go on, and now hunger pounced, urging me to move.

With the fifty cents to my name, I went to the little store

up the road, hoping to be able to afford something there. Strolling along the rocky, winding road, I made it to the nearby store. My eyes rested on some bollos—corn pastries—on the counter. Delighted to learn my choice was affordable, I completed my purchase, stepped out the door, and took a bite, slowly making my way back up the road while munching on my treat.

Two girls approached heading in the opposite direction. Their stare fixed on me. As they passed one said to the other, "She looks like she has gone crazy."

Acting as if I heard nothing, I continued on my merry way. Back home, crossing the small mirror hanging on the wall caused me to pause for a good look. The image staring back at me was unfamiliar, and I realized why the comment was made earlier. The long, thick head of curly black hair was now a tangled mess. It looked like a large bird nest sitting on my head. Not having the strength nor the inclination to comb it during my illness resulted in the disaster sitting on my head. Dark circles under my eyes stared back at me. My face was drawn and frail, my skinny arms weak and listless. That person wasn't me.

I made an attempt to clear my hair, but it wasn't working. The comb was not getting through the ball of knots. My arms were too weak to even bother. I arrived at the conclusion that the best solution would be to take the scissors to it, but then Granny's words came to mind.

"Don't ever cut your hair. Your hair is your beauty. You need to keep it clean and tidy."

With the scissors and comb in hand and a prayer on my lips, I ambled to the front door and took a seat on the step.

"Lord, you know I don't want to cut my hair, but there is nothing more I can do."

Placing my fingers at the base of my neck and under my hair, I pulled my hair away as far as possible from my scalp to see how far my fingers would go, but no, they could not go through the tangles very far. The hair would have to be cut pretty close to my scalp. Putting the scissors next to my fingers and about to cut, I heard a voice calling from across the road.

"No te lo cortes, No te lo cortes!" (Don't cut it, Don't cut it!)

Puzzled, I looked up, and running toward me through the wild, unkempt bushes along a winding narrow lane that seemed to lead to nowhere was a tall, skinny girl. She wore loose pink shorts and a baggy purple blouse. Her long, skinny legs dashed across the road as she waved her arms in the air.

"Why do you want to cut it?" she asked.

"Because I can't clear it," I said.

"Don't worry! I will clear it for you."

I frowned, wondering, *Is* she real?

She took the comb from my hand. She pointed to the lower step and said, "You sit here."

She sat behind me and took her time clearing out small sections at a time. It was not an easy job, especially for a girl not used to seeing curls like mine. She was used to the long, straight Native American hair, but she took her time and combed all the knots out.

Close to tears, I thought how nice it was of this girl to offer to do something like this for me. Without a shadow of a doubt, this was all the work of the Lord, sending this girl to help me when I needed it most.

When she finished, she handed me the comb. I thanked her, and she left as quickly as she came.

The next day, feeling well enough to go back to school, I reached for the one pair of shoes I owned, but they were badly torn. The front had lifted off the sole, making the perfect prop for tripping. When lifting my legs, the sole sagged like a dog's tongue after a long race. Since I had no glue, after a long search around the house in search of a solution to my predicament, a piece of yellow plastic rope came to my rescue. It would have to do.

Unraveling it into strings and punching holes through the

top and sole with an ice pick, I threaded the twine and tied the cord into perfect knots at the top and to the sides. The knots protruded in an unsatisfactory manner, making my repair clearly visible, but they did the job. The shoes held together nicely, and I did not have to worry about tripping.

While looking down at my feet, shame showed up, requiring me to give myself a good pep talk. *You need to swallow your pride and not let shame get the better of you. If people laugh, let them laugh. You have to do what you have to do. You can't stop going to school now.* After my pep talk and a deep breath, I stepped out the door with my head held high.

Strolling along the road, I gazed at a white cross at the top of the mountain. It was said that a healer lived near the cross. His name was Nando. The locals believed in his healing abilities and often went to see him for remedies for their ailments. Gazing at the cross, way on top of the mountain, I thought, *It must be so nice to be so close to God. That must be why God uses him to help so many people, because he is so close to God.*

Along the side of the mountain, people climbed up the narrow trail like ants. They meandered along the winding trail, arrayed in colorful garments, on their way to see the healer.

Oh, if I could join them to also be close to God!

One Saturday morning, the sun was bright but the wind blew cool and since I could not go all the way up to Nando's, I thought maybe climbing a nearby hill and getting to the top would be just the same. After surveying a nearby hill, I started my climb. Holding onto the tall grass, I wedged my foot into the crevasses. Gravel rolled down the side as I made my way up. People gathered on the road below me, watching me climb.

One lady said, "Look, that child is going to kill herself."

"Get down from there!" another lady yelled.

"It's dangerous to climb that hill, it's too steep!"

"No, I can climb this hill. I will be fine!" I yelled back.

Getting a good grip on a smooth rock and placing my foot firmly on another, I meandered between the shrubs. Determined to reach the top, up and up I went. After a while, there I was, exhausted but on top of the world under the branches of a majestic ceiba tree. Like an eagle, I surveyed the land.

The sun's golden overtone rested on the mountains, depicting its brilliance, through an array of greens and yellows. A soft haze of fog floated at the tip of mountain tops in the distance, and above, the rolls of fluffy white clouds floated along the gray sky. Nando's cross was clearly visible in the distance.

With folded arms I questioned, *How could this be?* I was high on top of the mountain, yet Nando's cross was still so far away; and why was the sky not any closer? Below, the red roofs looked small amidst the green shrubs. Somehow in my naivety, I thought being at a similar height would bring the cross and the sky closer to me, but this was not the case. I was still no closer to God. I was high on top of the mountain, but nothing else. My sadness was still there, my loneliness present and real. My thoughts drifted to Corn Island.

Tears rolled down my face and questions flooded my mind. *Why? Why does everyone hate me so? What did I do wrong?* Despite my best efforts to attain acceptance through good deeds and hard work, my actions fell short. Love eluded me, and I continued to fail.

Even though I was far away, my thoughts were still with Granny and Grandpa. They were the nearest thing to parents I ever had. But now, they lived only in my thoughts.

My parents came to mind. I wondered if they ever thought of me. I doubted that very much.

Why does my father never ask for me to spend a vacation with him?

Why do I never hear from my mother?

Questions I had, but no answers.

Up on a mountain in a little town in the middle of nowhere; that's where I was. This was my reality. I was alone with no one to care, trying to survive on my own.

Lord, it is just me and you. You are here with me. I know you love me. Because my Sunday school teacher told me so. Her words brought a smile to my face: "Do you know that Jesus loves you?"

Who is that lucky? I thought, and that lucky one turned out to be me.

Those words have been with me ever since, and it was something no one could ever take away from me. My reality is different now. At times, I may still feel alone, but I am no longer that defenseless child. I am now equipped with resilience and endurance. My determination paid off. The Lord has been a present help in a time of trouble, just like the first line in Psalm 46 says.

Being surrounded by the beauty of God's creation was relaxing. The mountains were lush and green, as were the large slopes and valleys in the distance. The view of the city was picturesque, like a huge Persian rug, beautifully crafted. "Lord, I know you are with me. You will never leave me nor forsake me," I said softly.

After a while, I made my way back down the steep hill. Each step took me back to my reality, but with a new perspective on life. I proved to the naysayers that I was able to make it up the hill.

At the top of the hill, I realized our perspective on life may not reflect reality. I thought going up the hill would put me at the same level as Nando and closer to God, but when I got there, I realized it was not being at the top of the hill that draws us closer to God, but that God is close to me no matter where I am in life.

Back in town, the locals busied themselves. People were all headed somewhere. I didn't know where, but there was excitement in the air.

I stopped a girl and asked, "Where is everyone going?"

"We are going to the John the Baptist celebration. It's being held by the Catholic church," she said.

In my attempt to satiate my emotional and spiritual hunger, I climbed the hill, and now I hoped they would serve food at this function in order to alleviate my physical hunger. Following the crowd, I made my way to the place and sure enough, they were serving chicha, a bright-pink drink made of fermented corn. The crowd sang choruses and chanted in honor of St. John the Baptist, who is the patron saint of Jinotega.

The population, most of whom were of the Catholic faith, hosted a celebration in June each year. St. John's statue was paraded on a pedestal held up by a group of men. I got a glass of chicha and then another. After a while, the men placed the statue down in front of the church, and people danced to the sound of drums and trumpets.

After a few glasses of the chicha, I felt nauseous, so I moved away from the crowd, and at the side of the road, I emptied myself of all the chicha. I tried to get far away, not wanting anyone to see me throwing up. I had no idea if I was sick because the chicha was fermented, or simply because I had too much of it.

On my walk back home, two boys carrying a bucket of freshly ground masa, a paste made of boiled corn used for making tortillas—a staple food in the region—passed me by. The corn mill was a few steps ahead. I stopped and peeped in the window. Inside, the experts were at work. There were barrels cut in half filled with boiled corn. A man poured ashes into one and stirred the boiling corn on the fire.

"What the heck?" I said under my breath. *They're putting ashes in the corn that they are going to eat?* This to me was very odd.

A huge mill with a large red funnel at the top and another protruding at the side stood majestically in the center of the dark room. A man filled the funnel with buckets of plump white corn and the machine spat out the freshly ground masa through the funnel at the other end, which fell into a plastic barrel. Another man took the dough and plopped it into a bucket, then handed it to a boy standing at the door. The sound of the engine muffled their voices as they yelled to each other. I imagined this was where the tortilla sellers came for their masa every day.

Early in the morning, people walked on the streets with their warm tortillas in one hand and in the other, a parcel wrapped in banana leaves carrying either cheese or *cuajada*, a soft, cheese-like savory ball eaten mostly with corn tortillas. Along the way, the coffee trees adorned the sides of the roads, covered in ripe red coffee beans. I picked a handful and sucked on the sweet beans while making my way home.

Chapter Twenty-Three

While I was making my bed one morning, Ruth came running upstairs.

"Bev!" she shouted excitedly with a big smile. "Do you know who is downstairs with Papá?"

"No."

"Your mom," she said, her eyes wide open, staring expectantly, as if eager for my response.

"Oh, good."

"Are you not coming down to greet her?"

"I will come down when I finish making my bed."

"Okay," she said, and ran back down the stairs.

It had been two years since I had last seen her.

I was puzzled, indifferent, and conflicted. I wondered what the reason was for her visit. I knew for sure it was not to see me. Perhaps Uncle Henry had summoned her to come and get me. He may have grown tired of me being there too. I had no idea of their arrangement or their plans and had no desire to engage in conversation with them to find out.

The sound of their chatter reached me in the room. I could tell they were sitting near the foot of the stairs. I finished making my bed and leisurely made my way down. Uncle Henry was now standing at the door.

"Hi," said my mother.

"Hi," I replied.

"I am coming to take you back to Bluefields. But I am sending you to Cayman, I hope you know."

"Oh, okay," I said.

Her words were as cold as a day in Antarctica. Her tone and demeanor toward me were as if I had done something to make her angry at me. A signal for me to keep my distance.

She remained seated, and I walked by and stood at the door. Jinotega is too close, I supposed. She had to get me even further away. Cayman? Wherever that is. Maybe it's time I write to Granny and Grandpa for that ticket. But then what? Leave again to be able to finish my studies? I wondered if Uncle Henry asked her to come and get me. I glanced over my shoulder. She was talking to him again.

"We are going back into town." Her voice pulled me out of my thoughts.

"Okay," I said.

They climbed into Uncle Henry's car and left.

Resentment welled up in my being, and the hope of ever having a relationship with her drifted away as the car faded into the distance. I still didn't have an answer. *Why did she come back? Just to send me further away? But why? Why does she want to send me so far away?* The way she looked at me was fresh in my mind. Cold, even spiteful. Her speed getting back into the car was as if she was delighted to put as much distance between herself and me as possible. There was no question about it. Would I ever get an answer to all this?

At the restaurant the following evening, I was about to finish my usual cleaning when, to my surprise, she walked in accompanied by Uncle Henry and Ruth. She wore an avocado-green dress and was deep in conversation with Uncle Henry.

As a stranger roaming in the shadows, I dillydallied around, extending my time to see what she was up to. It was getting late and in normal circumstances, I would have left by that time, but I sat in a dark corner taking in the movements. Some customers arrived. It was the first time I stayed late enough to see customers in the place.

A man went to the Roconola and made some selections, and the music started. The cook arrived and got set up in the kitchen. The lady at the bar served drinks. They turned on the lights in a small room that housed a casino table while folks gathered around. More people trickled in. They talked and laughed. Some ordered appetizers, others food. The aroma of the freshly made food awoke my hunger. The music was deafening.

My mother sat at the bar with a man next to her. She lifted her head and blew a whiff of smoke in the air followed by a drink of Flor de Caña, and she chuckled as they talked. They went onto the dance floor and she stole the show, moving to the beat and the claps of the onlookers. Being the only dark-skinned woman in the whole town, they cheered for the Morena—dark-skinned girl—to dance, and she showed them how it was done. She spun around, hands on her hips. Round and round she swayed to the music. Her dancing partner followed her around with his hands extended. The crowd gathered as the music blared, and another man joined, one man in front and one behind.

The crowd cheered, "Epa! Epa!" they roared.

"More merengue! More merengue!"

One man shouted to the guy next to the Roconola. The music paused, and the bartender poured more Flor de Caña. My mother put the glass to her mouth and gulped down a good drink.

The crowd hailed, "Wooo!" The music started again and back onto the floor she went.

After a while, I had enough and left. I walked quickly,

looking around in the direction of every sound as I trekked up the dark street, relieved when I stepped through the door.

The following day, I was about to walk out of the restaurant when Uncle Henry stepped in.

"Come here," he said.

Surprised that he even spoke to me, I stopped in my tracks, my brows tense. "Yes, sir?"

He looked down at the yellow strings holding my shoes together. "Come. I'll get you a pair of shoes."

Was I hearing right? Was he actually offering to buy me a pair of shoes? He stepped out the door and I followed in total surprise. We stopped at a nearby shoe shop, and he asked me to select a pair. I selected a brown pair with laces from a shelf on the wall. It was a style I saw most students wearing. The toe point curved from the big toe down to the small toe. After trying them on, I placed my old pair in the garbage in the store, delighted to leave them there. As we stepped out of the store, I thanked him. Even though I smiled, I fought the tears.

It had been two years since I had arrived there, and it was the first time I had received anything from him. I was grateful that he saw it in his heart to buy me that pair of shoes. It was truly a noble gesture. I wondered what prompted the desire in him, if it was simply a goodbye gift or if he noticed the yellow string in my shoe and wanted to do my mother a favor by paying for something she would then not have to pay for.

Two days later, I packed my few belongings and was ready for the long bus ride. The trip started at 4:00 a.m. at the bus stop. We got a cup of coffee and a corn tortilla with cuajada for breakfast before hopping onto the bus.

Daybreak was damp, dark, and cold. The fog meandered like smoke. We boarded the bus, and the sound of plastic ruffled as the passengers loaded their belongings overhead.

We did not say much to each other. I spoke only when necessary, and so did she. Two strangers strolling together, yet far apart. The bus departed, and the light of day peeped out on the horizon. The clouds floated over the mountaintops in the distance, close to the luscious, green coffee patches that zoomed by. Bags of fresh fruit and vegetables hung from stalls on the side of the road, while the thoughts in my mind silenced the sounds in the bus. *What next? Where will life take me from this point on? What will tomorrow bring?*

The road ahead was lonely, dreadful, and uncertain, but it was a journey I had to travel.

As the bus neared Managua, people stretched and yawned in anticipation of reaching their destination.

"I goin' look for your father as soon as we get to Managua. I have some papers I need him to sign to get your passport."

"Okay."

At her friend's house, we dropped off the luggage and headed to my father's. She got straight to the point.

"I have some papers for you to sign so I can get Beverly's passport. I am sending her to Cayman."

"I am not signing any papers to send this child out of the country. She is at an age now where she needs a mother. And you are talking about sending her out of the country. No, I am not signing any papers for that."

I listened quietly to the two strangers deciding my fate with no input of mine. My thoughts or opinions were irrelevant to them. I had no voice. I was grateful, however, that he spoke on my behalf, even though he showed no affection.

To him, I am nothing but a stranger, I thought. *How could these two people that gave me life behave as if I was a mere object of their discussion or worse, a fly on the wall? Why doesn't he say, no, leave her here with me? Wishful thinking,* I thought.

After his remarks, she walked away furious with the papers in her hands.

"He feels like he is the boss, but he is going to see who is the boss," she grumbled. She was upset for not getting her way and acted like a spoiled child throwing a tantrum. I shook my head and followed.

We did not linger long in Managua and headed to Bluefields the next day.

It was the middle of the school year. My mother enrolled me for half of the year at the local public school. Once again the stranger in the class, I put my head down and worked hard, not getting too settled, as I knew I would be leaving soon.

Surprised at the frequency with which my brothers and sisters missed school, I decided to work with them, and get them to understand the importance of education. My brother Charles, especially, only went to school if and when he wanted to.

I was twelve years old. He was a year younger than me yet in a much lower grade in school. It blew my mind. *How is this possible?* While being smart and able to achieve so much, he could barely read and write. He walked around in the neighborhood with no care in the world, barefoot, his shirt open, his chest bare, the sides of his shirt blowing in the wind.

He was free as a bird, but I wanted more for my siblings. How could I get them to understand that education was the path to a better life and that their futures depended on it? I saw no other way out, yet our views were so different. They lived for today. They saw the now, but I wanted them to look ahead. *How can I get them to think about tomorrow?*

My biggest obstacle was my mother. Education to her was a waste of time, and she was the matron, the one with all the say. And of course, my siblings loved the arrangement. They had all the freedom in the world and were the envy of the other kids in the neighborhood.

It was them against me, and I was losing the fight.

Even my brother Charles, whom I thought would be more accepting of me since I was told we shared the same father, kept his distance. I later discovered the reason for his resentment was he was told his father didn't want him, and the only one he did anything for was me. Little did he know that while I was living with my grandparents, I saw little of my father. I recalled him visiting the island once, and that was just for a day. And now I was being resented for him supposedly doing so much for me.

It was early morning. The sun floated overhead and illuminated the back of Gangan's house, casting a shadow on the side of the house and over a long trench dug to steer the water from the frequent Bluefields rains. I caught a glimpse of Charles as he jumped over the trench on his way to God knows where.

"Charles, come and get ready for school."

"No, I am not going to school today. I am going to catch cows with Delrin."

Delrin, my mother's live-in boyfriend and the father of two of my siblings, worked as a butcher in a meat shop. He worked Monday to Friday, and every weekend went on a drunken binge, spending most of the money he earned the week before. He became violent when drunk, oftentimes being physically abusive to my mother.

As soon as my mother heard me asking my brother to get ready for school, she came out in a huff and puff.

"Leave him alone, he is going bagosin'"—slang used for saying you are going to walk about. "Let them tie up their chickens, 'cause my rooster is loose."

Charles smiled in defiance and walked away. It broke my heart to see a young life going to waste. But each time I said anything, it was the same thing. On other occasions, it was, "Leave him alone. He is going to catch cows with Delrin." Or,

"He is going bagosin'. Let them tie up their heifers, 'cause my bull is loose."

The struggle was real. The sense of complacency and the lack of ambition around me was debilitating.

I was up the next morning early. The pile of dirty clothes was heaped up high in the corner of the room, but first, we had to have breakfast. I sent Charles to fetch the bread and cocoa from the store. By the time he got back, I had the water boiling. One by one, my brothers and sisters took their roll of golden-brown coconut bread and a cup of hot chocolate and found somewhere to sit and eat.

"Oh look," said Charles, looking through the window. "Crazy Rose is goin' up Big Field."

A lady, tattered and frail, strolled on the green grass.

"Why you call her Crazy Rose?" I asked.

"'Cause she crazy. If you walk close to her, she'll grab you."

"She going home. She lives in tha' house straight ahead in front the concrete walkway, just as you get off Big Field."

"Does she live alone?" I asked.

"No, she lives with her sister and her brother, but they 'fraid a her like puss. She fight them sometimes, you know."

"Bet you can't shout holy, holy," Lisa said, smiling.

They all looked at me.

"Unu, better stop teasing people," Yvonne said.

"Why would I want to shout holy, holy?"

"You better not," Charles said, laughing.

"One day she was walking up Big Field and her slip was showin', so Jojo shouted, 'Yuh slip holy, holy!' because it had a tear. And she spun round and said, 'Ih holy, holy, but Ih clean.'"

"He lucky she didn't make after him."

"Now if you tell her holy, holy, she get mad and cuss you out."

After washing the dishes and cleaning the kitchen, it was time to tackle the clothes.

"Charles, go and fill the wash pan with wata," Yvonne said.

While Charles filled the water, I sorted the clothes and then dunked the sheets in the galvanized wash pan perched on a wooden stand. The washboard with wooden trim and glass inlay rested on the rim. One by one, I soaped and scrubbed the garments against the washboard. The sheets were heavy when soaked. My little frame struggled to wring out the excess water, and it was a real workout to get them on the line.

On a piece of plastic, I spread out the whites for the rays to do their magic while the sheets blew in the wind. The dirty water was thrown out and clean water took its place for the second wash and rinse in blue water before ending up on the line as well.

Washing for seven people was a never-ending chore. Hours later, the process was still going. Sweat poured off me. My blouse and skirt were soaking wet from the constant splashing of the water while washing, rinsing, wringing, and hanging the clothes. My feet slipped and slid in my wet blue rubber slippers.

Yvonne placed the vintage Jamaican-style coal pot furnace on a stand next to the back door as she cut tiny pieces of wood and stacked them on the metal surface. She sprinkled kerosene and lit the match, then stacked pieces of coal around the tiny flames. The gentle breeze fanned the fire, and she squinted from the smoke that rose to her face. In no time, the coals burned red.

She took the furnace inside and placed it at the window, drizzled some coconut oil in a Dutch pot perched on the furnace, and waited for it to get hot.

On the counter, the meat Delrin brought from work the evening before, stuffed in his stainless-steel lunch container, had been marinating in vinegar. It was red from the achiote paste, covered in onion slices, and sprinkled with salt and black pepper. The hot oil sizzled as she dropped the pieces of beef into the pot, stirring to prevent the meat from sticking.

Katherine went to buy rice, green bananas, and cassava. Lisa went to Gangan's house to get two cups of boiled beans. Yvonne covered the pot on the fire and stood at the back door chipping a coconut with the machete before grating it, in preparation for the rice and beans. The delicious smell of the meat reached my nostrils, making my mouth water. When I heard lunch was ready, it was like music to my ears.

"Boy, food is the nicest thing when you are hungry," I said.

They chuckled. Ms. Yvonne had taken out a plate for everyone and placed it on the counter. Plates in hand, we headed for the living room to grab a spot. The gravy glided between the boiled green banana and powdery white cassava. I heaped my fork with the rice and beans and a piece of beef. The flavor burst in my mouth and I landed in Lalaland. The nice, cold Pinolillo accompanied the dish splendidly.

Around me, my siblings also enjoyed their meal. Today I sensed I was not a complete stranger, and tomorrow, perhaps they would get to know me better.

Chapter Twenty-Four

The next day, Charles came running into the house.

"What happened to you?" I asked.

"They bringing some cross cows, you better close the doors." Katherine jumped up and went to close the back door while Charles closed the front door. I had no idea what this meant or what was going on.

The slaughterhouse was next to the lake and in close proximity to our house. That was about all I knew, but this running from cross cows was another thing.

"What you mean, they are bringing cross cows?" I asked.

"They take the cows to the slaughterhouse all the time, but sometimes, they bring some cross ones, and you got to make sure you get out of the way. They will buck you, you know."

"Unless you like Mr. Taddy," Katherine said.

They all chuckled.

"Who is Mr. Taddy?"

"He's a man that lives in the house next to the slaughterhouse. He cleans the slaughterhouse. One time, they brought a really cross bull. Everybody ran into their house to get out of the way, everybody except Mr. Taddy, that is. He was in his house, but when he heard the commotion, instead of staying in his house, he ran outside, stood up at the corner of his house, an' shouted at the bull," Charles said.

"'You buck me, but don't buck my house!'" they all echoed and chuckled.

"Yeah, talk about being fool like fly," Charles said.

"You guys make things up," I responded.

"No, serious. The man is fool like fly, I tell you," Charles laughed. "It really happened. And here they come," Charles said. We peeked through the window.

A herd of cows came down the road. Two guys on horses kept them moving forward. "Whoa, whoa!" they shouted.

A brown bull took off up Big Field and then stopped suddenly, its head held high, its horns stuck straight up. A man on a white horse rode up behind him, a coil of rope in his left hand; a lasso in the right dangled off his leg. The edges of his straw hat curled up over his ears.

"Oh yeah, here comes Orlandito. He'll get him, you watch and see," Charles said.

"See the other guy there on the brown horse?" He pointed to another man.

"That's Pisco, and Tito is the other man coming behind him."

He knows everybody, I thought to myself.

"Let's hope they don't have to climb the light pole, like Orlandito the last time," Charles laughed.

"Why did he have to climb the light pole?" I asked.

"Orlandito was off his horse and a cross cow took after him. Man, I neva seen a man move so fast in all my life. Before you know it, he was up on the light pole. Man, I don't know how he climbed tha' pole so fast. Now that was a joke," Charles said.

Lisa and Katherine laughed.

"Yeah, we was on Granny Enid's veranda. People was shouting and laughing. Pisco came up and sling the cow. If not, Orlandito would still be up on tha' light pole," Lisa said, grinning. They all laughed.

I smiled.

Shortly after, Orlandito came down the road with the sling around the horns of the brown cow.

"You see wha' ah tell you. Orlandito could handle him, buay."

"Weh Delrincito?" I asked, realizing he was not at home. He spent most of his time down the bank side or by the slaughterhouse. Oftentimes he brought liver, heart l or other innards that were given to him by the men at the slaughterhouse.

"Where else? Slaughterhouse for sure," Katherine said.

When all the commotion ended, Delrincito stepped through the door grinning from ear to ear.

"It raining shrimps on water top this morning, man."

"What you mean, it's raining shrimps?" I asked.

"I mean the shrimps jumping up in the lake like rain."

I looked at him puzzled. "Yeah, right."

"You think I jokin'?" Delrincito looked at me, puzzled.

"I want to see that," I said.

"Come, come, let me show you," he said.

I went with him to the lake, skeptical of what I would see. As we approached the slaughterhouse, I noticed a bed of what seemed like cow fat glistening in the sun.

"What's that?" I asked, frowning.

"Oh, tha' Mr. Raymond tallah fat."

An old man shielded his dark skin under a straw hat. His yellowing, gray hair protruded over his ears and matched his once-white long-sleeved shirt, rolled up to below his elbows.

He sprinkled lye on the tallow fat, his prized source of income.

The putrid smell slowed my steps and scrunched my nose.

"Come on," Delrincito beckoned. "Tha' Mr. Raymond." He pointed to the old man.

His tattered gray pants were tied at his waist with a piece of rope, and his pants leg rolled up at the hem, exposing the flip-flops on his otherwise bare feet. Sheets of cowhide lay next to the tallow, buzzing with flies as he sprinkled handfuls of salt on his prized possession, surrounded by dingy black vultures perched on old stumps with their red, crumpled necks.

Children ran around without a care in the world.

"Look over there," Delrincito said, standing at the top of the bank.

I looked to the top of the lake where he pointed. I could not believe my eyes. The shrimps jumped in and out of the water, making tiny splatters on the surface. They gave the impression of rain, even though there was nothing but sunshine. Not a drop of rain, and yet out in the lake, it was raining indeed. I was amazed at the sight; a phenomenon incredible to watch.

A boy climbing up the bank shouted, "Delrincito, it rainin' today, boy!"

"Yeah, boy!" Delrincito shouted back. "See, I tell you," he said to me.

Under the trees, four men sat on a makeshift bench perched around a tree trunk. They shouted, and the wind took their voices up the bank, "Undah wata, undah wata."

"Why they shouting underwater?" I asked.

"Ah, that's 'cause the dory coming so full of shrimps. It's almost undah wata, man, you no see."

In the distance, a canoe glided toward the bank. A man stood with his feet on each side of the canoe as he balanced himself with a paddle. It was the closest thing to seeing a man walking on water.

"Undah wata, man, undah wata," Delrincito joined in,

laughing with the gap between his milk-white teeth and smiling back at me.

"Boy, they nah goin' make it, man," one man said.

"Boy, one more shrimp and they gone undah," said another.

As the canoe came closer into view, indeed it had about two inches of the rim visible above the water. As the canoe approached the bank, the guys clapped and shouted.

"Boy, you lucky!" one man shouted at the two men in the canoe.

A guy jumped in the water and waved his paddle. The men cheered, and another man seated at the stern got up and shouted back, "Man, I couldn't move!" He laughed.

Children gathered on the bank with gallon-sized paint cans.

"Why the children comin' with paint cans? They goin' give them shrimp or what?" I asked.

"No, they gettin' ready to work breakin' heads, man. We get paid ten cents a can. I got my cans too. I soon join them."

The smell of putrefied carcasses lingered in the air. Next to the slaughterhouse, from the top of the bank down to the water, the evidence of many years of existence was palpable. The collection of thousands of sun-bleached cow skulls and horns formed the gruesome scene, causing a feeling of eeriness and dread, as if walking through the land of the dead. Vultures flew overhead in search of their next meal.

At the back of the slaughterhouse, a large corral restrained the cows and pigs tied on posts awaiting their demise.

"Come see how the men butcher the cows," Delrincito said.

We approached the big open door at the front entrance and looked in. Men wearing rubber boots worked while they slid around in the fresh blood. The pungent smell of blood mingled with dung filled the place, but they joked and teased each other, not being affected by the smell in the least. Their laughter and chatter echoed off the unpainted concrete walls and the tall ceiling.

A man sharpened his knife on a hand-held file, then pulled the hide with one hand while he sliced off the skin with the knife in the other. He did this with such precision, it looked as easy as slicing butter. In no time, the big layer of cowhide touched the floor.

"Hey, Pisco!" Tito shouted to a man across the room. "You see, tha' how you supposed to keep your knife. Sharp!"

"Which butcha man you see walk without a file?" Pisco smiled and shook his head.

"Man, Pisco was working with a knife yesterday, tha' thing was so dull, I could ride on it from here to Managua and it couldn't cut me," the man laughed.

"And to top it off, the man claim he forget his file."

"Boy, talk 'bout going to war without a pistol."

"No, man, Pisco, you got to come better than that man," Tito teased.

"Yeah, you laugh, have fun at my expense, man. Today for me, tomorrow for you," he smiled as he continued to saw through a cow straight down the middle with his hand-held meat saw. He then took a knife and sliced it between the rib cage, rested the quarter slap over his shoulder, went to a truck parked out front, and dumped it in the back of the truck.

Close to the ceiling, a glimpse of light pierced through rows of decorative hollow blocks. Apart from the light coming through the big doors at the front and back of the building, this was the only source of light, as there was no electricity in the building.

"You see that little man there in the black rubber boots? That's Mr. Taddy," Delrincito said.

Mr. Taddy pushed the slurry mixture of blood and dung down a shaft with a big sweeper. Partly skinned cows hung from their two back legs on pulleys dangling from high beams.

I headed back up the road, inspecting the neighborhood,

aware of the inquiring look and staring eyes when I heard a boy shouting, "Hey, Delrincito, you goin' home go read though?"

I spun around to see Delrincito following me carrying a ball-shaped organ dangling at his side. He looked at the boy and shouted back, "Yeah, boy, this is the only kind a book I like to read!" They both laughed.

"See, I get a cow book, man."

"A cow book?" I asked, puzzled. I learned later this is the omasum, a spherical organ that's a part of the cow's stomach, also known as the bible because of its multiple leaflets resembling a book. That's why they call it a book.

"Yes, you never eat cow book before or what?"

"No."

"You going see how nice it is. You wait."

Chapter Twenty-Five

The days went by. My siblings all addressed my mother as Mamá, a word denoting a sense of closeness, love, and affection; something not offered to me. To feign the use of the word seemed awkward and hypocritical, a further indication that I did not belong. They did.

I was a mere stranger invading their territory. This was validated by my mother's deliberate intent to let me know how much she hated me, and the effort she placed into hurling hurtful words or expressions at me with malicious intent. Words to wound or to discourage.

"I picked you up in the garbage in Managua."

"You know when people put so many books in their head, they go damn crazy?"

"That old lady raised you old-fashioned, just like her."

How lonely I felt despite being surrounded by my family. Once again, I was a square peg trying to fit into a round hole; water trying to mix with oil. It produced a sense of isolation, despondency, and gloom, but overall, I kept a cheerful spirit, telling myself I deserved the air I breathed just as much as they. I made light of things, running jokes, and entertaining myself with the day-to-day events around the house, like watching them turn up the music and turn the living room into a dance hall.

One such evening, a merengue blasted from the cassette player. Katherine said to Charles, who was making his moves along with Lisa, "Come on, Manso—"Charles' nickname"—give me a split."

Charles's legs moved to the beat. He gave a quick split and slammed his palm on the floor. His pants were split from bow to stern when he got back up. The roar of laughter drowned the music, but he continued as if it were part of the show. Our cousin Aaron stood at the door looking on.

"Come on, Aaron," Katherine coaxed. "Show me a move!"

Aaron, shy but wanting to participate anyway, barely tapped his foot from heel to toe as he leaned his head from side to side.

"Come on, Aaron, that's all you've got?" Lisa teased.

Everyone laughed, but Aaron stuck to his move. More children trickled in as the laughter floated through the window. Delrincito broke away with Lisa.

"Come on, Lisa, you can't let Delrincito mash you up like that," I teased.

Lisa shouted, "Wait, wait, me back!" while grabbing her back like an old woman, encouraging the roar of laughter above the music as the children from the neighborhood filled the hall and joined in the dancing.

The following evening, we sat in the living room. My mother was seated in her usual spot at the window, combing Katherine's hair and conversing with my cousin Gladys. Lisa, seated on a bench, looked on.

"Do you know who my prettiest daughters are?" my mother asked Gladys. Before my cousin could reply, she answered herself, "Lisa and Katherine."

Gladys laughed. A sly grin came over my mother's face as she glanced at me. I was baffled by her efforts to inflict pain, but indifferent to her opinion of me or my looks. After all, I knew my worth was not found externally, it was within me, and I would not let her words convince me otherwise. I acted as though nothing was said.

Determined not to let her get under my skin, her comments rolled off me like water off a duck's back. I stuck to my agenda. There was still so much more to learn about myself, and I had no other way of knowing. My mother was my best source. My quest to uncover more propelled me to continue. To press on.

"Where in Managua was I born?" I asked.

"Who, you? I picked you up in the market in Managua. You were in a garbage bin with a runny nose and covered in coal and dirt."

Her nose lifted the sides of her lip in a snarl as she spewed her venom. More than her words, her tone and sly demeanor sliced my emotions as if whipped by a leather strap.

A roar of laughter filled the room. A fake smile camouflaged my pain to overcome her mocking and make light of her comments. The events of my life were nothing more than a joke to her. My jaw tightened, as if by the clenching of my teeth I could control my tear ducts, forcing my eyes to be moist, but not overflowing.

Despite my inner turmoil, my questions continued, not allowing her to puff out that little light of mine that shone from within. The little chorus we sang at Sunday school came to my rescue as I recalled the words in my mind.

This little light of mine,
I'm going to let it shine,
this little light of mine,
I'm going to let it shine,
let it shine, let it shine, let it shine.
Don't let Satan puff it out,
I'm going to let it shine.

Don't let Satan puff it out,
I'm going to let it shine
let it shine, let it shine, let it shine.

And so, I continued. "Who chose my name?" I asked.

"You? Not even your name I gave you. I was giving you up for adoption and Mrs. Hollingsworth, an American lady I worked for, agreed to adopt you. She came up with the name. If you were a girl, she said she would call you either Deborah or Beverly and for short, Debbie or Bev. When you were born, she decided your name would be Beverly."

I was transfixed by this new revelation while paying close attention to the underlying message, which screamed louder than her words. I was mesmerized by her lack of remorse, her tone, and her demeanor, which said you were never wanted, you were not important to me then, and neither are you now. She regurgitated her story, proud of her actions, while I questioned. How could a revelation such as this denote pride? How could someone be so cold and devoid of love for her own child?

Distancing myself from my emotions, I drifted away from my sense of sadness to a feeling of bewilderment as I studied her every move. I wanted to hear my story, but needed to leverage her words and actions to find out her feelings for me. Maybe, just maybe, I would be able to understand her.

"The day we left the hospital, you went with her and stayed in her room. She worked as a photographer taking pictures of butterflies, which she sold for making stamps. But one day, she was hit by a car while riding her motorbike and broke her back, which left her paralyzed. She was sent back to the US for treatment. That's the only reason she did not complete the adoption," she continued.

"After her accident, your father got you and took you to his sister Violeta. She took care of you then."

Gladys got up and stretched. "I'll be back soon," she said, and walked out the door.

I pressed on with my questions. "Who stabbed me in my head?" I asked. Her demeanor suddenly changed.

"I don't know. I wasn't there." Her look was cold, stern, and piercing, and she glared at me under her knitted brow. She stood, scanned me up and down, rolled her eyes, and walked away.

Startled by the expression of repulsion and rejection, the look of disgust written all over her face, her sudden change of mood, and her quick exit. It caused me to question her reaction. Was it her?

All those questions asked didn't seem to have an answer. One evening my aunt Vilma, my mother's sister, came to visit.

"Do you know how I got this stab in my head?" I asked.

"I don't know how you got it or who did it, but I was the one who took you to the hospital. I was walking towards the house when I heard you scream. I came into the house and found you with the knife sticking up in your head. I didn't ask any questions. I grabbed you and ran straight to the hospital. The doctor said you were lucky because the knife went through the bone and barely missed the soft spot at the top of your head."

Shocked to think she had actually seen me with the knife sticking out my head and awestruck to hear she was the one to take me to the hospital, I was glad she was even willing to speak to me about it.

"How old was I then?"

"You weren't even two years old. That's when your father came and got you and took you to his parents on Corn Island. You weren't even talking well yet." She paused. "I was told you had fallen down and the knife had gone into your head, but, child, I don't know."

This made no sense to me. I pictured a child falling with a knife in their hand. If the child fell forward, the instinctive move would be for the hands to go forward, not over their head. And the way the knife entered the bone, it seemed to me impossible for a child to do it on their own. My aunt spoke with a tinge of caution, not wanting to point fingers, and I didn't press further. The event remained a mystery and a topic every adult in the household seemed to want to avoid.

My mother had her favorites, with Lisa at the top of the list. She spent most of her time at her paternal grandmother's house across the road.

Katherine, Gangan's favorite, spent most of her time with her.

On the veranda, I was deep in thought, digesting my mother's comments and gazing at Gangan's house, perched high on its stilts. An old, broken canoe rested under the floor, gathering dust. Planks of thick wood formed the stairs at the back door. The open door split across the middle, allowing the bottom to be closed while the top remained open, but both pieces hung crookedly on their hinges resting on the side of the house. A light-blue chair at the side of the doorway allowed for a full view of the yard and big field.

People walked by all day long, as this provided access from one side of the town to the other. Ivette sat playing jacks on her front porch. I asked to join, and after a few games, she went inside. I tailed behind, taking the opportunity to peep into the empty kitchen.

Gangan was in an adjacent room ironing a dress. The iron was a massive, vintage cast-iron contraption with a wooden handle and holes on the sides, letting out a soft hint of smoke. The top opened wide, exposing its jagged edge, resembling a dragon's teeth. Inside, pieces of hot coal beamed red beneath a soft layer of ash.

In the corner of the kitchen, facing her chair, stood a big, black cast-iron wood-burning stove. I'd never seen one like that before either. On the side was a heavy door, with bits of wood protruding out. At the top, glimpses of red fire shot to the sides of the three pots sitting on the surface.

Gangan stepped towards the stove. A light-blue plaid dress flowed below her knee and the white cloth wrapped above her waist, keeping her hourglass figure in check. She was still shapely for an old lady of around eighty years. She removed a pot from the stove and poured the boiling water onto the washstand.

"This breadfruit looks nice and dry," she said.

The wisp of steam drifted over the breadfruit and plump green bananas. The intricate carvings at the front of the cast iron stove caught my attention, having not seen such antiquity before. Its four legs curved at the bottom like an antique table. She pulled out a piece of the burning wood and set it on top of the tobacco. In the bowl of her pipe, the tobacco turned red and each suck on the stem emitted a plopping sound from her lips. A puff of smoke shot above her tall chocolate frame. Her salt and pepper curls, cut about an inch long on her head, seemed effortless. Her countenance was serious, almost to a frown. The intense look on her face, cold and calculating, warned me to keep my distance.

She lifted the lid of a big pot and took the pot spoon and stirred. The smell of turtle meat filled the kitchen. Lifting the lid of the other pot, she stirred its contents with a fork. The rice and beans fluffed to the surface. She dropped some in her hand and into her mouth.

Turning around, she spotted me. "What are you doing here?"

My startled eyes met her snarl.

"Get out! You know I can't stand you!"

I scurried across the kitchen and through the door, then down the stairs in a flash. Once on solid ground, I paused to catch my breath and get over my fright. I took a seat on the steps.

What did I do to her? Why does she hate me so? I am hated everywhere I go. Something must be wrong with me. My thoughts were interrupted as I lifted my glance. In the distance, Charles roamed barefoot with no care in the world, heading nowhere in particular. Delrincito came towards me dangling a plastic bag.

"Where you coming from?" I asked.

"Down bank," he said, smiling.

"What you got?"

"Some fish roe. I goin' fry them right now."

"Fish roe? What's that?"

"Fish eggs, nuh," he said as if it was something I was expected to know.

"Can you fry it?" I asked, puzzled, wondering if this eight-year-old boy could do that.

"Yes, you watch me." He went around the back of the house, glancing back at me and smiling.

A while later, he came back with a plate and pieces of crisp brown fish roe fried to perfection.

"Taste a piece," he said with a wide smile.

"Mmm, nice," I said.

"See, I told you I could fry it."

He left again, and I made my way to the kitchen and froze. Plates, pots, and pans were scattered all over the kitchen counter, and the smell of raw fish was pungent. It was as if he used a separate pan to fry every piece of the fish roe.

"How did he manage to use so many dishes to fry a handful of fish roe?" I smiled, giving him credit for trying to help himself, and proceeded to wash the dishes.

In my effort to keep in touch with my father and grandparents, I had written to let them know I was now back in Bluefields.

In the meanwhile, my delving to find out more about myself continued. I had gathered that my father was seventeen years older than my mother and was actually her grandaunt's friend.

"Where did you meet my father?" I asked.

"I met him here in Bluefields, but we became better friends in Managua. When I got pregnant, I came to visit Gangan, but she gave me a good assing when she found out I was pregnant. She left me full of welts. I just took my march back to Managua after that."

Maybe that's why she hates me so much, I thought.

It was Sunday evening; my siblings were dressed to kill. Katherine and Lisa had on their mint-green skirts and white blouses with floral prints, their hair up in two ponytails, one plait over each ear. Charles and Delrin cleaned up nicely too, wearing long, dark pants and button-down shirts that were actually buttoned.

"Wow, you guys heading somewhere?" I asked.

"Yeah, we goin' by Brother Ray's Sunday school," Katherine said. "But it's not a real church, you know. He just put chairs in the yard, and we sing."

"Come nuh, you wah see," Charles said.

We strolled up Big Field. We hadn't gone far when to the right, under a big breadfruit tree, children sat on wooden benches and chairs spread out on the nicely swept red mole.

"See, that's Brother Ray," Charles said, pointing to a man of chocolate-brown complexion with a neatly shaped Afro.

The children sang a chorus. The mixture of races was well pronounced on faces, complexions, and textures of hair.

There were children with dark-chocolate complexions that sported their Afro or braids. Some Spaniards with dark-brown hair wore it loose or in ponytails, and some Miskitos or Ramas with their dark complexions and straight, jet-black hair let it hang loose on their backs. We took a seat in the shade of the tree. The breeze blew softly and was cool on my skin.

"We will sing, 'I will make you fishers of men' in Miskito first, then in Spanish, and then in English," Brother Ray said. "Sing after me." He started the chorus.

Inska waitna mino cabna,
mino cabna, mino cabna,
Inska waitna mino cabna ninibiques cabna.

Then they switched to Spanish:

Pescadores yo os hare,
yo os hare, yo os hare,
Pescadores yo os hare si seguis a mi.

Then English:

I will make you fishers of men,
fishers of men, fishers of men.
I will make you fishers of men if you follow me.
If you follow me if you follow me.
I will make you fishers of men if you follow me.

Brother Ray tried to make all children feel at home and included by allowing all to sing in their own language. This produced a warm feeling inside. And while he did not have the means to have a beautiful building, he made do with what he had. The time of worship was enjoyable.

Later in the evening, the children from the neighborhood gathered to play games, just as we did on Corn Island. From the corner of the porch, I had a good view. They played way into the night. Some games were familiar, others not. The light from Gangan's house shone through the back door and the open windows.

One game had a catchy song I had not heard before, "*Los pollos de mi cazuela*" (The chicken from my casserole). The children got into a circle holding hands as they skipped around. Following the words to the music, they put their hands on their hips as they swayed side to side. One child stepped in the middle and did a wiggle. It was hilarious when the girls got the boys to join in and reluctantly do the jig, being urged to move their hips like the girls. They sang it in Spanish, and it went like this:

Los pollos de mi cazuela no sirven para comer
Sino para la viudita que lo sepa componer
Se les echa ajo y cebolla, hojitas de laurel
Se sacan de la cazuela cuando se van a comer
Componte niña componte
Que ahí viene tu marinero
Con ese bonito traje que parece un carnicero
Anoche yo te vi, en la esquina de Windsong—a popular store in Bluefields
Meneando tu cinturita, param pam pam pam pam.

The translation is:

The chickens in my casserole is not good to eat
but for the little widow, that knows how to fix it.
You put garlic, onion, and little bay leaves
They're taken out of the casserole when they are going to be eaten. Fix yourself, girl, fix yourself,
because here comes your sailor,

in his fancy suit, that looks like a butcher,
last night I saw you, on Windsong's corner
shaking your waist, param pam pam pam pam.

They held their stomachs, threw their heads back, and roared in laughter as the boys moved their hips awkwardly to the beat of the music.

My thoughts drifted back to my days on Corn Island and the evenings I played with my friends back home. I wondered what Granny and Grandpa were doing.

Were my friends playing in the yard as we did so many times before? How big was my pig now? She must be a sow by now, and perhaps even had piglets of her own. Who knows?

Chapter Twenty-Six

My gaze floated into the distance. It had been months of living with my mother, doing chores to the best of my abilities, and being the best person I could be. I kept hoping that with good behavior and hard work, I could gain her love.

How wrong of me to think that time could fix everything. Would things ever change? I was doubtful. Wanting to hold onto hope and not be negative was commendable, but I could not live in denial.

I did not place the length of time it would take into my equation. Now the questions were: How long do you live with someone for them to get to know you? How long do you wait to gain someone's love? Especially the love of a mother.

I was not aware of anyone else that shared my dilemma, struggling to attain their own mother's love. A love that for others was never earned. It was obtained freely, with no effort. It was rumored to be unconditional, but in my world, it wasn't.

In front of a window, around a makeshift kitchen sink—a stand extended outside the window built of scraps of wood—I rubbed the bar of soap on a small rag and washed the plastic cups, plates, and bowls. The suds floated on the surface of the water and I dunked them in a blue plastic basin filled with water for rinsing.

"Beverly, someone is here to see you."

Startled by my mother's voice, I jolted to attention and dried my hands. Who would be looking for me? I had no friends or acquaintances that would stop by to see me. I raced to the living room. There stood a lady I had never seen before.

"Hello," the strange lady greeted with a smile. "Your grandmother and grandfather asked me to come and see you."

Her words were like a warm hug on a cold night. To hear "your grandmother and grandfather" was so soothing. How I wished they were there! That it was them who came instead of this lady. But it was comforting to hear of them, nonetheless.

"They wanted me to give you this." She had the biggest roll of money in her hand I had ever seen. I extended my hand to receive the money when my mother reached in and snatched the money from the lady's hand. Shocked at her speed, I froze.

The lady looked at my mother and then back at me, also visibly startled at the turn of events. How I wished she had taken me outside to speak to me privately before handing me the money! But now it was too late.

"Your grandparents said to tell you it's the money they got from selling your pigs. They didn't have time to write. I was on my way to the airport when they saw me." She glanced at my mother again, who had a tight grip on the money. "It was nice meeting you. I will let them know I delivered the money."

"Thank you," I said, and the lady left.

"Well, this money comes in good for me to enroll you and those children in school," Yvonne said, smiling.

I knew it was enough to enroll me and my siblings for a

couple of years, but didn't bother to ask how much money it was. It was the last I saw or heard of it.

The buzz of Christmas filled the air. Neighbors went into cleaning mode. Yards were cleaned and walls were painted. A big star made of poster paper hung by an electric cord in the corner or in the center of the porches. The rays of light depicted from the red, blue, or yellow bul shot through the decorative holes along the ridges.

Christmas trees shimmered, covered with a web of artificial snow that peeked through windows and doors, and lights twinkled around the frames announcing the joyous occasion.

On my knees, I scrubbed the floor. When it had dried, Yvonne pointed to a pint of diesel oil.

"You need to oil the floor now," she said.

My brow knitted. This was new to me. *Surely this is dangerous,* I thought.

"What do you mean? To put the diesel oil on the floor?"

"Yes, that's the tradition. We oil the floors on the twenty-third."

"Oh, okay."

She handed me a piece of rag and I went back onto my knees. Even though this was new to me, I liked the effect in the end. It brought novelty to the atmosphere; the bare wood took on the appearance of being varnished.

We did not have a Christmas tree, but we got a pair of new curtains that billowed from the open windows, and the dark look of the wood floors and the newness in the air whispered Christmas. The smell of freshly baked cakes floated from the kitchen while a big pot of beef soup boiled on the furnace. It was the evening of the twenty-fourth and the atmosphere was exhilarating.

The sound of fireworks, the clouds of thick smoke, and

the evocative smell of sulfur filled the air. Amidst the smoke and the dusk of night, faint images of children ran back and forth on the streets, and screams of laughter were faintly heard through the deafening sound. The shattered paper fell from the sky like confetti. People dressed in their finest went door to door visiting friends. The music drifted through the windows and wide-open doors, and impromptu parties started here and there.

"I can't wait to see what Santa brought for me," Lisa said with a big grin.

"I can't wait either," Delrincito replied as he bounced about excitedly.

My cousins Gladys, Luisa, and Barbara dressed for the occasion.

"Hey, Bon,"—they called Yvonne, Bon.

"Merry Christmas, cuz."

"What do you think of the look?" Barbara asked of her light-blue bell-bottom pants and matching blouse.

"Looking good, cuz. You all mean businessman, unu well dolled up."

"Well, you know when I step into GG"—a popular nightclub—"heads must turn." With her left hand on her hip, Barbara took her right hand and flicked her auburn, chin-length bob, glanced at Yvonne, and laughed.

"Well, you know that's right," Luisa followed, stepping around in a circle, modeling her hot-pink, one-sleeved jumpsuit, her shoulder-length, light-brown hair with a tinge of red falling gently against her white cheek.

"You'll see me when you see me!" Luisa shouted over the music as she glided through the front door.

"We're hitting the road, cuz," Gladys said.

"Have fun for me and you, and don't do anything I wouldn't do!" Yvonne shouted back with a grin.

It was my first Christmas in Bluefields and the first

Christmas I was spending with my mother and siblings I could not wait for Christmas morning. We had a late night on Christmas Eve, getting to bed at around 2:00 a.m., but everyone was up at the crack of dawn on Christmas morning, eager to see what Santa had brought.

I entered the living room to the sound of screams and excitement. A stack of Christmas gifts sat on a small, iron-rimmed center table; a piece of plywood replaced where there was once glass. My brothers and sisters could not contain themselves, jumping and laughing as Yvonne handed them each a gift.

"Charles, Santa brought this for you. Katherine, Santa brought this for you." And so she went, handing out the gifts. Pieces of Christmas wrapping flew in the air amid the screams.

"Look, look, look at my playthings!" Lisa said, showing off a box containing a set of white plastic cups and saucers with dainty pink flowers around the rim.

"Look at my guns!" Delrincito shouted, showing a box containing a cowboy pistol set with bullets and all.

They were all happy with their gifts, excited to open the boxes for closer inspection, when Yvonne said to me with disdain, "Santa didn't bring anything for you. He stops bringing gifts for children once they turn twelve."

While everyone laughed and cheered, a dark shadow of sadness flowed over me. Energy oozed through my fingers like sap from a tree. My first Christmas with her was another tool to inflict emotional pain. Would she not spare me even for Christmas? The subtle grin on her face as she glanced at my siblings bursting with joy and then back at me relishing my anguish; it was her moment of joy.

Pressing through the mush of emotions, through that dark, creepy forest of despondency, I ducked to avoid the feeling of going under, as if gripped by quicksand. But reaching up, I attempted to grab hold of something as a branch or to see a glimmer of light, in my effort to control my emotion. I would not be swallowed up in dejection. I searched for optimism, determined not to break. All I had was me, and I had to be enough.

Her actions screamed her message—repugnance. There was no doubt. I had jumped out of the frying pan and into the fire. The questions lingered in my head. *Why? Why such indifference? Why such hate?* There was not even an attempt to be subtle. Her willful intention to cause pain was transparent and shone through her demeanor and gentle grin. A faint smile veiled my face, camouflaging my pain, and I walked away.

As was my custom on Corn Island when wanting to think or get away, I drifted outside under the mango tree and the star apple tree, but they were not there. They were my place of refuge where I would stand and look through the branches often, hoping for answers. Now, I went to the outside toilet instead, away from prying eyes, a place where I could get away and let my tears flow.

"Accept it," I told myself. "You have failed. You were wrong. You cannot get someone to love and accept you. They either do or they don't." In my assumption that if my mother got to know me, she would love me, I did not equate in my logic that she would have to *want* to know me. And I could not force her.

The voices of my cousins resounded in my head, *I told you so.* Their mocking grins were pictured in my mind. How I wanted to prove them wrong, to show them that my family loved me! But it was time to accept the reality. My cousins were right. How foolish of me to think otherwise.

The truth was, I didn't belong there with them. But I didn't belong here in this family either. The question was, where? Where did I belong? It was time to accept that I belonged nowhere. I had to learn to live with that realization.

Take my cross and bear it. Learn to find love within and learn to love *me*, look out for *me*, and take care of *myself*.

I wondered what Granny and Grandpa might be doing. I hoped they were having a good Christmas with good food, health, and strength. I was no longer there, but hoped they found someone to run their errands and help with the chores.

I wiped my tears, faked a smile, and went back to the house. As my mother once said, it was my responsibility to keep the place clean, since I was the eldest. So after clearing away the torn gift wraps and empty boxes, I went on to clean the dishes, all the while trying hard to reach deep down to get a hold of my strength, my reason to exist, my joy.

Later that evening, some of my mother's friends gathered to play dominoes. The loud laughter drowned the music as they slammed the dominoes on the small table. They shared a bottle of Flor de Caña, Nicaragua's signature local liquor. When the bottle got low, one of them called to me.

"Hey, you wah earn two córdobas? Go buy a bottle of Flor de Caña."

I was underage, but there were no restrictions on selling liquor to a minor there. Money in hand, I dashed up the road on the high concrete pavement and jumped off the two-foot drop and across the road to the little store. In no time flat, I was on my way back with the bottle of golden liquid swinging in my hand.

I didn't like the idea of them drinking, but the opportunity to earn some money was appealing. If I didn't go, someone else would. Therefore, I became the errand girl, making several trips to buy cigarettes, Flor de Caña, Coca-Cola, or whatever they fancied.

After Christmas, the pace slowed down, the smell of sulfur faded, and the smoke blew away. People caught up with their sleep. Christmas came and went, and the routine of daily life showed its face again. Everyone complained of being broke, as if they went to bed rich and woke up a pauper, wondering what happened.

I smiled, knowing I had more money than I did at the start, but kept my delight to myself, cognizant that I had to look out for myself and needed to spend wisely.

Chapter Twenty-Seven

It was the start of a new year. We were enrolled in the Anglican school and for the first time, I would attend with my siblings. On the first day of school, I approached the small, navy-blue building skirted with red. I was conscious that I would not be there very long. I did not want to get too comfortable, since I would be leaving soon.

The unkempt front yard with patches of high grass, weeds, and the bare red mole was encased by a short concrete fence. Boys in blue pants and white button-down shirts ran playfully around while the girls busied themselves in search of their new classrooms. The big white collars draped on our backs floated in the wind. The white sleeves peeped through the arms of our crisply pleated navy-blue dresses.

At the center a paved, Spanish-style hacienda courtyard faced the doors to each classroom. A long string banged on a flagpole as it dangled from a pulley in the middle of the courtyard. The bell rang, and everyone gathered in front of the classrooms, facing the flagpole. An older lady, short and plump, with glistening, loose black curls cut short in a bob above her neck appeared and addressed the students. Her skin was the color of cinnamon and her smile was captivating.

"Good morning, everyone. I am Ms. Perdita. For those of you who are new, I am the principal of the school. Welcome to your first day of class. We meet here each morning for devotion to give reverence to the Lord, and to thank him for his goodness. It is always good to start our day with thanksgiving in our hearts. You are expected to be punctual as we start our day."

The cool breeze floated through as we stood quietly in the shade.

"Our first order of business is the hoisting of our national flag—Nicaragua boasts a beautiful, blue, white, and blue flag—and you are required to be reverent and respectful. Those assigned to do the honors will proceed with the formalities," said Ms. Perdita.

At the far corner near the entrance stood four girls. One held the national flag, folded in the shape of a triangle, depicting the national coat of arms.

The triangle signifies equality. The arch above the center of a rainbow depicts peace, and at its center like a heart, a Phrygian cap symbolizes liberty. Underneath, five volcanoes rise to express the unity of the five sister republics: Costa Rica, El Salvador, Guatemala, Honduras, and Nicaragua.

"Attention!" the girl commanded. She then handed the flag to the girl in the middle of the three. The three girls spun around in unison, facing the flagpole. They marched forward, and one stepped to the pole and loosened the cord while the other two unfolded the flag. They tied the first string at the upper corner of the flag to the string on the pole, while the student pulled the cord up slightly, giving room for them to tie the remaining strings.

As the flag was hoisted, we sang the National Anthem. Girls held their right hand—four fingers straight and thumb—over their heart while the guys held four fingers against their temple, looking as stiff as a board. As the flag blew in the wind at the top of the pole, the students marched back to the girl standing at the entrance and reported back.

"The insignia of the homeland was hoisted without any incident."

"Your reports were received. Take your places," she commanded in army style. This was followed by a number of catchy choruses, most of which I had not heard before.

The classroom was poorly lit but clean. The chairs boasted a built-in armrest that allowed for comfortable note-taking and were arranged in perfect rows. At recess, students lined up in front of a small window to purchase snacks. In the passageways, they caught up with friends and enjoyed their nibbles, as there was no cafeteria. Some walked around with mouth-watering mini lemon pies filled with dainty yellow filling. The golden-brown tips of the fluffy white meringues screamed deliciousness.

I wished I had the money to indulge, but Granny's words came to mind—*"If you have, you have, and if you don't have, you do without."*

And so, I swallowed hard and took the time to familiarize myself with the new surroundings. Around the back, the sun blazed over the unkempt backyard covered by high grass and weeds but void of trees and the chirping of the birds and of children. It was clear why they preferred to hang out in the paved courtyard.

I made my way back through the corridor and peeked into the classrooms one after the other. They were similar in size, shape, and content, and not much to see.

On our way back from school, I came upon a group of children gathered and staring at a tree.

"What are they looking at?" I wondered.

On the branch, moving at a crawl, was an animal I had never seen before. Trying to figure it out, I stared at the furry creature covered in coarse, brown fur with patches of beige highlights. His dark, round eyes shone through his beige brow with a raccoon-looking stare fixed on his target. Its long arm reached for the branch as if in slow motion. Three long claws protruded through its fist, and he had legs like daggers. His nose was that of a bear and his mouth a neat line depicting a tender smile. Not paying any attention to its spectators, it did its own thing. Its demeanor was serene and peaceful, as if in a world of its own. *Is it a bear? Or a monkey?* I asked myself. It was as if it was a combination of the two with a hint of raccoon.

"What is it?" I asked Charles, who came and stood beside me.

"Oh, they're watching a sloth. It's going from one branch to the other." He walked away.

"Wait! I want to see it."

"Gyal, if you wha see that sloth cross to the other limb, you goin' be there till tomorrow. I gone." He laughed and walked away.

"You see how slowly it moves, they say they only move fast when people nah watching. They move really fast in the night, you nuh," one boy said.

"Yeah, right. They can't move fast. No way," a little girl said, and walked away.

At home, I told of my awesome experience seeing a sloth for the first time.

"You know the joke about the sloth?" Katherine asked.

"No."

"Well, a woman had a sloth for a pet and one day she got sick, so she told the sloth to go and get help. The sloth said okay and left. One week later, the lady still didn't get any help and heard nothing from the sloth, so she said, 'Man, it's been a whole week and this sloth can't come back. Man, if my life depended on that sloth, I would die.' The sloth heard her and said, 'You better hush before I don't go anywhere.' He was still on the porch." We all laughed.

"Talk about slow," I said.

I was taken by surprise one evening when my mother approached me.

"Delrin asked me to marry him. What do you think?"

I frowned, puzzled by the question, but believed maybe she thought enough of me to want my opinion of something as important as this. Could this mean her opinion of me was changing? I thought my answer might not be what she may want to hear, but if I asked someone a question, I would like an honest response, and therefore I replied, "From what I have seen in my short stay here, I think you can do better. To me, he is not a good provider."

She listened in silence. I was perplexed by her lack of response, but thought perhaps she was considering what I had to say. I went on to do my chores.

The house was in need of most of the basic necessities and I didn't see him making any efforts to provide for the home, for her, or for the children. Therefore, I believed my comments spoke for themselves.

A few days later, I went to Aunt Amalia's store. It was a two-story building, which doubled as her dwelling house. The first floor was concrete, and housed the store, but the second was the dwelling area. It was a white wooden structure encased by a front porch with flat baluster railings. A door was smack between two large windows trimmed in burgundy red. Aunt Amalia was actually my mother's mother, but they called her Aunt Amalia, which seemed odd to me.

There she stood behind the counter, her hair parted down the middle with two buns wrapped loosely over each ear. Her dark-chocolate skin glistened in the heat of the poorly lit room. I approached the counter.

"Good evening, Auntie Amalia, can I have two loaves of bread, please?" I placed the money on the counter.

"You just came here and already start to make trouble. Why did you tell Yvonne that Delrin is not good enough for her?"

Floored by the confrontation and puzzled by her question, and more so by her tone, I froze.

"I didn't just tell her that," I said in my defense. "She asked me for my opinion and I told her what I thought."

"You should not be causing problems. You only just got here." She growled in anger like a dog defending its bone. Her look was stern and piercing as she reached for the money and shoved the bread across the counter. I took the bread and left the store bewildered. I was puzzled about being the subject of discussion and being talked about negatively behind my back. The sharp look and harsh demeanor directed my way was an indication that being thrown under the bus did not fare well for me. So many things ran through my mind. When did she have a conversation with Yvonne?

Up the road I drifted, trying to make sense of the event. *Why would she ask for my opinion only to use my response against me?*

Confusion, despondency, and disappointment floated along with me. It was a blatant betrayal. Why would my own mother do something like that?

The many times she hurled her venom at me flashed through my mind as though pressing a replay button. I shook my head as if the back-and-forth motion would erase the events. I tried to let them slide, not to let them get to me. Thoughts of the moment she asked me the question in the first place filled my mind. How puzzled I was. How naive and stupid of me to think there would be a chance, however slight, that my opinion mattered. My opinion on something as important to her as her wedding.

I smiled and shook my head. "How gullible could you be? Beverly, you know that lady only wants to hurt you. How could you fall into her trap?"

This, however, taught me something. It dawned on me that not only did she hate me, but that her intent was for others to hate me as much as she did. The transformation on Aunt Amalia's face revealed that she was successful.

Chapter Twenty-Eight

After school, my siblings got out of their uniforms and went off to play. This was puzzling to me, as my habit was to get out of my uniform and get to my homework.

"Delrincito, come and do your homework," I said.

He rolled his eyes and continued on his way.

Outside, Charles roamed, barefoot, in a pair of dark-green shorts with the threads dangling from the uneven cut of the once-long pants. His button-down shirt was wide open, the flaps blowing in the wind, depicting his carefree existence with no sense of urgency, no plans for a future, and no care in the world. There was no guidance, no one to show the way. Concerned for their future, I wished they would take my advice.

"Charles, come on inside and do your homework." He glanced at me in total defiance, and Yvonne rushed out to his defense.

"Leave the boy alone. Not everyone has a book in their head like you." Charles smiled sarcastically, gave me a side look, and continued on his way.

A sense of sadness washed over me like a cold draft. The

hope for a better future floated away like liquid down a drain. I wanted to save them from a life of want, steer them into a life of plenty, to be successful, respectable, and worthy of admiration. It had been said that if you made your bed soft, you would sleep in it. And if you made your bed hard, you had to sleep in it also. *Why couldn't they see I wanted to help them to make their bed soft?*

Downcast and wallowing in a sense of defeat, I tried hard to contain my frustration and my sense of incapacity. I felt like my hands were tied and no matter how hard I tried to wiggle myself free, my efforts were useless.

The mailman in his uniform—an aqua-blue shirt and navy-blue pants—approached on his bicycle. The front basket was full of light-blue envelopes with red parallelograms lining the edges. A small box was strapped on the rear rack of his bike. He hopped off and leaned his bicycle on the side of the house and removed the parcel. From the label, he read, "Beverly."

I perked up and held onto the letter and the small box. On the top of the box, I saw the name of the remitter. It was Granny; but I could have guessed that it would only be Granny or Grandpa. As if he had flipped my switch, I lit up.

I dashed inside with my package and carefully cut the tape to expose two avocados, six ripe mangoes, three golden-brown buns with a heavenly smell, and four small balls of coconut cakes. My mouth watered as I sniffed the coconut cakes. I could not resist biting into one. It had been years since I had tasted one. The gooey taste of coconut stewed in sweet cane syrup and spiced with fresh ginger burst into my mouth. It was the taste of Corn Island. The taste of home.

On the porch, I took my sweet time reading their letter. Like magic, I was transported home, if only in spirit.

My mind was racing, considering I was growing up, but were they getting older? Or maybe for them, time stood still, and they remained as I left them. The same Granny and

Grandpa. This was wishful thinking, and to consider the alternative was upsetting. In this instance, it was best to live in denial.

A few days later, my cousin Gladys came over.

"Bon, yuh have wrapping paper? I need to wrap Marvis's present," Gladys said.

"Oh yes, today is Marvis's party."

My mother turned to me. "Go and put some makeup on your face and go to that party."

Makeup! I thought. *Does she even know that I am twelve years old and don't wear makeup?*

"No, I am okay. I don't want to go anywhere."

"No, you want to stay in this house and *vestir Santos*"—dress saints—a term used to indicate a person would stay home and be a spinster. I could not believe she thought it was fine for me to put on makeup and go to a party being held at night at my age. I watched her reaction to my pushback. She showed frustration and disapproval of my not being in agreement with her command.

"You rather stay in this house and become a *niña vieja*? An old maid?"

Her disparaging remarks were frequent. Her derogatory comments followed my every move. Our differing opinions on life, in general, were the reason for disagreements. Her views on life were to live for today, have fun, eat, drink, and be merry.

My views were to improve our circumstances, set targets, and strive to achieve them. To live a better life, and not live wondering where our next meal would come from each day. We had contrasting points of view. We would never see eye to eye.

Was I to blame for my upbringing? For being sent to live with a family that had a different outlook on life? Having a glimpse at both worlds opened my eyes, and the former was more appealing. To have been given the opportunity to see a different perspective on life filled me with gratitude. Perhaps there was justification for clinging to my woe.

But there was a choice. I could hold onto the negative or continue to press on, strive for the positive, and cling to the hope of a better tomorrow, as small as that hope may seem. At times, it felt as though I was hanging on for dear life, dangling at the end of a cliff, trying to feel for that tiny toehold on a ledge. With no offer of help in sight. But I knew the Lord would somehow open a way for me and I held onto that hope.

The next morning, someone shouting: "Fastito!" echoed in the room.

Yvonne looked out. "Something happened to Dull-Dull," she said. "What happen'?" Yvonne shouted at a guy passing.

"Dull-Dull ketch the biggest snake you wah see, man."

In a stampede, my brothers and sisters sped out the door and I followed.

"He has it down Step-Step," the guy said.

The row of concrete steps led down to the lake in another area of the Barrio. There, hanging from the limb of a mango tree, was the biggest snake I had ever seen.

This must be what Grandpa talked about, I thought. A snake so big, the body looks more like a tree stump. Even though thrown across a branch, the tail rested on the ground in a coil. Delrincito stood next to me.

"See, that's Fastito." He pointed to a tiny man that they called Fastito or Dull-Dull interchangeably. I was about five feet tall, and he was shorter than I was. He gazed at his catch. His brown pants were tucked into rubber boots that reached his knees. His blue cap was set backward on his head, the visor on his neck and the strap across his forehead. He smiled from ear to ear. A pack of dogs paced closely around him. He signaled and spoke with a muffled tone, using hand gestures.

"They call him Dull-Dull 'cause he is deaf and dumb," Delrincito explained. "That's why he can't talk well, but he understands his dogs and his dogs understand him."

"Them boys say, the snake attack one ah the dogs and he shot the snake clean in the head."

"Dull-Dull say he goin' skin it."

"He is so small. How did he manage that snake? It is no way he could lift that snake by himself."

"He dragged it to his dory, man."

"You see him? He small but he strong."

My eyes drifted to the lake, calm as a sheet of glass, with not a ripple on its surface. A row of trees and mangroves formed a perfect hedge. Scattered here and there, tiny islands floated on the horizon. "Bahia de Bluefields," I whispered.

A few days before, while in class, we sang this song. I thought of the words that said:

It was a little door to the ocean,
Its clams and oysters, its natural riches.
On a warm night of silvery moon and sentimentality,
The Creole girls like none other
In their canoes, they paddle along and
At daybreak, your islets appear.

The songwriter, Mr. Beltran Bustamante, came to mind. Perhaps he stood in a spot like this when these words rang in his head.

Back home, the talks continued.

"He is really lucky the snake didn't attack him instead of the dog. He wouldn't stand a chance," Charles said.

"Good thing he shot it. He had a good shot though."

"Yeah, like Dido's daughter and the jaguar," Lisa remarked.

"Who is Dido? What jaguar?" I asked.

"Ms. Dido is a lady that lives a few houses down, across

the road. Her daughter lives in Kukra Hill," Delrincito answered. "One day she went to hang out her clothes and spotted a huge jaguar. She said she eased back inside and got her rifle, then got a good aim at him. One shot she gave him, and he dropped," Delrincito continued. "She brought the skin for Dido, and Dido has it on her living room floor."

"I can show it to you if you want. She is like my granny, you know," Lisa said.

It was Easter, and everyone was getting ready to go on a picnic over at Cookra Pint, as it was the custom, I gathered.

"Where is Cookra Pint?" I asked.

"If you stand up by the slaughterhouse and look straight across the lake, over the other side. That is Cookra Pint," said Charles.

"Oh, so we have to go in a canoe?"

"We could go in a canoe if we had a canoe, but we don't, so we goin' on number eleven."

"What do you mean, number eleven?"

"Your two-foot, noh," Katherine laughed.

"We have to walk all the way down the canal and go all the way around. So, get ready to walk, girl," Charles said.

"Girl, put on this bikini and let's go," Gladys said. After trying on the bathing suit, I slipped on a pair of shorts and a big T-shirt.

"Girl, what you doin'?" Gladys asked.

"I'd rather wear my shorts and T-shirt."

"You see what a' tell you. That old lady raised her old-fashioned just like she," my mother said.

"Girl, take off that T-shirt and shorts. If you have it, flaunt it," Gladys said.

I walked away deep in thought. I may have been raised old-fashioned, but I would much rather be old-fashioned than live with blindfolds over my eyes and have no hope for the future.

How could they be so blind? Why couldn't my mother see the blessing she had in the form of her children? They were healthy, strong, and smart. They needed guidance, someone to say they can do it. Someone to encourage them to set a goal in life and to help them achieve that goal. But unfortunately, that was not happening.

On the road, the blistering sun had no mercy. The red, blinding dust rose up like smoke each time the cars zoomed past. Relieved when a truck stopped and offered us a ride, we piled in the back to complete our journey.

At the picnic, people looked around for the best spot they could find. Most carried huge watermelons, bags of mangoes, jars of stew plums, and loaves of buns, as Easter is not Easter without buns.

The children ran around playing under the tall coconut trees as the leaves swayed back and forth from the cool breeze next to the lake, while others swam in the fresh water. The shallow, murky water barely reached knee-high even after walking a good distance out. The dark-brown sand was a slimy slush that looked more like mud than sand.

Others shoveled oysters and placed them in small buckets. This was a novelty to me. I had no idea oysters were collected this way. The day was filled with giggles and laughter.

On our return from the picnic, the celebration continued with a party at Ms. Enid's house across the street. The music blared, and dancing and drinking ensued. Yvonne and some of her friends had a competition going. The bet was who could drink the most rum in one go. They had no shot glasses but drank straight from the bottle.

"Bottoms up!" one guy teased, and Yvonne put the bottle to her mouth and gave a long gulp.

"Whoooo!" The crowd echoed.

"Go deh, Yvonne, easy does it," a guy said. She took a

long pull on her cigarette and slowly let out the smoke into the air. They passed the bottle around as the crowd cheered. A now familiar Maypole song produced by a local group boomed from the record player. The crowd sang along:

Tululululu, pass undah,
gial an buay them pass undah,
all a them goin' pass undah,
gial an buay them pass undah,
Seferina, pass undah,
gial an buay them pass undah
all a them goin' pass undah
gial an buay them pass undah.

Hands waved in the air as she wiggled her hips to the beat. The crowd cheered when a lady dropped to the floor and a guy lifted his leg over her as they chanted.

"Pass, pass, pass under, girl, and boy them pass under."

Across the road, two houses down, a lady came out on her porch. A lady shouted at her.

"Sefe, come pass under!" someone shouted.

"Yes, Sefe, come show them how it's done!" another one shouted.

"That's Seferina," Charles said.

"You mean the person they mentioned in the song?"

"Yes. If you want to see how to dance Maypole, check her out. She is the best dancer in Bluefields, man."

The tall, slender-built lady stepped off her porch. Her white blouse and white pants were a clear contrast to her coffee-toned skin. Seferina stepped onto the porch and someone shouted, "Come again, come again!" The song started again.

The lady put her hand on her hip and stamped one leg on the ground, teasing.

A man shouted, "Wait, wait, gi' my way, gi' my way!"

Seferina made a move and the crowd went wild. When the song ended, she walked away. "See you guys later."

Someone offered her a drink. "Take one for the road, Sefe, one for the road."

"Later, man," she said as she went up the road.

Yvonne took the bottle and took another gulp. My brothers and sisters stood watching.

Gladys looked at me and said, "Yvonne, look at Bev's face."

"Who, her? She too damn old-fashioned like her grandmother." They laughed.

Walking away, I questioned the example continuously set for her children and was disappointed that not even her so-called friends and family cared enough to point out to her the disservice committed to the detriment of her children's future. Frustration gripped me. The inability to change the course of their impending doom produced a sense of despondency.

Alone in the living room, I sat on an unpainted wooden stool and glanced around. A green wooden chair with a high semi-reclining back in desperate need of a new paint job stood in the corner of the room. The big open seams on the floor were a clear indication of the builder's inexperience. There was no dining table—or dining room, for that matter. A plywood partition, also in need of a new paint job, separated the living room from the bedroom.

Oh, how I wished I could finish school and get a job! I would fix all that was screaming to be fixed. Set things right and better our living conditions. If only I could get everyone on board. Little by little, we could do it. I was certain of it.

If my mother didn't want to participate, perhaps my siblings would; but how to get them to see the light? Unfortunately, they looked for the easy way out and shunned hard work. Children need guidance, and my efforts were being sabotaged. Reaching my siblings on my own was futile. I was fighting a losing battle.

Chapter Twenty-Nine

My last year at the Anglican school rolled around quickly. I was now thirteen years old. A group of students gathered in our new classroom like a hive of bees. The buzz and laughter floated in the air while they caught up on stories of who went where and who did what.

"Guys, you realize this is our last year?" Thelma announced. "We are going to need to plan graduation."

"We will have to start a committee and start planning. That's what the sixth-grade class did last year," I said. "We have a whole year to plan, but we need to start early. We need to make a list of who would like to be on the committee," I added.

The bell rang and interrupted our conversation.

The weeks flew by, and we formed a fundraiser committee and decided it would be fun to organize an excursion to Managua for the graduates.

This had never been done before, and we wanted to be different. We would leave sixth grade with a bang. Raffles and pastry sales were organized, but our biggest fundraising project would be a comedy show. Luis and Henry, our class clowns, were both native Spaniards who always had the class in stitches. They would be the main actors. We knew they could play the part. It was right up their alley.

The planning for the show began. We would sell tickets for the event, and also had to consider who would be invited to be the speaker at our graduation.

"Why not ask Alexis Arguello?" Henry asked sarcastically.

We laughed.

"Yeah, right, like he would want to come and speak at our graduation. Besides, we wouldn't even know how to get in touch with him," Vilma replied.

"Let's find out the address of his boxing committee and write to them. All they could do is say no, or completely ignore us," I said. We all laughed

"Nothing beats a failure but a trial," I said.

"Yeah, seriously, let's try," Henry agreed.

We did some investigation, spoke to the principal, and prepared a letter to invite Alexis Arguello, our boxing champion and national hero. He was a person we had only seen on black-and-white TV, and only by those lucky enough to have a TV. It was wild and far-fetched, but we would try.

After class, on my daily walk back home, I slowed down to take a look at the only color TV in Bluefields, which was strategically set to be visible through the living room door. Students slowed down to a crawl and leaned against the railing on the porch to take it all in, in awe of the vivid colors, the true likeness of characters, and the color of their clothes.

One particular evening, the buzz was out. Alexis was to fight Jose Fernandez. No one wanted to miss the epic event, and spectators gathered at homes with TVs. The roars echoed at the delivery of every punch and when his opponent was knocked out, my gosh, the place was flooded with shouts and roars of laughter.

The fight did not last long. The opponent was knocked out in the first round, but the shouts and laughter went on. Men gathered outside with hands in the air. Cassette players boomed with the song, "Alexis Punched Him Right Out Of The Ring," a chorus chanted by the crowd. It was yet another excuse to throw a party. Music blared and the bottles of Flor de Caña came out. It was Christmas in August. The celebration went on all night.

At school, in anticipation of the yearly Independence celebration, we practiced for our march to be performed on September 15. The school band drummed up the popular marching sounds. We marched around the school in three perfect rows, keeping proper posture as we learned the correct way to make our turns. The sounds of the drop of our feet were in tune with the music as our steps synchronized.

I gazed at the *palillonas*—cane dancers—their white hats resting neatly over their brows. The sequins on their uniforms twinkled, their stockinged legs peeped below their miniskirts next to the rim of their white boots above their knees, and their poles glistened in the sun, resting at the bend of their elbows. How I wished to be a part of such a majestic-looking group! But the price of the uniform prevented this aspiration.

At the entrance of the park, I gazed up at the statue of Anastacio Somoza Garcia. Impressed by the craftsmanship of the monumental sculpture, I continued on.

Under the shade of the giant mahogany trees, the gentle stir of the luscious branches evoked a sense of peaceful serenity. I inhaled, feeling as light as a kite as I enjoyed the moment. Children ran and played on the grass with no care in the world. Their laughter floated through the air like music.

On my way home, the folkloric sound of the marimba caught my ears. The sound came from a building to my right. A group of girls dressed in colorful costumes, with frills across their shoulders and wide, flowing skirts, swirled to the music. They glided across the floor, heads held high, their arms reaching to the ceiling. Their fingers gracefully extended, gently enfolding the frilled hem of their skirts in a swirl.

I gasped. *Yes, maybe I could join a dance group like this!* A girl came to the door. I inquired about the class, but after she mentioned the cost of the costume, which was over two hundred córdoba, my heart sank and I walked away. This, too, would be only a dream. Overshadowed by gloom, my eyes trailed the cracks in the pavement as I made my way home.

After another day of chores, I looked at the freshly washed living room floor. The smell of Pine-Sol lingered in the air. After a long, deep breath and a sigh, I smiled. It was one more chore done.

In the kitchen, Yvonne busied herself making bread. Her fingers were covered in the thick paste as she incorporated the flour into the big wad of dough. I stood quietly at the corner of the counter, taking in the master at work, when suddenly, *Wham!* The sound echoed in my ear. The force of the slap caused my head to turn, and my hand instantly covered my cheek to frame the sting as tears welled up in my eyes and my jaw dropped. My brows furrowed in disbelief as I stared.

"What?" I asked.

"Standing there with your mouth pushed out," she said.

Her pouted lips, frowned brow, and fierce look puzzled me. As the saying went, if looks could kill, I would be a dead girl.

Shocked, I walked away, tears rolling down my face. I sat on the bed and stared at the wall, wishing I was anywhere but there.

A few weeks later at school, we were shocked and amazed at the response we received from Alexis Arguello's office. He accepted to be the guest speaker at our graduation! We were blown away, and we jumped for joy. This was a further push to continue with the sale of tickets for our comedic event, and all the tickets sold out.

The first night of our show was nerve-wracking but exciting. The Anglican church hall was filled to capacity. On stage, the lights bounced off the polished oak desk in the interior of an executive office. The manager's chair, tucked under the desk, looked out at the audience. One chair set across the desk on a slant allowed for a clear view of the spectators. The lights on stage shone brightly while the audience sat in darkness. The show began.

The manager (Luis) sat at his desk as the cleaning lady came in. "Ms. Francine, would you get me a cup of coffee and a pastry please?"

"Okay, sir," she replied.

"And call the new secretary for me. I need to dictate a letter."

"Yes, sir," she said as she left.

Shortly afterward, she entered the room and rested the cup of coffee and the pastry on the boss's desk. The secretary entered.

"Thank you, Ms. Francine," the boss said as she walked out the door.

At the time of the event, there were talks of war throughout the country. The Sandinista Rebels fought against the then-dictator President Somoza Debayle. Soldiers were everywhere; some even came from Cuba. There were a lot of nurses and doctors who came from Cuba as well.

Rumor had it that if a riot broke out, you would see how quickly the nurses and doctors would slip out of their white uniforms and right into the green ones, as they were known to be versatile. It had been decided that a soldier would play the role of the secretary in the play, to display that versatility.

The secretary (Henry) stepped in, dressed in a green combat uniform, with a rifle thrown over his shoulder. The manager, dressed in navy-blue pants, a long-sleeved white shirt, and a tie stood up and addressed the secretary as he placed his hands behind his back and gazed into the distance.

"I need to dictate a letter, but I think better when I'm standing. You may have a seat and take notes."

The secretary fumbled around behind him, trying to decide where to sit, as it was his first day on the job. He took a seat in the boss's chair, causing the crowd to chuckle. The boss started his dictation.

"Secre apunte," he said—Secre is short for secretary and apunte is a play on the word meaning to take note or to take aim.

The secretary stood up from his seat and pointed his rifle at the audience. The audience roared. The boss, not knowing what was going on behind his back, walked around seriously.

"Dear Ms." he paused. The secretary realized he was supposed to be taking notes, so he sat down quickly and started to take notes.

Then the boss said, "Beba"—Beba was the name of the person he was writing to, but also means to drink—the secretary took a sip of the boss's coffee. The audience chuckled.

"Coma," the boss said—meaning a comma, or to eat. The secretary took a bite of the boss's pastry and the audience rumbled. The whole letter went on like this. Each time the boss said coma, the secretary ate his pastry, and each time the boss said Ms. Beba, the secretary drank his coffee.

The audience thundered and the whole event, masterly crafted with the use of play on words, had the audience in stitches. It was a huge success and got standing ovations. The show was put on the following weekend as well and was sold out again. We gathered enough funds to pay for our excursion, but we had to cancel our trip as it was deemed too dangerous with the war going on in the region.

The graduation date approached. Alexis Arguello, true to his promise, arrived in Bluefields. The whole town came out to greet him. Over their shoulders, they carried him through the streets amid chants, shouts, and laughter.

The graduation was an event to remember, despite my

being there alone. I invited my mother, but she declined my invitation as if my trying to make something of my life or succeeding in any way was adding salt to her wounds.

We opted to use the money we raised to enjoy a huge banquet at a nice restaurant instead of the trip. We had enough money for everyone to order from the menu. As usual, Henry and Luis stole the show by ordering a whole chicken each. We laughed so hard to see the waiter put a whole roast chicken in front of them. They tore off the legs with their bare hands, going against all table manners and protocols. After our meal, they asked for music and we danced, laughed, and acted crazy. We had so much fun.

Granny and Grandpa came to mind and the tears welled up in my eyes. I knew Granny would be there had she been in Bluefields, and now understood better the meaning of the words she uttered—she was all I had.

Chapter Thirty

It was the beginning of the new year and I got ready for my first day of school. I would be attending the Cristobal Colón school. Dressed in my white blouse and burgundy-red skirt, crisply pleated and pressed, I strolled across the green grass to the park.

After a few days, we were told the school was in bad need of repair. We would have to move to a new location at the San Jose school building. Each student was required to carry their own chair to the new location almost a mile away.

Some wore their chairs as shields, others carried them on their heads as hats, and some rested their chair in the middle of the road and sat, just to be funny. Like leaf-cutter ants we went down the road, holding our seats.

The move was successful, but the new school was smaller. This required the classes to be split into two rotations, morning and evening, and two locations to accommodate everyone. Academic classes were held at the San Jose building, and trade classes consisting of cooking, woodwork, electricity, metalwork, car repair, and sewing were held at a building across the town, near the airport.

My first trade class was woodwork. The classroom was

equipped with heavy machinery lining the peripheries. Electric saws, a huge machine to do wood carving, and an assortment of chisels lined the walls. Armed with my piece of four-by-four, I stepped in, ready to make the perfect baseball bat for my brothers. On a machine in the center of the hall, I clamped both ends of the four-by-four, trapping it in position to start paring the wood to size. The loud noise of the machines filled the room. My four-by-four spun at full speed, when all of a sudden, like a missile, it flew over my head and across the room at lightning speed. I ducked just in time.

In shock, I spun around to see if anything was damaged or if anyone was injured. Luckily, everyone was spared, but they all burst out laughing, including the teacher.

"Girl, what are you doing?"

"You trying to kill us or what?" one of the boys asked.

I put my hand on my chest as if to slow down my racing heart and chuckled nervously. "Man, I don't know what happened."

"Well, this is a good example of what not to do," our teacher said.

Everyone laughed. This gave our teacher an opportunity to train everyone in the proper use of the machine.

"Okay, guys, come over here." He proceeded to show us the parts of the machine. "Make sure, and check carefully, that the wood is securely clamped on both ends. We don't want to knock someone out with a flying four-by-four."

After the fiasco, I went on with my carving. The square angles disappeared into a cylinder and my bat began to take shape. After several sessions at school and much sanding and polishing, I presented my brothers with a beautiful bat made with my own hands.

I then had to move on to the electricity class. A square piece of board was assigned to each student with the goal of wiring the board, installing a bulb, and then configuring the wires to be operated by a switch.

Before the class began, our instructor went through some safety tips. This required us to touch a live wire to get familiar with the shock and also to know what to do and what not to do when working with live wires. Monica, the girly girl in our class, was furious. Her pink hairband held her light-brown hair neatly in place as she pouted, standing in the corner of the classroom with her hands folded across her chest.

"I don't know why we are forced to take this class. Prof—teacher—do you really think you will see me on a light pole fixing a light on the street when I leave this class? This is a complete waste of time."

"Monica, I understand your frustration, but this is a class you need to pass in order to pass the year, and the quicker you accept that fact, the better it will be for you."

"Well, I don't see why they have to make this class a requirement. Do you really think I am going to ever need this skill? No, I don't think so," she growled with a knitted brow and folded arms.

"I don't have any say in that regard, but as a student in this class, you have to fulfill the requirements, and you need to go through the safety training. Therefore, please join the line. When working with electricity, you need to know what you are working with and what it feels like."

He turned to the class.

"If someone is being shocked and is stuck, do not grab them, or you will get shocked too. Your first instinct may be to grab the person and pull them off, but that would be the wrong thing to do. You would also put yourself in danger. What you need to do is, if you have a belt on, take the belt off, put it around the person, and jerk the person away from the electrical source. Or use another object like a shirt, but never use your bare hands."

He looked at each of us. "Avoid stepping in water when doing this, or the shock can be even more severe."

One by one, we approached a live wire sticking out of a

wall to feel the effect of the electric current. Monica, the last in line, acting pampered and girly as always, was reluctant to touch the wire, but as soon as she did, a boy in the class put his foot in a small puddle of water on the floor and touched her.

She screamed; the water caused her to get an even stronger shock than everyone else got. She was fit to be tied! She stomped across the room and everyone was in stitches, laughing.

After class, on our long walk back home to get ready for academic class at the other building in the town, a group of us girls walked together.

"Let's take a shortcut," Mayra said.

"If we take this road"—pointing at a narrow lane—"we can save a lot of time."

"What road, that one?" I asked, pointing at the lane with a big pool of muddy water extending from one side to the other. "Girl, we would have to swim through that to get across."

"No, we can hold onto that plant over there and cross on the edge."

The water came right up to the root of the plant.

"Come on," she said, holding onto the plant as she tiptoed across.

Two other friends followed and went across fine. When it was my turn, I held onto the shrub and felt the branch slowly go down, and down. Before I knew it, I was sitting in the puddle.

"No, man, Bev!" They held their stomachs as they laughed.

"I can't believe this. Why me? You all passed fine, and the branch held you up." I was covered in mud. "How am I going to get this cleaned now? How am I going to walk through town looking like this? I knew I should not have followed you girls."

We walked a little further along a luscious green pasture,

my skirt stuck to my legs, wet and yucky. Straight ahead, to my amazement, there, propped up on a wooden frame, was an old canoe, filled with clear rainwater. I dashed ahead, pleased at my fortune. I cupped my hands and started rinsing my skirt and legs.

My friends called to me as they ran off.

"Hey, wait for me! Why are you leaving me here before I finish rinsing off?"

"Look, look!" they yelled.

I looked behind me, and to my shock, a herd of cows was heading my way. The canoe! It dawned on me that the canoe must have been their drinking water. I took off like lightning, trying to catch up with my friends, who were running way ahead of me as they shouted, "Cows, cows! Run, run!"

When we got to the main road, they were bent over laughing.

"Man, no wonder the dory was propped up so neatly. I should have known. Girls, you better not come up with any other bright ideas. No more shortcuts for me."

They threw back their heads, laughing. "Bev, but you can run though."

"Yeah, like how you ran off and left me behind with the cows." Hurriedly, I headed home.

While getting ready for my next class, I was conscious of my thin white blouse, keenly aware of my desperate need for undergarments and other female essentials. I had to figure out a way to earn some money. Even though I now lived with my mother, the reality was that I was on my own and had no one to turn to.

In the town, the sale of raffle tickets was common. This gave me an idea. The numbers were read on the radio every Saturday evening. Surely, I could sell raffle numbers as well, but there was a drawback. Most people carried booklets with tear-off coupons, which cost money—money I did not have.

So instead, I took out my notebook and wrote 00 to 99 to offer a chance to win 50 córdobas, one córdoba a piece.

On my way to and from school, I stopped random strangers and went from door to door selling my numbers. I jotted down their names and made sure all the numbers were sold before Saturday. It was a relief every time the last number was sold. This meant I earned 50 córdobas for the week.

One week I sold eighty-seven numbers and was disappointed when Saturday came, knowing my earnings would be short, but relieved I would have enough to pay the winner.

As luck would have it, the winning number was one that was not sold. I jumped with excitement in awe of my good fortune. At the market, I shopped for a bra, but the only affordable one was bright yellow. Conscious of the color being clearly visible through my thin white blouse, and knowing it would be worn daily until I could afford another, caused me to hesitate. But it would have to do while I collected more money to buy a white one.

After a couple of weeks, I reinvested my earnings and bought cassava and cheese, and made buñuelos. On Saturday evenings, around a small makeshift table, in the cool shade of my neighbor's soursop tree, I sold my buñuelos drizzled with homemade syrup, served on almonds or sea grape leaves.

Soon afterward, I was able to buy a pint of light-green paint and a small paintbrush and began my project of painting the main wall in the living room. Patiently trying to achieve perfection when doing the edges and trims, it was like learning to write between the lines all over again.

Once finished, I stood back and admired my handiwork. It boosted my confidence and I went on to tackle the other walls, bit by bit, feeling proud of my accomplishments.

In my effort to produce an income, I decided to set up a shop on the porch. We closed a small section off with lumber. The section of the wall facing the road was left with a big opening. This was fitted with a door that was installed horizontally. It opened outward and was sustained by a rope on each corner, forming a floating counter. This allowed for a good view of the items on the shelves, and doubled as a display counter for coconuts, cassava, and plantains. Next to the door, another counter allowed for the proper serving of the customers.

At the market, I searched for affordable items at wholesale prices. Specifically, items easily displayed on shelves or hung on the walls, such as snacks packed in small bags like Cheetos and chips. Candies were placed in big glass jars to attract the children. Each week, I added something new.

One week, I bought a large scale, which I hung from the ceiling next to the counter. The following week, I could afford a sack of one hundred pounds of sugar. This was the minimum sold at a wholesale price, and I was bursting with excitement.

I bought clear plastic bags of different sizes and inquired how much it would cost to have someone take the one-hundred-pound bag of sugar home. This proved to be too expensive, so after getting assistance from a random man to put the bag on my head, off I went, praying the sack would not fall off along the way and hoping that the journey would quickly end.

Breathless, I reached the stairs after lugging the bag for more than a mile. Relieved to have made it home, I unloaded the burdensome baggage off my small frame, surprised that I had accomplished the feat.

Taking my time, weighing out bags of one and two pounds, I stacked them on the shelves. Soon afterward rice, beans, and flour were added, followed by boxes of small cans of Carnation milk and bars of washing soap. All of these were brought home on my head to save on transportation fees.

Little by little, the stock increased with an assortment of things. The resale price was well calculated to produce a profit, and the business grew. My mother tended to the store in my absence, but I noticed she was bent on sabotaging my efforts.

One morning, my brother walked in. "Ma, I want chips."

"Go in the shop and take it," she said as she glanced at me to see my reaction. I said nothing.

Soon afterward, a neighbor's child came over. "Ms. Yvonne, my mom says if you would let her have a pound of sugar and a pound of rice, she will pay you later."

"Okay," she said. Soon we had a book with a list of names of people who got things on credit, and the list got longer and longer.

"The store needs to be registered," my mother said. "I will get that done today."

"Okay," I said, pleased with the offer and delighted with the prospect of progress. Later that evening on my way back from school, my mother greeted me.

"I got the store registered, and I had a sign painted." She handed me the paper and showed me the registration and the newly installed sign hanging over the door. It read, "Pulperia Lisa"—(Lisa's Variety Store).

Awestruck that she chose to name the store after my sister and repulsed by her deliberate intent to hurt me once again, I shook my head. *How must my other siblings feel? Seeing their sister's name displayed on the store. How could she be so insensitive to her children's feelings? How could she feel good about herself, knowing that every penny that went into the store was from all my efforts? How could she feel she was doing the right thing?* I shook my head in disbelief and continued my efforts.

While on the bottom bunk of the bed, I laid reading my assignment when Lisa came into the room.

"You know your father is a bum. He's good for nothing," she said, staring at me as if waiting for my reaction.

"And yours?" I asked.

I glanced up at her, then back at my book and continued reading. She walked out the door. Two minutes later, my mother barged into the room, grabbed me off the bed, and punched me in my back.

"What did you tell Lisa?" she screamed as the belt slammed against my back, her fury and vitriol gushing like hot lava, not giving me a chance to respond.

Crouched forward in my attempt to avoid the blows, I made it to the living room while keeping close to the wall for shelter. Amidst the blows, I fell and lost consciousness. Outside on the grass, I regained awareness. A number of people were gathered around.

I was told her brother Richard came into the house and pushed her away from me, picked me up, and took me outside. I was covered in welts and bruises and had a cut on my inner thigh, which left a permanent scar.

"Why do you hate me so much?" I asked her one morning.

"Because you are you!" she barked.

I shook my head with a wry smile, expecting her to maybe deny the fact by saying it was all in my head, my reluctance to let go of my illusion of a loving mother slowly raveling away. Her need to hide her dislike of me was remote and there was nothing to be done. I was who I was.

Had she said because you are lazy or have no manners, maybe I would have been given an opportunity to remedy the issue. But to say, "Because you are you," indicated finality. I would always be me.

I was on the veranda when a young man came and asked, "Are you Beverly?"

"Yes."

"Ms. Julia says to tell you, your father and your sister are at the house and asked for you to come there."

"Thank you," I replied.

Right away I went to change and looked for Charles, but I had no idea where he was.

Across Big Field, we strolled through the twilight, excited

to see my sister more than anything. The last time I saw her, she was a tiny baby in a crib in Managua. Oh, I could not wait to meet her, expecting that perhaps she was excited to meet me as well.

Thoughts rushed through my head like a top in motion, feeling sure she would love to have a sister also. While living on Corn Island, I longed to have a sister. Perhaps I would be able to have a better relationship with her. She would accept me, and I would not be an intruder trying to fit in.

"Good evening," I said as I walked into the kitchen.

My father was deep in conversation with Ms. Julia. He turned around. "Hi, my child," he said, giving me a hug.

I glanced around, looking for my sister. "Where is Carolina?" I asked.

"She is in the living room," Ms. Julia said. "You can go and look for her."

I dashed through the familiar corridor. There she was, sitting in the living room. "Hi, Carolina," I greeted cheerfully.

"Go away, because my father is not your father, and you are not my sister."

The venom spewed by my six-year-old sister caught me by surprise. I tried hard to maintain my composure. She stared, her expression piercing, stern, and cold.

In my mind, she would crave having a brother or sister, as she was an only child in her household. But then, there I was, being gullible as always. *Is she thinking she is better than me?* Here it was again, this rejection, this *Go from here, you are not good enough* message.

Turning away, I headed back down the dark corridor, telling the tears welling up in my eyes to go back. *No, you are not going to cry.*

Before entering the kitchen, I made every effort to control my emotions, not wanting them to see me upset. Taking a deep breath, I entered the kitchen.

"That was quick. Did you see Carolina?" Ms. Julia said.

"Yes, ma'am, I already said hi. I will leave now. It was good seeing you," I said to my father.

"You are leaving already?" he asked.

"Yes, sir. I have some things to do, so I have to get back."

"Okay, I will walk you back," he said.

I tried to discourage him, but he would not take no for an answer. He called Carolina to accompany us. She came out and held his hand as innocently as if nothing had ever happened.

We headed back under the moonlight. She stood on the left holding his hand and I on the right, keeping my distance.

"I'm taking Carolina to Corn Island tomorrow," he said.

"Tell Granny and Grandpa I say hi, please. I don't have time to write them now but tell them I will write them later."

Blinking away my tears and being inconspicuous while wiping my eyes, I tried to keep my composure. We strolled along the field, but what I really wanted to do was run. They stood at the entrance to the yard and I bid farewell. I was eager to head straight to the room, hoping not to see anyone. I just wanted to be alone.

A few days later, I stood at the back door when I heard one of my mother's friends say to the other, "Do you know Yvonne is expecting?"

She had been sick most mornings, but I had not made the connection. Somehow, I was hopeful at this prospect. Maybe this child would accept me, as I would be in his life from the beginning. No one would be able to turn this child away from me. This new possibility filled me with encouragement. With the other members of the family, I was at a disadvantage, as they met me later in their lives. This now would not be the case. To them, I was a stranger, but this child would meet me as a baby. He would know me from the get-go. This thought was pleasing. A noble possibility indeed.

Chapter Thirty-One

I was now fourteen years old, and during this time, rumors of war increased. After school, the students organized manifestations and marched in the town and in the parks carrying banners. The chants resounded.

"Free homeland!" a leader shouted.

"Or death!" the students replied. "Homeland or death!"

"Victory is ours!" came the students' jubilant response, fists waving in the air.

"Guardias! Guardias!" (National soldiers! National soldiers!) Voices echoed through the crowd.

Like ants from a troubled nest, the students scattered in all directions as the soldiers approached in full green uniforms, bearing arms. It was time to get away or bear the consequences, which were to be arrested and incarcerated, or even shot. The *Novedades* newspaper carried news supporting the then president, Somoza, announcing the president's remarks about the horrific deaths of those fallen from the rebel groups.

The *Prensa*, the other newspaper, which was more supportive of the rebel forces, spoke of the massacres of innocent people said to have opposed the government. The director of the *Prensa*, Dr. Joaquin Chamorro, was gunned down in front of his office on his way to work. The country mourned his passing.

Rumors of the intensification of the war increased. War broke out in many districts on the Pacific side and in the mountains. This caused most farmers to flee the rural areas, resulting in a shortage of onions, tomatoes, beans, and rice. These were items previously so plentiful that they were exported to other countries. Now they were in short supply within the country.

We stood in long queues to purchase them. The fighting intensified throughout the country. We were careful not to wear the colors black and red at the same time, or it was viewed as a declaration of support for the rebels, which could have dire consequences. The Sandinistas—the rebels—declared their colors to be red and black and oftentimes were pictured wearing the banners covering their faces or carrying a flag in these colors.

Classes were suspended because of the war. Men who grew their hair were harassed by the Guardias, as they were suspected of being rebels coming from the mountains. The papers were filled with gruesome scenes of attacks on villages, horrific pictures of bodies covering the pages, innocent victims, and some not-so-innocent. The custom of singing our National Anthem before class, the words, "The voice of the cannon no longer roars," or, "Nor is your glorious multicolored banner stained with the blood of brothers," became wishful thinking, the opposite of our truth.

In July 1979, the Sandinistas claimed victory, and Somoza fled the country. People busied themselves spreading the news.

"You heard; the Sandinistas won."

"They said Somoza escaped in a helicopter," others claimed.

"Thank God, the war is over and we can finally live in peace."

"Well, you never know what tomorrow will bring," said another.

Classes were still suspended.

A couple of days later, the Sandinistas announced they wanted everyone to support the cause. This could be done by getting involved in the first nationwide project called "Operation Clean-Up." Clean-up committees were organized, and the town got busy trimming trees and collecting garbage. Heaps of garbage appeared at the sides of the roads. Garbage trucks went from district to district, road to road.

A few days into the Operation Clean-Up drive, I got sad news. My old classmate, Henry, had been helping on one of the garbage trucks. He was holding onto the back and lost his grip. The truck was reversing. The driver did not know he had fallen and accidentally ran over him. He died on the spot.

The community was overshadowed by this sadness. Students from the Anglican school, the Colón school, as well as the people who attended the show, were all devastated and mourned his loss. Both schools joined to commemorate his passing by participating in a funeral procession. The bands from each school followed the casket. Students marched to the somber beat of the drums to take his body to its final resting place.

After a short lull, classes resumed. The hallways buzzed with excitement and questions such as, "Where did you go?"

One professor welcomed the class and someone asked, "Prof, what did you do?"

"Well, if I must tell you, I went to the mountain"—a familiar phrase used to indicate joining the rebels in the fight —"and, class, while I always respected women, I must say, I now have even more respect for women than I did before."

The class stared quietly, taking in his every word. He leaned against his desk, his legs extended, as he went on to address the class.

"One night, in the middle of a shootout against the

Guardia, our leader was shot and he fell. We didn't know what to do. The sound of bullets rang out all around us; we were surrounded by heavy fighting, and we had no leader. A young girl stepped up. She was no older than twenty. 'I am the new leader,' she said. We stared at her quietly. The fear was clear on most faces. Some trembled. The bodies lay motionless all around us. The forest was dense and dark, there were no roads, and we had no idea where we were.

"One man said, 'I am leaving. I have to get out of here.' She looked at him swiftly and said, 'You are going nowhere. You can't leave now, or you will expose us all. I can't have that. And please don't attempt it, as I don't want to have to kill you. Don't make me.' She proceeded to loosen a rope that hung at her side. We watched as she tied the rope around her waist, tied the other end around the man's waist, and said, 'Don't try anything funny, or I will kill you.'

"The sound of heavy shooting around us continued. 'We will stay here until daybreak,' she said. 'Sit here and get some rest. We will need it in the morning.'

"At the crack of dawn, we were up. The shooting had subsided. 'Okay, get moving,' she said. 'Follow me.' We walked quietly along a ditch when suddenly, the man she had tied around her waist slipped down the ditch. With lightning speed, that girl wrapped herself around a tree trunk, dropped to the ground, and braced her foot on the tree root as the man dangled below. She pulled with all her might and got him up. We helped him over the bank. His legs were shaking so badly, he could hardly stand. 'You better not try that again,' she said. We shook our heads and kept walking.

"It was thanks to that young lady that I am here today because I am sure we would not have made it out alive without her. It was horrific, and a truly humbling experience. I am glad I have the good fortune to be able to tell you this today. Many don't have this opportunity."

My cousin Yvette and Uncle Richard returned from their trip to Jinotega. They went to visit our Uncle Henry.

"How come you guys came back so quickly?" I asked.

"Girl, you are lucky you left Jinotega when you did. You left just in time. Girl, we had to run out of that place."

"What you mean?"

"The riots there were crazy. One night we were at the restaurant, and we heard shooting all around. We had to hide under a table. We heard people outside, and Richard decided he wanted to see what was going on.

"He barely cracked the window to peep. He saw a girl, and you know him, he decided he had to get a better look and opened the window wider. That girl spun around and pointed her M16 right in his face. Girl, the only reason she didn't shoot him is because she must have been so shocked to see a Black man. You know, they are not used to seeing Black people in Jinotega. He shouted quickly, 'I am a visitor, I am a visitor!' 'Well close that window and don't try that foolishness again. You might not be so lucky next time,' she told him.

"When he closed the window, he was white as paper. Uncle told him, 'You see, girls going to be the death of you. You see, that girl could have blown your head off just like that.' We decided to get out of that place fast.

"Girl, you should have seen all the bodies on the streets. There were tires smoking everywhere. You know, they use tires to burn the bodies. Girl, what a gruesome scene! When the heat hits those bodies they make all sorts of shapes, hands and heads protruding out the top of the tires, frozen in all sorts of distorted ways. The place was gray with smoke and the stench was awful. The streets are all destroyed because they dug up the blocks to make barricades. You would not recognize the place. I don't want to live through that experience again."

"And Uncle Henry stayed there? He should have left too."

"We told him to leave, but he didn't want to. He claims he will be fine because everybody knows him. You believe that foolishness? We told him, you never know. This is war."

Rumors had it that Operation Clean-Up was being used not only to clean the nation's garbage, but that people took the time to take revenge, to come against people who were previous Somoza supporters. People were disappearing. Homes were being confiscated. People were fleeing the country.

It was a bad omen to be a teen or older. You could be called upon at any time to bear arms. If you refused, you could be branded as a traitor and your family could even be in danger. The passport office was busy. Each time I asked for someone I had not seen, the response was they went to Costa Rica or they went to Honduras. Whole families were leaving. A sense of fear hung over the country like a dark cloud.

My mother was far along in her pregnancy, but I saw no preparation and decided to make some baby clothes. I had one problem. I had no material, nor did I have any money, but I had a pair of light-blue pajamas. I proceeded to cut the pajamas up into little shimmies from patterns I drew on a piece of newspaper, making sure the size was big enough to have room for growth.

This material was not stretchy; therefore, it had to be opened in the front to make it easy to go on. I used the press snaps on the original garment, so there was nothing to waste. On the front of the shimmies, I drew ducks on one, bears on the other, and on another, alphabet blocks and pacifiers, which I embroidered from my pencil drawings in various colors. I was proud of my handiwork.

One evening, we sat watching *Cannon*, a popular detective series at the time. My mother got up and went to the bedroom.

"Call Gangan," she said to Katherine.

We continued watching the show when Gangan went into

the room with my mother. A few minutes later, we heard a baby cry.

"The baby is born?" I asked.

Shortly afterward, Gangan walked out of the room and I heard my mother say, "Open the door, let me finish watching *Cannon*."

This was incredible to me. At the end of the show, as the names were rolling up, my mother said, "Yep, that's the name. Hubert Sterling."

My mouth dropped. Just like that, my brother was born and his name was chosen.

My mother had not bought anything for the baby, and therefore, the clothes I made were the clothes he wore.

Our cousin Midgett was visiting and walked in after Gangan left. "Where is this baby boy?" she asked, laughing as she walked into the room.

"Cuz, you're something else. Just had that baby just like that. Man, that's what you call a woman," she chuckled.

Hubert started crying.

"Bring the janny cake, man, you see the boy is hungry," Midgett said. We all laughed.

As the months went by, I took care of the child to the point where I had to hide whenever I needed to leave for school. He cried after me whenever I left. I thought it was funny. My mother could come and go as she pleased, and he did not make a fuss, but he did not want me out of his sight.

My dream was finally a reality. My baby brother loved me. I was not a stranger to him.

Chapter Thirty-Two

It was a perfect day for washing. The morning was bright and vibrant. While in the process of spreading my washing on the grass, an unfamiliar voice drew my attention.

"Hey," a Spanish-speaking lady called. Dressed in a full army-green uniform, she stood at the gate with a baby in her left arm, and over her right shoulder, a Galil pointed toward her black soldier boots. She beckoned for me to come closer. Her dark-auburn curls brushed the nape of her neck and an olive-green canvas belt cinched her waist, with a bandolier of bullets across her chest.

I looked away, puzzled, wondering if she was talking to me or someone else.

"Come here," she said, and I approached in obedience.

"Do you want this baby?"

Wanting to make sure I heard what she said correctly, I drew closer.

"What did you say?" I asked, baffled.

"I asked if you want this baby," she repeated. "Ask your mother if she wants this baby."

The baby boy fussed and squirmed. Discomfort was

written all over his face. The frown, the knitted brow; he was uncomfortable and restless. His hand reached behind his head to his back, constantly scratching, his nails clearly infected.

"Hold on," I said, and ran to call Yvonne. "There is a lady with a baby outside, and she is asking if we want the baby."

"What?" she asked. Yvonne came out to the lady. "What did you say?" she asked.

"I asked if you want this baby."

"Yes, man," Yvonne said as she snatched the child out of the lady's arm and stormed away.

"Where you going?" I shouted.

"To the hospital, man. You watch those children!" she shouted back.

The lady stood motionless.

"What is the baby's name?" I asked.

"He does not have a name yet."

I thought this was odd, as the child seemed to be about a month or two old.

"When is his birthday?" I asked. The thought going through my mind was, *I bet this child was born on April 19. Mothers don't seem to want you if you are born on this date.*

"His birthday is April 29," she replied. It was not the date I expected, but it was close enough.

"Are you his mother?" I asked.

"No, he belongs to my cousin, but she doesn't want him. She cannot take care of him."

"Oh," I replied. "And who is his father?"

"I don't know. She didn't tell me."

"And how come you have him?"

"I have him because she gave him to me and asked that I find someone I could give him to."

"Oh, would you like to come in?" I asked as I pointed to the house. She nodded and followed me into the house.

Delrincito's gaze followed her to the table and could not hide his excitement as he stared at the gun and all the bullets.

"Can you take that gun apart?" he asked.

It was rumored the Sandinistas were experts at taking their weapons apart in a flash and could even do it blindfolded. She dropped the gun off her shoulder. It hit the floor and before I could squint, the gun was up on the table. In no time, it was dismantled. Amazed at her speed and agility, our jaws dropped.

"There," she said.

As fast as she had taken it apart, she set it back up, stood up, hung the gun over her shoulder, and headed through the front door as she waved her hand in the wind.

We watched her back as she went up the road. It was the last we saw of her.

A few hours later, Yvonne returned from the hospital, the baby in one hand and some medication in the other.

Following an old lady's instructions, we collected a plant with dainty yellow flowers each morning and washed and squeezed the plant into his bath, producing an oil-like consistency. This was followed by the application of the ointment received from the hospital to ease the terrible rash that covered his frail body from head to toe. In a few days, his rash slowly disappeared.

Elvis Presley had recently died, and his music was frequently played on the radio. I suggested we name the baby Denis Elvis, in memory of Elvis Presley, but later learned the idea was dropped.

Needless to say, with the arrival of not one, but two babies, there were always bottles to wash and the pile of dirty clothes grew.

The baseball season had begun and on the weekends, the stadium was full. The games were announced over the radio and there was excitement in the neighborhood. The bets on favorite teams were on.

Yvonne decided selling snacks at the stadium was a good idea. She sold Vigorón and Frito. Prep work started the evening before. I had never cut more cabbage and tomatoes and peeled and boiled more cassava in my life. Tons of chicharrón were diced, and lots of green plantains were peeled. The big plastic basins made their way to the living room, as there was no space in the tiny kitchen. Big, round plastic tubs filled with well-seasoned chicken and pork, red with achiote, ready for cooking at the crack of dawn, marinated in wait. The work was backbreaking but necessary.

Yvonne made her way to the stadium accompanied by Charles for the weekend sale. I stayed at home to look after my siblings. Each time, she returned with empty containers and a look of pride. Sales were good. Watching her count the money was even better.

One day, she mentioned someone was selling a table and she would buy it. We were so excited when the table arrived. This was followed by a renovation to the house. She wanted to add an upstairs. The roof was lifted, and we had the semblance of a second floor. The roof was low and not conducive to standing, even though we were short. We crouched over to walk around.

We gained access with a ladder. On one of my ascensions with Hubert on my hip, just before we reached the top, the ladder slid and down we came, evidencing the force of gravity. My body cushioned him, which proved to be an adequate shield. I was bruised but grateful there were no broken bones.

In my efforts to gain the family's acceptance, I decided to try my luck at winning Gangan over once again. Up the stairs I went, but was halted by her snarl as soon as I came into view.

"Get out! You know I can't stand you. Yvonne! Don't you have anything for this one to do?" I dashed down the stairs, but with all the commotion, Yvonne came out and stopped me in my tracks.

"How many times do I have to tell you not to go over there? When you goin' get in your thick skull to stay away? Why don't you go to the neighbors, or anywhere else! Just go!"

Her screams shocked me into full attention—if I had been a caricature, the drawing would be me on my heels, arms and legs sprawled, eyes bulging and hair spiked. But it was not comical. I lowered my head and stepped back, feeling as low as the dirt beneath my feet.

I glanced around at the nearby houses in search of that place of acceptance, to find someone who would see the good in me while trying to accept that my place of belonging had to be somewhere out there. Outside of my home, outside of my family, and perhaps even outside of my country.

My mother's words burned through me, melting away my blindfold and revealing a truth that was so hard to accept. She wanted me to go, go away, get out of her sight, out of her space, out of her life.

My steps led to Ms. Jane's. I stared at the TV screen in my attempt to dull the numbness within. The images crossed the screen and the sound floated above my head, but the story eluded me.

Sometimes I went over to Ms. Aldith, our neighbor across the road. I enjoyed her company, especially on Saturday evenings. Most times it was only her and I as her family, while big, was often out and about. We enjoyed the music shows, with special guests such as Julio Iglesias, Mocedades, El Puma, José José, and Abba, to name a few.

My time in Bluefields was drawing to an end. My mother continued to investigate ways to go through with getting my passport without the need for my father's consent. Someone told her she would need an affidavit from a lawyer, and she was trying to figure out which lawyer to use.

Before long, it was time to celebrate Hubert's first birthday.

While there would not be a party, I was eager to do something special for this joyous occasion. I baked a cake, but waiting for the cake to cool was too long a wait. The icing had to be nice and different. Not the customary blue for boys, but deciding on a color was another challenge. Many colors were added in my effort to come up with something unique, resulting in a dingy gray. Not quite the color I was looking for, but unique it was.

Chapter Thirty-Three

Shortly afterward, my mother made an appointment with a lawyer. Outside his office, we stood at the door.

"Now, you be quiet. I will do the talking."

"What can I do for you?" he asked after we entered.

"I am here to ask if you could do an affidavit for me. I need to apply for her passport, without needing to get her father's signature."

"And where is her father?" the lawyer asked.

"He left the country for many years and is presumed dead. I would like to get her passport for her to go and visit my aunt."

I glanced at her in disbelief, listening to all the lies being fed to the lawyer. He took note.

After the meeting, at the door, she blurted, "And you better not let your father know anything about this, or it will be me and you."

I listened quietly and continued on my way.

The affidavit was soon issued, followed by the attainment of my passport. Her face glowed with pride. To her, it was a great achievement, deserving of a pat on her shoulder. She was ecstatic. The glee on her face said it all, but the biggest accomplishment was what she was now able to do—get rid of me for good. She could do her spring cleaning at last. Get rid of the clutter in her house. That's all I was to her, the waste she picked up from the garbage in Managua. The time had come to throw it out.

In the days that followed, I moped aimlessly, devoid of emotion, depleted of energy, as if the fight in me had turned away and vanished.

The Cayman Islands—I had no idea where this place was. In my social studies class, I asked my professor, "Have you heard of the Cayman Islands?"

He frowned. "No," he replied.

We went over and gazed at the world map on the wall to locate the place, but to no avail.

I was saddened at the thought of leaving my two young brothers, the thought of them growing up around me now fading away.

I was about to turn fifteen, becoming of age—a big event in a young girl's life in Nicaragua, and often celebrated in a big way.

Most families saved for years for this big celebration. The young ladies wore fancy ballroom dresses, the selection of which is as intense as selecting a wedding dress. The color and style are given much attention, as is the size of its flared skirt in order to achieve that Cinderella appearance.

A fancy ballroom is selected to host the guests and the place is decorated to shimmer and shine. But my birthday came and went. I knew not to expect anything special.

But to my surprise, as I got ready to leave the country, my mother came up with the bright idea that since my birthday had passed a few months earlier, and since I was about to leave the country for good, it would be a good idea to celebrate.

She blurted out, "We can have a party, and we can call it a farewell quinceañera party."

A wry smile crossed my face. Repulsion washed over me. Her comment was an insult to my intelligence. Did she really believe I would buy into her false pretense? Pretending this was my big quinceañera party? This party was not for me. It was for her. It was a party to celebrate her achievement, the fulfillment of her goal. It was a celebration of my departure. I would leave the country and neither I nor my father had a say.

The plans for the party went on. A random date was picked and invitations were distributed by word of mouth. Our neighbor, Ms. Cora, made me a cake. The music played and everyone danced and laughed. We took pictures to remember the occasion. I smiled along with everyone else. By now I had learned quite well how to smile on the outside even though I was sad or angry on the inside.

On two occasions, I had been invited by Maria, Ms. Aldith's daughter, to attend a youth group they called Fellowship. A group of young people my age gathered together and played games and sang choruses. Maria asked if I would be going to the youth fellowship the following evening. I agreed. After all, it would be my last meeting with them. For the first time, I was part of a group, but that was short-lived.

Maria informed the group it would be my last visit as I was moving away. At the end of the evening, while holding hands in a circle, the leader of the group spoke. "We will not consider your leaving a goodbye. It is just a farewell."

He led them into an unfamiliar song and the group followed. My eyes welled up with tears that rolled down my face as I listened to the lyrics.

No es más que un hasta luego,
No es más que un breve adiós,
Muy pronto junto al fuego

Nos reunirá el Señor.—
It is no more than a farewell,
It is but a brief goodbye,
Soon, close by the fire.
Reunited by the Lord we'll be.

After we sang, I was presented with a little notebook as a token to remember the group. It was a cherished gift that I kept for years.

The day came for me to leave. I packed a small bag with a few belongings. Wanting to leave something of myself with my siblings, I searched, but I didn't have much to leave. I had sold my shells to a jewelry store long ago. I had taken good care of my doll and my set of chairs and table. They were a remembrance of my childhood and the only gift of toys I had ever received. They would make the perfect gift.

My doll went to Katherine and my table set went to Lisa. I had a gold bracelet, which I'd had for as long as I could remember. It bore my initials, "B A W." I took it off my hand and put it on Hubert's hand. I asked my mother to please tell him what the initials meant when he got older and could understand. I had nothing else to give to my other siblings but my goodbye hugs.

My first visit came to mind as my eyes roamed the living room, my siblings not knowing of my existence. In a few years, would Hubert and Dennis feel the same way? Maybe not. Now that everyone knows of me.

My cousin Gladys was also taking the trip. We headed to Rama and then to Managua. We would take a bus to Costa Rica and then a flight to the Cayman Islands. My mother warned me not to let my father know of my travel plans; therefore, neither he nor my grandparents knew I would be leaving the country. After our long travel, we spent the night in Managua.

The following morning, we took yet another long bus ride

to Costa Rica, where we spent a couple of days at a family friend's house. Walking on the streets of San Jose early one morning, the sun beaming yellow against the pavement, my eyes followed the spindles of an ornate black metal fence, the bars tall above my head.

Granny and Grandpa were constantly on my mind. I seemed to be going further and further away, with no idea when I would see them again. My eyes welled up with tears as the muscle on my chest squeezed to suppress my sadness. I was eager to write to them and my father and let them know of my new location.

Walking behind me, Gladys made fun of my avocado-green hand-me-down dress. "Watch her with her low ass," she said to her friend, and they giggled.

I continued on as if I heard nothing.

The following morning, we boarded Lacsa Airline, and the flight took off. Having no idea what life had in store for me, I looked to God for comfort. He had been there with me always. He had taken me in the palm of his hands. I consoled myself in knowing he would be with me always, no matter how far away I went.

I looked out at the clear blue sky as the plane took off, marveling at the snow-white clouds floating near the window and wondering, *What will tomorrow bring?*

The End

About the Author

Beverly Bernard lives and works in the Cayman Islands. She and her husband, Anthony, have been married for over forty years and are proud parents to three exceptional children, each accomplished in their own right.

Beverly draws from decades of personal experience in her writing, including both the triumphs and the struggles that have shaped her life. She writes honestly about loss, resilience, and the unexpected moments of grace that emerge from hardship.

Readers will find in her stories not just one woman's journey, but universal truths about facing adversity and finding strength in life's most challenging seasons.

www.beverlybernardbooks.com

Made in the USA
Coppell, TX
09 June 2026

79968099R00177